PERSUADING GOD

Hebrew Bible Monographs, 73

Series Editors
David J.A. Clines, J. Cheryl Exum

Editorial Board
A. Graeme Auld, Marc Brettler, David M. Carr, Paul M. Joyce,
Francis Landy, Lena-Sofia Tiemeyer, Stuart D.E. Weeks

Persuading God

Rhetorical Studies of First-Person Psalms

Davida H. Charney

Sheffield Phoenix Press

2017

Copyright © Sheffield Phoenix Press, 2015, 2017

First published in hardback, 2015
First published in paperback, 2017

Published by Sheffield Phoenix Press
Department of Biblical Studies, University of Sheffield
45 Victoria Street
Sheffield S3 7QB

www.sheffieldphoenix.com

All rights reserved.
No part of this publication may be reproduced or transmitted in any
form or by any means, electronic or mechanical, including
photocopying, recording or any information storage or retrieval
system, without the publisher's permission in writing.

A CIP catalogue record for this book
is available from the British Library

Printed by Lightning Source

ISBN 978-1-909697-80-5 (hardback)
ISBN 978-1-910928-21-9 (paperback)

ISSN 1747-9614

In honor of my parents

Rabbi Lawrence H. Charney (ז״ל)
Lillian U. Charney

Contents

Preface	ix
Tables and Figures	x
Acknowledgments	xi
Abbreviations	xii

INTRODUCTION	1
Psalms as Arguments in the Israelite Public Sphere	1
Beyond Psychologizing the Speaker	5
Beyond Presuming Piety	8
Distinguishing Rhetorical and Literary Analyses	10
Ancient and Contemporary Rhetorical Theory	11
Toward a Rhetorical Theory of the Psalms	12
Stances Toward God	14
A Note on Translations	16

Chapter 1

PRAISE AS DIVINE CURRENCY	17
Praise as Negotiable Currency	20
Psalm 71: Extending the Supply of Praise	25
Praise as a Charged Current	29
Psalm 16: Balancing with God's Guidance	30
Psalm 26: Ongoing Refinement	32
Psalm 131: Bragging on Quietism	35

Chapter 2

INSTRUCTIONS FOR KEEPING FAITH	39
Two Pieces of Rhetorical Theory: Amplitude and Identification	39
Psalm 4: A Seven-Step Recovery Program	41
Psalm 62: Restoring the Expletive	47
Psalm 82: Persuading Gods	52
Conclusion: Bait and Switch?	54

Chapter 3

THE LAMENT AS PROPOSAL	56
Psalm 54: Invoking Action	58
Psalm 13: Questioning Absence	59
Absence of Amplitude	61

Chapter 4
SONGS OF INNOCENCE — 65
- Psalm 44: God's Breach of Covenant — 65
- Psalm 22: From Worm to Champion — 71
- Psalm 17: Assertions of Godliness — 76
- Conclusion — 81

Chapter 5
THE KAIROS OF CURSES — 83
- Psalm 7: Measured Innocence — 86
- Psalm 35: Paying Back in Kind — 92
- Psalm 109: Returning Curse for Curse — 98
- Conclusion — 109

Chapter 6
RECOVERING FROM GUILT — 111
- The Discourse of Guilt — 112
- Psalm 130: Proclaiming Patience — 113
- Psalm 38: Eloquently Inarticulate — 116
- Psalm 51: An Action-Oriented Confession — 120
- Conclusion — 125

Chapter 7
SELF-PERSUASION AND WISDOM — 127
- Psalm 77: Reimagining the Past — 128
- Psalm 73: Speaking Internally and Externally — 135
- Discipline and Persuasion — 142

Bibliography — 143
Index of References — 150
Index of Rhetorical Terms — 154
Index of Authors — 155

Preface

I am a scholar of rhetoric by title with over thirty years of intellectual debts to teachers, colleagues and friends such as Chris Neuwirth, Marie Secor, Jeanne Fahnestock, Jeff Walker, Jack Selzer, Carolyn Miller, Dave Kaufer, Rich Enos and Richard Young. There is no good term for how I have gradually become a scholar of Hebrew Bible. 'Auto-didact' is not only clumsy but inaccurate. I gained a love of sacred texts from my parents and grandparents. I studied for six years at the Solomon Schechter Day School in suburban Chicago and took a few classes in Near Eastern and Judaic Studies as an undergraduate at Brandeis. I read drafts of Bernie Levinson's dissertation and sat in on seminars led by Gary Knoppers and Baruch Halpern as a faculty member at Penn State. I participated in many study groups over the years discussing the weekly Torah portion or the Talmud. I learned a lot from teaching Biblical Hebrew and Jewish adult learning classes on Moses, King David and Ruth in Austin, Texas. While on sabbatical in Cambridge, England, I enjoyed Diana Lipton's deeply engaging classes, conversations and sermons, and learned much from arguing with Meira Polliack—and from finally listening to her. Eventually, even without having a card to carry in my wallet, I came to believe that I have something to contribute to biblical studies. Since then, I have benefited from the support and insights of these friends and many others. By championing the study of Jewish rhetoric in print and in deed, Michael Bernard-Donals and Jan Fernheimer have created a supportive environment within rhetorical studies. Michael Bernard-Donals, Jeff Walker, Jeanne Fahnestock, Adele Berlin and Gary Knoppers wrote in support of several less-than-successful grant applications as I have spluttered and mumbled my way into speaking the language of a new discipline. The Department of Rhetoric and Writing and the College of Liberal Arts at the University of Texas granted me a crucial Dean's Fellowship that I spent in Tel Aviv in 2009. Above all, I am indebted to Meira Polliack, Diana Lipton, Adele Berlin and Jeffrey Walker for their feedback on drafts of this book. And I am deeply grateful to Chris Neuwirth for pushing my buttons and to my mom for her constant encouragement.

TABLES AND FIGURES

Table 1 Frequencies of Language-Related Words in Psalms	3
Figure 1.1 Structure of Psalm 71	27
Figure 1.2 Structure of Psalm 26	33
Figure 2.1 Structure of Psalm 4	43
Figure 2.2 Structure of Psalm 62	49
Figure 2.3 Verse-Initial Words in Psalm 62	51
Figure 2.4 Structure of Psalm 82	53
Figure 3.1 Structure of Psalm 54	59
Figure 3.2 Structure of Psalm 13	60
Figure 4.1 Structure of Psalm 44	67
Figure 4.2 Chiastic Structure of References in Address and Complaint in Psalm 44	68
Figure 4.3 Structure of Psalm 22	73
Figure 4.4 Structure of Psalm 17	77
Figure 5.1 Structure of Psalm 7	88
Figure 5.2 Structure of Psalm 35	95
Figure 5.3 Structure of Psalm 109 for Speaker-as-Curser Reading	101
Figure 5.4 Structure of Psalm 109 for Opponent-as-Curser Reading	105
Figure 6.1 Structure of Psalm 130	114
Figure 6.2 Structure of Psalm 38	118
Figure 6.3 Structure of Psalm 51	122
Figure 6.4 Parallel Structure of Divine and Reciprocal Action in Psalm 51	123
Figure 7.1 Structure of Psalm 77	130
Figure 7.2 Kselman's Chiastic Structure of Questions and Answers in Psalm 77	133
Figure 7.3 Structure of Psalm 73	138

ACKNOWLEDGMENTS

An earlier version of Chapter 2 appeared in 'Keeping the Faithful: Persuasive Strategies in Psalms 4 and 62', *Journal of Hebrew Scriptures* 12 (2012), pp. 1-13, http://dx.doi.org/10.5508/jhs.2012.v12.a16.

Portions of the Introduction and Chapter 4 rework material originally published in 'Maintaining Innocence before a Divine Hearer: Deliberative Rhetoric in Ps. 22, Ps. 17, and Ps. 7', *Biblical Interpretation* 21.1 (2013), pp. 33-63 and in 'Performativity and Persuasion in the Hebrew Book of Psalms: A Rhetorical Analysis of Psalms 22 and 116', *Rhetoric Society Quarterly* 40 (2010), pp. 247-68.

Translations of the psalms are from *The Book of Psalms: A Translation with Commentary*, translated by Robert Alter. Copyright ©2007 by Robert Alter. Used by permission of W.W. Norton & Company, Inc.

Unless otherwise indicated, all other translations are reprinted from *Tanakh: The Holy Scriptures* by permission of the University of Nebraska Press. Copyright ©1985, 1999 by the Jewish Publication Society, Philadelphia.

ABBREVIATIONS

AJP	*American Journal of Philology*
AOTC	*Abingdon Old Testament Commentary Series*
Bib	*Biblica*
BibInt	*Biblical Interpretation: A Journal of Contemporary Approaches*
BSac	*Bibliotheca Sacra*
CBQ	*Catholic Bible Quarterly*
ClQ	*Classical Quarterly*
HBT	*Horizons in Biblical Theology*
HTR	*Harvard Theological Review*
HUCA	*Hebrew Union College Annual*
Int	*Interpretation*
JAAR	*Journal of the American Academy of Religion*
JANES	*Journal of the Ancient Near Eastern Society*
JBL	*Journal of Biblical Literature*
JEA	*Journal of Egyptian Archaeology*
JHS	*Journal of Hellenic Studies*
JSOT	*Journal for the Study of the Old Testament*
JSOTSup	Journal for the Study of the Old Testament, Supplements
KJV	King James Version
NJPS	New Jewish Publication Society of America Tanakh
PMLA	*Proceedings of the Modern Language Association*
ResQ	*Restoration Quarterly*
RevExp	Review and Expositor
RSV	Revised Standard Version
SBL	Society of Biblical Literature
TynBul	*Tyndale Bulletin*
VT	*Vetus Testamentum*
VTSup	Vetus Testamentum, Supplements
WW	*Word and World*
ZAW	*Zeitschrift für die alttestamentliche Wissenschaft*

INTRODUCTION

Psalms as Arguments in the Israelite Public Sphere

Arguing with God is a key theme in the Hebrew Bible. David Frank writes that '[t]he God of the Hebrew Bible is, by nature, argumentative', and goes so far as to say that '[a]gonistic speech is the beginning of Jewish theology'.[1] Great figures including Abraham, Moses, Jeremiah and Job are celebrated for their give-and-take with God. Apart from the dialogues between these figures, contentiousness is a recurrent theme in the narrative. The Israelite tribes, whose forty years of wandering complainingly through the Sinai takes up most of the Torah, overwhelmed Moses with their disputes to such an extent that he had to set up echelons of elders in what amounted to municipal and superior courts (Exod. 18.13-26).

Of all the parts of the Hebrew Bible that might spring to mind in association with persuasion and argumentation, the book of Psalms might be among the last. '"The Lord is my shepherd"; "by the rivers of Babylon"; "out of the mouth of babes" (*sic*); "the valley of the shadow of death"—that's probably about the extent of what the average post-religious reader carries around from the Book of Psalms', as Christopher Tayler notes in his *Guardian* review of Robert Alter's translation of the psalms.[2] Readers who frequent a church or synagogue can do a bit better than that, having become familiar with the hymnic hallelujahs that make up parts of the liturgy. But they may be surprised to learn that only about a fifth of the 150 poems in the book of Psalms are straightforward hymns of praise or other expressions of a religious assembly.

In fact, a much larger proportion of the psalms, over a third, have an individual first-person speaker who directly addresses God to convey thanksgiving, petition or lament. The speakers in the psalms are beset by opponents, some other Israelites, some aliens. The speakers are the victims of false accusations, threats from neighborhood bullies and slanders from gossips. They are caught in the trials of daily life—they are aging or sick,

---

1. David A. Frank, 'Arguing with God, Talmudic Discourse, and the Jewish Countermodel: Implications for the Study of Argumentation', *Argumentation and Advocacy* 41 (2004), pp. 71-86 (73).

2. Christopher Tayler, 'In the Vale of Death's Shadow', *The Guardian* (21 December 2007).

they face temptation, see the wicked prosper and lose faith in God's abiding presence. The problems have political, legal and philosophical implications but they are primarily personal and social. The speakers deal with their problems by arguing with God, attempting to persuade God to intervene in their lives to relieve the crisis in which they find themselves. They ask for divine reassurance, for vindication, for their opponents to be swept away. They give thanks and praise to God, seeking to stay close to God and retain God's favor. They promise to remain faithful, to broadcast God's praises in public and to call on others to praise.

As speakers seeking to persuade a hearer to enact a proposed solution to a serious problem, the psalmists are engaging in rhetoric. Aristotle defined rhetoric as the art/faculty of choosing from among the available means of persuasion in any given situation.[3] From a rhetorical perspective, texts serve practical purposes in real-world situations. For a situation to be a rhetorical situation, a speaker has to experience a sense of exigence or urgency that can be addressed productively with language. The speaker fashions a spoken or written text and delivers it in such a way as to maximize its influence on an appropriate set of hearers, those who can take steps to reduce or perhaps even resolve the problem. Considerations of purpose and audience influence the choice of claims, the amount and kinds of supporting evidence, the style, forms of address and even the length of the text.[4]

One sign that persuasion is a central purpose of the psalms is the high concentration of language about language. Across the Hebrew Bible as a whole, Margaret Zulick found a wide array of terms for speech, eloquence, argument and persuasion (legal and theistic) as well as terms for 'active' listening.[5] Though she found no active, transitive, value-neutral Hebrew verb meaning 'to persuade', Zulick argues that in Israelite epistemology, persuasion is determined by the hearer rather than by the speaker. A speaker can try to influence the hearer, but being persuaded is 'an independent motion of the will on the part of the hearer'.[6] As intricately wrought poetry, the psalms are, if anything, even more highly focused on persuasion than the rest of the Bible, bringing to bear all the enchantments of sound and form. The psalms are suffused with terms connected to language: the speech organs,

---

3. Aristotle. *On Rhetoric: A Theory of Civic Discourse* (trans. G.A. Kennedy; New York: Oxford University Press, 1991), p. 1355b.

4. For a discussion of how considerations of audience influence the shape of an argument see Carolyn Miller and Davida Charney, 'Audience, Persuasion, and Argument', in Charles Bazerman (ed.), *Handbook of Research on Writing: History, Society, School, Individual, Text* (New York: Routledge, 2007), pp. 583-98.

5. Margaret D. Zulick, 'The Active Force of Hearing: The Ancient Hebrew Language of Persuasion', *Rhetorica* 10 (1992), pp. 267-380.

6. Zulick, 'Active Force', p. 378.

the varieties of vocal utterances and the goals of speech. Herbert Levine notes that psalmists show a 'heightened awareness of their own acts of expression', naming a 'striking number' of speech acts, especially as their opening and closing verses.[7] As indicated in Table 1, speech acts are named in more than six verses per psalm on average. Considering that the psalms are relatively short poems (averaging about 16 verses), this is a remarkably high concentration.

Table 1. *Frequencies of Language-Related Words in Psalms*

Category	Word List*	No. Verses	Verses per Psalm
Speech Organs	Ear, lips, mouth, tongue, voice	170	1.1
Speech Acts	Answer, ask, bless, boast, call, chasten, complain, cry, curse, declare, despise, exalt, extol, groan, honor, inquire, language, loathe, magnify, mention, mock, name, noise, plea, praise, proclaim, say, scorn, shout, sing, speak, tell, word	984	6.6
Hearing	Attend, hear, heed, listen	232	1.6
Sound	Aloud, mute, dumb, silent	18	0.1

* Word counts include variants (e.g., tense, number, verbal/nominal/adjectival forms)

Using the psalms to persuade God reflects how Israelites viewed their relationship. When Israelites engage in discourse with God, they know that they are unequal in the power needed to resolve the issue. But they do assume that both sides are open to argument and capable of persuasion. From a theological perspective, God's willingness to listen to argument rather than just lay down the law bespeaks an extraordinary generosity toward humanity, for 'it is sometimes a valued honor to be a person with whom another will enter into discussion', as Chaïm Perelman and Lucie Olbrechts-Tyteca point out in *The New Rhetoric*.[8] The belief that God is open to argument is constantly in tension with the knowledge that God may decline to respond or may deny the request of even the most righteous and eloquent speaker. It is this feature that distinguishes the psalms from magical incantations that need only be pronounced or performed correctly to be effective. Arguments,

---

7. Herbert Levine, *Sing unto God a New Song: A Contemporary Reading of the Psalms* (Bloomington, IN: Indiana University Press, 1995), p. 102.

8. Chaïm Perelman and Lucie Olbrechts-Tyteca, *The New Rhetoric: A Treatise on Argumentation* (trans. J. Wilkinson and P. Weaver; Notre Dame, IN: University of Notre Dame Press, 1969), p. 16. While Chaïm Perelman and Lucie Olbrechts-Tyteca were partners in researching and writing *The New Rhetoric*, for convenience, I will refer just to Perelman hereafter.

like conversations, can be picked up at any time by either party; a disappointed Israelite can try again with another perhaps more persuasive psalm. Psalms may have been designed expressly to keep the Israelite community engaged in divine discourse even when the hoped-for response is not forthcoming.

Israelites presumably interpreted God's response from subsequent events.[9] An ill person recovers or dies; a fearsome opponent prevails or relents. Those who see events turn in their favor move from lament to thanksgiving; they credit God for their success rather than themselves or other human agents. Those whose troubles persist may go on petitioning and lamenting, making their very persistence a sign of their faithfulness and worthiness for rescue. As Andreas Schuele suggests, it is useful to conceptualize a '*lament process* that could unfold over an extended period of time'.[10] The psalms have social as well as individual import. As Walter Brueggemann and Carleen Mandolfo have recognized, the laments sanction protest against injustice, putting God at risk of failing to live up to God's own standards.[11] Thus, as a sanctioned public way to celebrate successes and protest injustice, the psalms spell out and promote such cultural values as צדק ('justice') and חסד ('loving-kindness'), while discouraging arrogance, greed, baseless hatred and apostasy.

While God is the primary audience of most psalms, speakers also seek to shape public opinion. Psalmists simultaneously promise, call for and articulate public praise of God. Public performance is dynamic; it influences, underscores and maintains loyalty to God and the cultural values that God represents. However, the speakers of the psalms also use their public performances to adjust their standing in the community. In ancient Israel, trouble in daily life was quickly taken as a sign of divine displeasure; to preserve

---

9. The recourse to 'wait and see', which also applies to distinguishing between a true and false oracle, has much wider implications across the Hebrew Bible, as Baruch Halpern says: 'In devoting itself thus to a cosmic personal god who rules the universe, Israel worships Fate. Israel accepts history as judge.' See Baruch Halpern, 'YHWH the Revolutionary: Reflections on the Rhetoric of Redistribution in the Social Context of Dawning Monotheism', in Alice Ogden Bellis (ed.), *Jews, Christians, and the Theology of the Hebrew Scriptures* (Atlanta, GA: SBL, 2000), pp. 179-212 (209).

10. Andreas Schuele, '"Call on me in the day of trouble…": From Oral Lament to Lament Psalms', in Annette Weissenrieder and Robert B. Coote (eds.), *Interface of Orality and Writing: Speaking, Seeing, Writing in the Shaping of New Genres* (Tübingen: Mohr Siebeck, 2010), pp. 322-34 (329); original emphasis.

11. Walter Brueggemann has described the daringness of the challenge in 'The Costly Loss of Lament', *JSOT* 36 (1986), pp. 57-71 and more recently in 'The Psalms in Theological Use: On Incommensurability and Mutuality', in Peter W. Flint and Patrick D. Miller (eds.), *Book of Psalms: Composition and Reception* (VTSup, 109; Leiden: Brill, 2005), pp. 581-602. See also Carleen Mandolfo, 'Psalm 88 and the Holocaust: Lament in Search of a Divine Response', *BibInt* 15 (2007), pp. 151-70.

their own standing, neighbors might desert or even denounce the afflicted. Performing a psalm helps the speaker fight back and regain a respectable standing. As William Morrow notes,

> a primary goal of the complaint psalms was to rehabilitate the individual to the larger group (who also worship Yhwh) by affirming the undeserved suffering of the petitioner, an affirmation that is intended to arrest both his social exclusion and also the justification of group violence against him.[12]

Beyond Psychologizing the Speaker

A rhetorical approach, I argue, opens up new ways to address long-standing puzzles concerning the psalms: how to deal with the long string of imprecations in Psalm 109, whether Psalm 4 is best read as protesting a false accusation or as countering apostasy, why so many verses in Psalm 62 begin with the expostulation אך ('ach'). A particularly prominent puzzle is the abrupt shifts in mood that characterize the laments. As Andreas Schuele says,

> the shift from lament to praise as a defining characteristic of lament psalms is the most challenging aspect of their interpretation. What would enable someone who presents herself in a situation of utter distress and need to switch—literally from one second to the next—to the opposite end of the emotional spectrum?[13]

Many psalms scholars have resorted to psychologizing the psalmist as overwrought, swinging between despair and hope while composing or reciting the lament. They take the characteristic final shift to praise as a sign of the therapeutic power of composing a lament (or articulating a lament composed for them); eventually, the activity enables the speaker to affirm trust in God. Cecil Staton, for example, sees Ps. 13.6 as a sign that 'honest prayer may bring aid and hope to the desperate pray-er'.[14] Even if the prayer is not answered favorably in the immediate future, the speaker recuperates enough over the course of the psalm to remain faithful. Therapy is rarely so efficient, however. As Herbert Levine notes, 'Behind these and other psychological explanations lies the faulty assumption that the real time it

---

12. William S. Morrow, *Protest against God: The Eclipse of a Biblical Tradition* (Sheffield: Phoenix Press, 2006), pp. 53-54.
13. Schuele, 'Call on me', p. 324.
14. Cecil Staton, '"How long, O Yahweh?" The Complaint Prayer of Psalm 13', *Faith and Mission* 7 (1990), pp. 59-67 (65). He notes: 'Commentators have often expressed amazement at the transition from lament to praise found in this and similar psalms' (p. 65).

takes to recite a psalm must correspond to the inner changes it reports in its speaker'.[15]

In addition to assigning therapeutic benefits to the speaker, many scholars also see psychological benefits accruing for subsequent hearers and readers. Drawing on Bakhtin's notions of dialogism and confessional self-accounting, Patricia Tull describes how individuals across the centuries have co-articulated/co-authored the psalms in their own reading, writing and praying.[16] By engaging deeply with the text, a sensitive reader enters into the moment-by-moment play of thoughts and feelings of a troubled individual moving from an isolated internal struggle with his or her misdeeds to an external encounter with the divine. Tull writes,

> In one and the same act of empathetic reading we both aestheticize the speaker of the Psalm, perceiving artistic beauty where the psalmist only sees pain, and by projecting ourselves into the *subiectum*, identify the psalmist's tones and petitions with our own.[17]

Performance amounts to creation of something original. While Tull's view of the enduring power of the psalms is compelling, she only sees one role for the speaker in a lament, that of a penitent who seeks and finally achieves reconciliation. She closes off the possibility that innocent people seeking redress for perceived injustice may very well remain dissatisfied, despite ending the psalm with praise. By identifying individual passages with swings in mood, psychologizing justifies a psalm's apparent shifts in mood without explaining them.

A different approach to the puzzling shifts in mood is to assign them to separate voices. Carleen Mandolfo, who also draws on Bakhtin's dialogism, demarcates the shifts in a lament as turns in a conversation—at times even a quarrel—between a voice speaking from harsh worldly experience and a more didactic voice of faith.[18] Mandolfo observes that the worldly

---

15. Levine, *Sing unto God*, p. 146.
16. Patricia K. Tull, 'Bakhtin's Confessional Self-Accounting and Psalms of Lament', *BibInt* 13 (2005), pp. 41-55; Mikhail M. Bakhtin, 'Author and Hero in Aesthetic Activity', in Michael Holquist and Vadim Liapunov (eds.), *Art and Answerability: Early Philosophical Essays by M.M. Bakhtin* (Austin, TX: University of Texas Press, 1990), pp. 4-256. For Bakhtin, literary texts mediate the essential relationships of individuals across time, to each other and to the divine. Dialogic texts set out multiple perspectives by depicting self-reflection, introducing multiple voices and alluding implicitly or explicitly to other texts. Readers entertain multiple interpretations simultaneously and become co-authors by bringing to bear their knowledge of similar texts, related texts and commentaries as well as by refracting their readings through their own experiences.
17. Tull, 'Bakhtin's Confessional', p. 54.
18. Mandolfo, 'Psalm 88'. See also Mandolfo's 'Dialogic Form Criticism: An Intertextual Reading of Lamentations and Psalms of Lament', in Roland Boer (ed.), *Bakhtin and Genre Theory in Biblical Studies* (Atlanta, GA: Society of Biblical Literature, 2007),

voice challenges faith itself, God's commitment to justice and adherence to the covenant. The characteristic final turn to praise gives the last word to the didactic voice, signaling that the speaker achieves reconciliation with God. Only in one psalm, Psalm 88, does the speaker remain on the offensive. Mandolfo sees Psalm 88 as completely monologic, the only psalm in which 'the supplicant does not explicitly request or expect redemption, only God's ear and perhaps an accounting for God's failure to live up to the standards he has projected'.[19] In the other laments, the speaker comes close to but never 'unequivocally charges God with faithlessness or breach of covenant'. Mandolfo's approach goes further than Tull's in accomplishing what Brueggemann has called a 'redistribution of power' in favor of the petitioner in a way that puts God at risk.[20] She makes sense of Israelites' continued faithfulness in the face of injustice.

However, Mandolfo ends up muting the challenge to God by locating the dialogue completely within the text. If the speaker has a conversational partner, his or her isolation from an unresponsive God is far less poignant; it is, in Mandolfo's terms, 'mitigated' or 'tempered' by the intervention of the didactic theodic voice.[21] Except in Psalm 88, the petitioner ends up seeming reconciled because the didactic voice so often gets the last word:

> within all of these psalms, except one, a defense of God is integrated into the discourse of the supplicant, diluting the complaint, and thus hinting that the supplicant's negative experience is either deserved, or that God's perceived absence is only a temporary aberration, soon to be rectified if the supplicant maintains faith.[22]

The laments are structured this way, Mandolfo concludes, to serve as an institutional response to restiveness, with the dialogue presenting a 'verbal image of the contentious social dialogue taking place outside the text'.[23] While I agree that the laments serve as what Baruch Halpern would call 'steam valves for the state',[24] assigning passages to separate voices risks caricaturing the two sides. On the one hand, the worldly voice comes across as single-minded and self-interested, never articulating the prevailing

---

pp. 69-90 and her reading of Psalm 7 in 'Finding their Voices: Sanctioned Subversion in Psalms of Lament', *HBT* 24 (2002), pp. 27-52.

19. Mandolfo, 'Psalm 88', p. 165.
20. Brueggemann, 'Costly Loss', p. 59.
21. Mandolfo, 'Finding their Voices', p. 49. Andreas Schuele also sees the final shift to praise as seeming to 'tame' or 'domesticate' the lament though God remains held to the promise of rescue ('Call on me', p. 334).
22. Mandolfo, 'Psalm 88', p. 158.
23. Mandolfo, 'Finding their Voices', p. 52.
24. Halpern, 'Yhwh the Revolutionary', p. 190.

cultural values. On the other hand, the didactic voice comes across as odiously pious, oblivious of the complexities of living in the real world.

Taking a rhetorical perspective, I see the speaker as neither over-wrought nor narrow-minded but rather as the shaper of an argument, the parts of which sometimes go unrecognized. The task of a rhetorical approach is to spell out how apparent digressions actually build a connected line of argument in a given psalm and contribute to a coherent and persuasive reading of the text as a whole. As the readings here will show, the passages that Mandolfo identifies with the didactic voice can often be viewed as efforts by the speaker to hold God accountable to divine principles and pronouncements. It is actually a common persuasive strategy for speakers to reflect back to hearers their own previous words, views and self-images. By doing so, a speaker demonstrates that she agrees with or shares those views or at least has heard and understood them. For these purposes, the views must be presented in a form that the hearer will recognize and agree to, thus producing in the psalms what Mandolfo detects as shifts in voice. The theodic points, then, may not be intended to mollify or respond to the *speaker's* suffering but rather are pointed reminders to *God* of the attributes and conduct that God has publicly promulgated. God is being challenged to intervene on behalf of the speaker to reaffirm those divine attributes and values. Challenging God does not seem presumptuous because, as Harold Fisch puts it in the case of Job, 'the challenge is itself made possible only by the having been fashioned by a creator God in such a way as to be able to ask such questions'.[25]

Beyond Presuming Piety

Until now the puzzle of the shifts has been treated psychologically—as a problem in understanding or resolving the feelings of the speaker. From a rhetorical perspective, the problem is broader and entails understanding what beliefs and attitudes the speaker wants to inspire in the hearers, namely God and other public onlookers. Shifting the focus shakes up the traditional picture of the speakers of the psalms, their character, their social standing and their stances toward God. This is an important corrective to taking the speakers at face value. When the speakers of the psalms are taken to be the psalmists themselves or Temple functionaries or kings (let alone King David), it is too easy to see them as uniformly virtuous and pious. From a rhetorical perspective, however, a speaker's *ethos* or character is constructed for the occasion (at least in part), and is signaled by choices in the content and form of the text. The character that is constructed is a

---

25. Harold Fisch, *Poetry with a Purpose: Biblical Poetics and Interpretation* (Bloomington, IN: Indiana University Press, 1988), p. 32.

self-representation—a far from disinterested one—that is key to the speaker's persuasive strategies. A psalm that depicts the moment-by-moment play of thoughts and feelings, then, is one that has been constructed with great artistry to do so as a persuasive strategy. Detecting these strategies reveals a full range of characters across the psalms, from tolerant to smug and from heroic to vindictive. In some cases, in fact, the speaker's character seems to be set up by a distinct person or persons—the psalmists, perhaps—for a critical purpose (for example, Psalm 7, Psalm 116 and Psalm 109).[26]

In this book, I examine how the speakers of the psalms represent themselves by deducing a rhetorical situation from the content and form of the text. The rhetorical situation is the starting point, the exigence that prompts the text. It often involves some kind of conflict or dispute, from simple issues that arise in everyday life to those requiring formal judicial adjudication. In a dispute, all the parties may believe themselves to be in the right—or at least partly in the right—even when they are wrong. They all strive to present themselves in the best possible light. The psalms only present one side of a dispute—the speaker's side. Within the rhetorical situation, the speaker attempts to seize the 'right moment' or *kairos* for speaking. The kairos depends on the speaker's current sense of security and well-being as well as his or her aspirations. It depends on his or her faith-history of relations with God, a relationship that is apparently intimate, dynamic and far from uncritical on either side. And the kairos involves the speaker's current standing in the social sphere, with friends and neighbors as well as with rivals and opponents. The contribution of taking a rhetorical perspective is two-fold. First, it puts aside the presumption that the speaker is innocent. In many cases, innocence is exactly the issue being debated. Second, rhetoric teases out the claims to which the speaker seems to be responding, allowing a broader perspective. A speaker who characterizes opponents as arrogant, lying and sinful may be deliberately countering the claims of other Israelites appealing to God for justice against him. With scanty historical evidence available, the rhetorical situations that I describe and the readings that I derive from them are necessarily speculative, but they are not undisciplined.

---

26. The distinction between the speaker and the psalmist is discussed by William Brown, 'The Psalms and "I": The Dialogical Self and the Disappearing Psalmist', in Joel S. Burnett, W.H. Bellinger and W. Dennis Tucker (eds.), *Diachronic and Synchronic: Reading the Psalms in Real Time* (Proceedings of the Baylor Symposium on the Book of Psalms; New York: T. & T. Clark, 2007), pp. 26-44. See also Schuele, 'Call on me', p. 330. For my reading of Psalm 116, see Davida Charney, 'Performativity and Persuasion in the Hebrew Book of Psalms: A Rhetorical Analysis of Psalms 22 and 116', *Rhetoric Society Quarterly* 40 (2010), pp. 247-68.

Distinguishing Rhetorical and Literary Analyses

A rhetorical analysis is akin to a literary analysis. Both rely on the technique of close reading, which leads to readings of a text that can be plausible and coherent but not definitive. The plausibility and coherence of an interpretation depends on accounting for as many features of a text as possible. Both literary and rhetorical analysis take a first-person speaker or narrator as a construct that cannot be equated with a specific writer or writers. While some literary theories dispense with the historical context in which a text was produced, the context is essential to a rhetorical analysis, even though such contexts can be understood only partially at best. While a literary analysis may take up any of a wide array of critical paradigms, a rhetorical analysis focuses on persuasive strategies, as articulated over rhetoric's long history. Rhetorical theorists recognize that arguments do not carry the force of formal logic, cannot guarantee a just or valid outcome, and no matter how well crafted, cannot compel the assent of any hearer.[27]

Within Biblical Studies generally, rhetorical approaches have been applied much more commonly to the New Testament than to the Hebrew Bible, and, until recently, much more frequently to the books of the prophets than to any other book.[28] While James Muilenberg famously called for rhetorical analysis of the psalms in 1969, he and his followers adopted a rather narrow conception of rhetoric that focused on structural and stylistic elements and that did not seek to identify persuasive or argumentative strategies.[29]

Recently, however, a substantial case for viewing the psalms as prayer-arguments was made by William S. Morrow who draws on the work of Erhard Gerstenberger and Rainer Albertz to trace the rise of domestic prayers in pre-exilic Israel and their eventual eclipse by theological developments in the late Second Temple period.[30] Morrow depicts the complaint psalms as arguments but does not analyze in depth the persuasive strategies of specific psalms. Around the same time, Robert Foster and David M. Howard, Jr published a collected volume devoted to the rhetoric of the

---

27. See especially Perelman and Olbrechts-Tyteca, *The New Rhetoric*, pp. 26-31.

28. See for example Yehoshua Gitay, 'Prophetic Criticism—"What are They Doing?": The Case of Isaiah—A Methodological Assessment', *JSOT* 96 (2001), pp. 101-27 and Meir Sternberg, 'The Bible's Art of Persuasion: Ideology, Rhetoric, and Poetics in Saul's Fall', *HUCA* 54 (1983), pp. 45-82.

29. James Muilenberg, 'Form Criticism and Beyond', *JBL* 88 (1969), pp. 1-18.

30. Morrow, *Protest against God*; Erhard Gerstenberger, 'Theologies in the Book of Psalms', in Peter W. Flint and Patrick D. Miller (eds.), *Book of Psalms: Composition and Reception* (VTSup, 109; Leiden: Brill, 2005), pp. 603-25; Rainer Albertz and Rüdiger Schmitt, *Family and Household Religion in Ancient Israel and the Levant* (Winona Lake, IN: Eisenbrauns, 2012).

psalms.³¹ Several chapters trace a rhetorical theme or topos across a variety of psalms, while another set of chapters each examines strategies in a single psalm. However, most of these scholars continue to adopt a rather narrow conception of rhetorical theory. The chapter that comes closest to my approach is 'Persuading the One and Only God to Intervene' by Dale Patrick and Kenneth Diable. They compare the usual stance of the Israelite speaker as an aggrieved innocent to the stance of speakers in other ancient Near Eastern prayer-songs who are usually conscious of having offended one god and appeal to another to intervene on his or her behalf.³²

Ancient and Contemporary Rhetorical Theory

Contemporary rhetorical theory traces its roots to ancient Athens. There the emergence of democratic forms of governance meant that decisions would be made on the basis of arguments rather than force or ancestry. Civil and criminal judicial cases, legislation and public policy issues alike were debated in the public forum and voted on by the assembled citizens. As a result, the skill of speaking eloquently and persuasively took on a high social value. Speakers perceived as wise and eloquent were at a decided advantage, so teachers of rhetoric were eagerly sought. By the fourth century BCE, theories of argument were developed in explicit enough form to be taught in academies by such figures as Isocrates, Socrates, Plato and Aristotle.³³

Much of contemporary theory follows from the Aristotelian definition of rhetoric as the faculty/art of choosing from among the available means of persuasion in a particular situation. In ancient Athens, civic argument occurred in at least three public forums. The judicial or 'forensic' forum deals with questions of what happened in the past. The legislative or 'deliberative' forum deals with questions of policy and action, what should happen in the future. Civic or 'epideictic' forums evaluate the current state of affairs, as in a dedication ceremony or state of the union address, often

---

31. Robert Foster and David M. Howard, Jr (eds.), *My Words are Lovely: Studies in the Rhetoric of the Psalms* (London: T. & T. Clark, 2008).

32. Dale Patrick and Kenneth Diable, 'Persuading the One and Only God to Intervene', in Robert Foster and David M. Howard, Jr (eds.), *My Words are Lovely: Studies in the Rhetoric of the Psalms* (London: T. & T. Clark, 2008), pp. 19-32. Additional important scholars who have taken rhetorical approaches to the psalms include Amy Cottrill (*Language, Power, and Identity in the Lament Psalms of the Individual* [New York: T. & T. Clark, 2008]) and Patrick D. Miller ('Prayer as Persuasion: The Rhetoric and Intention of Prayer', *WW* 13 [1993], pp. 356-62).

33. For an accessible history of rhetoric, see George Kennedy, *Classical Rhetoric and its Christian and Secular Tradition from Ancient to Modern Times* (Durham, NC: University of North Carolina Press, 2nd rev. edn, 1999 [1980]).

celebrating and reinforcing important cultural values. Contemporary rhetorical theory extrapolates from these forums to a wider array of professional, academic, civic and personal discourse. When texts developed in such contexts are perceived as successful, other speakers may use them as models or templates when faced with similar situations leading to the formation of productive genres.[34]

While prose argument in the traditional arenas developed most fully in the classical period, arguments in poetic form evidently had an important social function even earlier in archaic Greece.[35] Poetry was used in public and private settings to sum up the life of the deceased, to praise prominent citizens and even to seduce potential lovers. Poetic discourse was influential because it was easy to memorize and repeat, it articulated what the culture accepted as wisdom, modeled high standards for eloquence and elevated the status of skilled orators. By demonstrating that important issues could be resolved through discourse, poetic arguments helped to lay the social and cultural underpinnings for democratic governance. As compared to prose arguments, however, the texts of poetic arguments from this period are scarce. The psalms therefore represent a valuable repository of texts combining poetic and rhetorical arts.

Toward a Rhetorical Theory of the Psalms

In undertaking this project of comparative rhetoric, I am not assuming contact between Israelite and Greek societies and do not see Greek styles of argument as superior. The cultural differences in the two societies' conceptions of persuasive discourse may be epitomized by their conceptions of wrestling. In Greece, the wrestling arena was both figuratively and literally a site for practicing rhetoric.[36] Greek citizens wrestled/argued with their peers, some stronger and some weaker. Physical victory brought prizes, rank and glory. Rhetorical success brought a reputation for eloquence and wisdom and raised the speaker's influence over public policy.

---

34. Readers interested in how these terms comport with related terms in Bakhtin may consult Don Bialostosky, 'Aristotle's Rhetoric and Bakhtin's Discourse Theory', in Walter Jost and Wendy Olmsted (eds.), *A Companion to Rhetoric and Rhetorical Criticism* (Malden, MA: Blackwell, 2007), pp. 393-408.

35. Bruno Gentili, *Poetry and its Public in Ancient Greece: From Homer to the Fifth Century* (trans. A. Thomas Cole; Baltimore, MD: Johns Hopkins University Press, 1988); Jeffrey Walker, *Rhetoric and Poetics in Antiquity* (New York: Oxford University Press, 2000).

36. For a discussion of the relationship between wrestling and rhetoric, see Debra Hawhee, *Bodily Arts: Rhetoric and Athletics in Ancient Greece* (Austin, TX: University of Texas Press, 2005).

In contrast to Athenians, citizens in Israel do not seem to have gained prestige or social advancement through any form of public competition. Theologically, an Israelite wrestled not with peers but with God, emulating the patriarch Jacob who fought God to a draw—as good a result as a human being can hope to achieve. The very name 'Children of Israel' alludes to the divine wrestling match (Gen. 32.24-32), after which Jacob was renamed ישראל (*Yisra-el*), which can be translated as either 'will fight God' or 'God will fight'. For Israelites, decisions are to be made by consulting God and God's laws, not through the skill of persuasive argument. While judicial and even public policy disputes were brought to priests or elders, there is no evidence that persuasive skill was decisive in shaping the outcome. With the priesthood defined by tribe and the monarchy passed by direct descent (or military overthrow), no putative Israelite rhetor would be in a position to win political standing, fame or rank. Under these circumstances, it is not surprising that the psalms are not attributed to specific writers. Nor would it seem necessary to preserve verbatim texts that detailed the particularities of any given situation. With human crises recurring on a daily basis, it would instead be of practical benefit to skilled poets to frame psalms in ways that would allow them to be reused in whole or in part in a variety of situations.[37]

While the rhetorical concepts of rhetorical situation and kairos bear some relationship to the notion of *Sitz im Leben*, my goal is not to connect a psalm to a particular biblical episode, nor to a putative cultic ritual or festival. The writers of the psalms may have written them for themselves or on commission from others, perhaps as part of the feast following a free-will offering.[38] As Tull notes,

> it is not at all clear that every individual Psalm originated from personal experience; in fact, it seems more likely that they did not. Some Psalms may have been written non-autobiographically: perhaps on behalf of someone else (such as the king), or perhaps on behalf of many worshippers in similar straits, for their use and edification.[39]

Morrow suggests that informal complaint prayers began in tribal and domestic settings; at least some of the more formal psalms may have been

---

37. Morrow suggests that the psalmists were a heterogeneous group: 'the expert poets involved in composing lament, certainly in the stage of oral tradition, could have been skilled lay persons as well as identifiable functionaries of the religion of the large group such as temple singers or prophets' (*Protest against God*, p. 68).

38. For a persuasive case that the psalms were the work of pre-exilic guilds that became part of morning and evening incense offerings at various locations, see Nahum Sarna, 'The Psalm Superscriptions and the Guilds', in Siegfried Stein and Raphael Loewe (eds.), *Studies in Jewish Religious and Intellectual History* (Tuscaloosa, AL: University of Alabama Press, 1979), pp. 281-300.

39. Tull, 'Bakhtin's Confessional', p. 54.

composed and performed in 'liturgical services conducted on an *ad hoc* basis for individuals in need'.⁴⁰

Patrick and Diable argue that the psalms reflect a 'circumscribed period' in Israelite theology when monotheism had prevailed: 'But in Israel, Y<small>HWH</small> was the only deity to whom prayer could be addressed. Even if Y<small>HWH</small> was angry or appeared unresponsive, there was no other court of appeal. The petitioner had to come to Y<small>HWH</small> to make a case.'⁴¹ However, an assumption of an early or pure state of monotheism within Israelite culture is not necessary to my analysis. The psalms may have been designed to foster and promote Yahwism at a time of competing theologies.

The readings offered here challenge the view that the psalmists are a homogeneous, pious and faithful lot who conclude a psalm confident that justice is forthcoming. Arguing is a process of rehearsing the roles that speaker and hearer should play in a rational and orderly world. The psalms may have been intended to foster rather than simply to reflect the roles that Israelites and God should ideally play in an ongoing covenantal relationship in a world where good and evil co-exist. In the course of persuading God to live up to the covenant, the psalmists might well have promoted these ideals for the speaker and an assembly of spectators. Without some impetus for continuing to engage with God, Israelites suffering injustice could succumb to the temptation to slip out of the community altogether. Habituating Israelites to continue arguing and struggling with God, regardless of the outcome in any given case, rehearses the cultural commitment to justice, keeps alive the expectation of eventual deliverance and wards off apostasy.

Stances Toward God

While each speaker's rhetorical situation is distinct, this book is organized around a small number of recurring stances that ancient speakers take vis-à-vis God and the rest of the community. These stances include: maintaining good relations, arguing an innocent's right of redress, denouncing others, balancing dissenting views, acting as a model for others (keeping adherents faithful and warning off the wicked), appealing to God's self-interest and convincing one's self. These stances are akin to the functions that Walter Brueggemann describes as orienting, disorienting and reorienting and associates with psalms of trust, lament and thanksgiving.⁴²

Each of the stances is treated in its own chapter. Each chapter provides fresh readings of two or three exemplary psalms, analyzes their key

---

40. Morrow, *Protest against God*, p. 70.
41. Patrick and Diable, 'Persuading the One and Only God to Intervene', p. 22.
42. Walter Brueggemann, 'Psalms and the Life of Faith: A Suggested Typology of Function', *JSOT* 17 (1980), pp. 3-32.

rhetorical strategies and establishes the stance as a sub-genre based on their commonalities. In my readings, I consider previous form-critical, philological and theological studies of each psalm as constraints on possible readings, but I do not provide a comprehensive or detailed review of the literature on each psalm. Chapter 1, 'Praise as Divine Currency', draws from a variety of psalms to show that Israelites conceived of their relationship with God as a reciprocal one in which both parties have a stake in perpetuating faithful behavior, exhibited by Israelites through observance, ethical action and praise-giving, and exhibited by God through protecting and answering Israelites in need. Chapter 2, 'Instructions for Keeping Faith', introduces two key rhetorical strategies, amplitude and identification, to produce new and more coherent readings of psalms that have not previously been seen as similar or related. While Psalms 4 and 62 have previously been classified as laments, I argue that they—as well as Psalm 82—should be read as efforts to persuade backsliders to return to faithful, ethical practice.

Chapter 3, 'The Lament as Proposal', introduces several key elements of deliberative arguments, arguments that alert an audience of stakeholders to the existence of a serious problem and propose a solution. Two of the shortest and simplest laments, Psalms 54 and 13, are used to illustrate how the traditional sections of a lament can be aligned with the sections of a public policy proposal. The chapter also addresses the absence of amplitude in these two psalms, considering whether their brevity is a sign of deficiency or fitness for certain kinds of situations. Chapter 4, 'Songs of Innocence', considers more complex laments that all turn on the speaker's argument for innocence and worthiness for rescue. Despite the similarities of their goals, the speakers in Psalms 44, 22 and 17 take widely different stances toward God, reflecting their different social standing and previous prayer histories. Chapter 5, 'The Kairos of Curses', considers three psalms, Psalms 7, 35 and 109, that use curses to force God to choose between the speaker and his opponent, thereby implicating God in the justice or injustice of the outcome. Chapter 6, 'Recovering from Guilt', analyzes psalms in which the speaker admits to wrong-doing, complicating the case that he deserves divine rescue. The three psalms, Psalms 130, 38 and 51, increase in the explicitness of the speaker's confessions as well as in the reformative actions the speaker vows to take.

Chapter 7, 'Self-Persuasion and Wisdom', takes up the use of psalms for creating the disposition to overcome crises of faith; the speakers in Psalms 73 and 77 employ internal strategies such as recalling memories and songs, rehearsing cultural values and changing venue, in order to persuade themselves to maintain their faith, leading to the experience of communion with God. These psalms provide an appropriate closing to the book in illustrating how the psalmists' program to persuade God cultivated an appreciation for challenge, critical inquiry and self-discipline, all the elements of wisdom.

A Note on Translations

While I often compare multiple translations of key verses, all translations of the psalms are from Robert Alter's *The Book of Psalms: A Translation with Commentary*, copyright ©2007 by Robert Alter and used by permission of W.W. Norton & Company, Inc. More than any other translator, Alter conveys the poetry—the 'rhythmic compactness' and the sound patterns—of the Hebrew, without sacrificing accuracy or sensitivity to the historical, cultural and textual context. The *poetry* of the poetry is perhaps its most persuasive aspect. Jeffrey Walker attributes the 'psychagogic power' of poetry:

> to the bodily and subliminal effects of acoustic rhythm and even tonal quality acting on the central nervous system and/or the sheer aesthetic pleasure and sense of 'rightness' created by the skillful arousal, complication, and fulfillment of rhythmic and formal expectancies.[43]

For a book that I hope will attract readers with various backgrounds, translations that do full justice to the persuasive power of the psalms seem most appropriate.

Unless otherwise indicated, all other translations are reprinted from NJPS, *Tanakh: The Holy Scriptures* by permission of the University of Nebraska Press, copyright ©1985, 1999 by the Jewish Publication Society, Philadelphia.

---

43. Walker, *Rhetoric and Poetics*, p. 12.

Chapter 1

PRAISE AS DIVINE CURRENCY

The overwhelming purpose of the psalms is to praise God. Many psalms are designated in their superscriptions as תהלים *tehilim* 'praises'. The same root, הלל *hll*, recurs in the refrain הללויה *hallelu-yah*, 'praise God', that simultaneously expresses and commands praise from the multitudes. The psalms abound in verbs for praising: bless, declare, exalt, extol, honor, magnify, proclaim, shout, sing, speak, tell, and so on. In short, as Patrick Miller notes, 'praise is not one item on a long list of elements that belonged to the proper or normative prayer in the Old Testament, it is the very heart of the matter'.[1] The point is so obvious that we seldom question its underlying assumptions. Why is praise so important? Why does God need or desire praise? Doesn't omniscience render praise unnecessary for distinguishing the righteous from the wicked? While these theological questions go beyond the scope of this book, I contend that the psalms themselves provide important evidence of how ancient Israelites conceived of God's need for praise and how they leveraged praise to persuade God to intervene in their daily lives.

Many biblical scholars see the praise of ancient Israelites in psychological terms, as a natural, instinctive and perhaps irrepressible human outpouring of emotion, gratitude and awe. But Moshe Greenberg goes further to trace through the psalms a growing sophistication in how Israelites conceived of the divine, moving away from the beliefs of neighboring societies that the gods depended on sacrifices for nourishment and were susceptible to flattery. In Israel, Greenberg writes, 'prayer became a vehicle of humility, an expression of un-self-sufficiency, which, in biblical thought, is the proper stance of man before God'.[2] Pointing to psalms that rate sacrifice lower than public praise (e.g., Pss. 40.7-11, 50.13, 51.17, 69.31), Greenberg argues that, for Israelites, what God desires is the public proclamation of this dependency, for each person to publish abroad 'how he called

---

1. Patrick D. Miller, '"Enthroned on the Praises of Israel": The Praise of God in Old Testament Theology', *Int* 39 (1985), pp. 5-19 (6).
2. Moshe Greenberg, 'On the Refinement of the Conception of Prayer in Hebrew Scriptures', *AJS Review* 1 (1976), pp. 57-92 (90).

upon God in distress and how God heard and delivered him'.[3] The purpose of praise, as Greenberg sees it, is to shape and release the emotions of individual speakers and hearers; even when a psalm was composed long ago under different circumstances, the prayer 'gives shape to the feelings of later generations and conserves in them the values of the founders'.[4] In this view, composing psalms, delivering them in public, hearing or reading them, singing them or hearing them sung, reinforces the proper Israelite stance of humility and gratitude before God and perpetuates it by passing it down through the generations. Individuals devoted to praising God may strive to emulate God's qualities and cherish God's commandments, fostering lawful, ethical behavior and adherence to distinctly Israelite rituals and practices.

The idea that praise shores up a culture's traditional values is a familiar one for scholars of rhetoric, who use the term 'epideictic' for the public discourse of praise and blame. In Aristotle's formulation (from fourth century BCE Athens), *epideictic* rhetoric focuses on the current state of affairs whereas *forensic* rhetoric, the discourse of the courtroom, deals with arguments over what happened in the past, and *deliberative* rhetoric, the discourse of the legislature, deals with arguments about what should happen in the future.[5] For modern scholars, Aristotle's tidy formulation is flawed because it discounts epideictic relative to forensic and deliberative discourse; confines epideictic too narrowly to staged ceremonial occasions such as funerals, dedications of public spaces and pageants for victorious athletes or warriors; over-emphasizes showiness in epideictic speeches while downplaying their ideological impact; and positions the audience as passive spectators with nothing to decide on except the entertainment value of the speech and the virtues of its highly paid author.[6] In the ancient Greek democracy, audiences at epideictic ceremonies are less engaged than those in a courtroom or assembly because epideictic presents no issues for them to debate further and decide by means of a vote. Nothing vital seems to be at stake except for the prestige of the speaker and the size of the purse he or she can command.

The limited public situations in which epideictic occurred in ancient Greece, mainly formal ceremonial events, make epideictic seem less challenging than deliberative or forensic discourse. The art of persuasion lies

3. Greenberg, 'On the Refinement', p. 78.
4. Greenberg, 'On the Refinement', p. 89.
5. Aristotle, *On Rhetoric* 1358b.
6. For recent discussions see Jonathan Pratt, 'The Epideictic *Agōn* and Aristotle's Elusive Third Genre', *AJP* 133 (2012), pp. 177-208; Edward Schiappa and David M. Timmerman, 'Aristotle's Disciplining of Epideictic', in Edward Schiappa, *The Beginnings of Rhetorical Theory in Ancient Greece* (New Haven, CT: Yale University Press, 1999), pp. 185-206; Laurent Pernot, *Epideictic Rhetoric* (Austin: University of Texas Press, 2015).

in changing a hearer's attitudes, beliefs or actions, but little change seems needed in praising values that the society already accepts. As Jonathan Pratt puts it,

> The epideictic spectator is expected to have his mind made up, or, at the very least, to be inclined to go along with the speaker's every argument. His job is not, it would seem, to offer resistance. This being so, how could the auditor be said to exercise judgment at all? If nothing is easier than praising Athenians in Athens, as Plato's Socrates puts it, then what need is there for an art of epideictic rhetoric?[7]

The biggest risk for the speaker, according to Pratt, is being judged against speeches that others might have made or did make in similar situations: 'the *theoros* [spectator] decides among a single delivered speech and other, imagined or remembered speeches advancing the same thesis'.[8]

In ancient Israel, however, the range of public situations available for epideictic is broader and reveals more of its potential. Obviously, many psalms were performed in cultic situations in front of spectators, situations that called for what Claus Westermann designates as descriptive praise of God's essential nature.[9] As in Greek epideictic, hymnic psalms assume agreement on the ultimate value of the object of praise, namely God. These psalms are sometimes addressed to God directly and sometimes to the spectators, exhorting them to praise God. In either case, God serves both as the object of praise and as audience; it is God's judgment of the praise that counts. At stake is God's relationship with Israel because praise is one of the primary means whereby Israel maintains its status as a faithful partner in the covenant. As Pratt notes, 'Well-wrought praise enhances the status of giver and recipient alike, to the point of assimilating the former's words to the latter's deeds'.[10] Performing the psalms in public is both a faith activity and a spot of regular maintenance work, continually rehearsing the key values that must be adhered to by both parties to the covenant, God and the Israelites.

A more complex form of praise is offered in the first-person psalms, including what Westermann called declarative praise of God's actions on behalf of individuals. In ancient Israel, the course of an individual's life was taken to reflect his or her relations with God. Illness, defeat, failure

---

7. Pratt, 'The Epideictic *Agōn*', p. 190
8. Pratt, 'The Epideictic *Agōn*', p. 203. Archaic Greece did have some situations in which epideictic discourse from a variety of speakers was addressed to the object of praise: in private symposia, a potential lover might be solicited by a variety of suitors. For example, see Walker's discussion of the 'Speech of Lysias' in *Rhetoric and Poetics*, p. 146.
9. Claus Westermann, *Praise and Lament in the Psalms* (trans. Keith R. Crim and Richard N. Soulen; Atlanta, GA: John Knox Press, 1981).
10. Pratt, 'The Epideictic *Agōn*', p. 202.

and disgrace were taken as signs of God's punishment or at least abandonment. Therefore an Israelite's relationship with God was a matter of everyday concern; much was at risk. In good times, they took care to stay on good terms with God through freewill offerings, celebrating and maintaining the relationship with what scholars call 'psalms of trust', such as Psalm 23. If they got off track, they sought to regain their standing through purification rituals or expiation offerings; these rituals seem rarely to have been accompanied by psalms, though there are a few that plead for forgiveness, such as Psalm 38. The majority of first-person psalms either appeal to God for help or thank God for help received. The former, termed 'laments' or 'petitions', seek God's intervention in everyday affairs in times of conflict and in dire crises. At these times, all that Israelites have to offer in return for rescue is thanksgiving and praise. Laments promise future praise when rescue is secured; thanksgivings often describe a past crisis along with praise and gratitude for rescue.

This alternation from steady state to crisis to repair work, all via psalms, is what Walter Brueggemann terms orientation, disorientation and reorientation. Yet, even while he fully appreciates their psychological importance, Brueggemann finds laments and thanksgiving psalms more interesting than the orientation psalms,

> for there is in them no great movement, no tension to resolve. Indeed what mainly characterizes them is the absence of tension. The mind-set and world-view of those who enjoy a serene location of their lives is a sense of orderliness, goodness, and reliability of life.[11]

The goal of this chapter is to complicate this picture by demonstrating that Israelites placed little value on complacency and serenity; rather, even at the best of times, Israelite speakers are well aware of the precariousness of their paths and the need to use praise actively to maintain their balance. As a result, these psalms underscore a continuing need for engagement between individual Israelites and God. This point is developed by exploring two different senses in which Israelites treat praise as currency, the first in which praise is treated as a negotiable medium of exchange and the second in which praise extends a relationship that is current, that is timely, that is ever-present.

Praise as Negotiable Currency

In treating praise as a negotiable currency, speakers leverage God's need or desire for praise; on the one hand, they tender praise as a reason for God to help or save them; on the other hand, they threaten God with the cessation

---

11. Brueggemann, 'Psalms and the Life of Faith', p. 6.

or absence of praise. The threat is veiled but it is there and it is most palpable in a speaker's references to death, to wicked opponents and to God's world-wide reputation for justice and faithfulness.[12]

Death: Depriving God of Praise
For Israelites, the silence of the grave deprives God of praise. Like their neighbors in the ancient Near East, Israelites had a conception of an afterlife, though several of its qualities are unique. The dead reside without possessions or rank in a realm called Sheol where God has dominion but where the dead do not have access to God's presence and cannot communicate with God. This conception of death puts a premium on life both for God and for Israelites. As the following verses indicate, only the living can supply the praise that God needs or wants.

Ps. 6.6	For death holds no mention of You. In Sheol who can acclaim You?
Ps. 30.10	'What profit in my blood, in my going down deathward? Will dust acclaim You, will it tell Your truth?'
Ps. 88.11-13	Will You do wonders for the dead? Will the shades arise and acclaim You? [selah] Will Your kindness be told in the grave, Your faithfulness in perdition? Will your wonder be known in the darkness, Your bounty in the land of oblivion?
Ps. 115.17-18	The dead do not praise the LORD nor all who go down into silence. But we will bless Yah now and forevermore, hallelujah.

Death in these verses is not the terrifying danger or unfair punishment that it is elsewhere; instead death is what prevents God from receiving praise, from public oral celebration of God's truth, God's wonders, God's faithfulness, God's kindness. Thus the death of the speaker threatens God with the loss of praise. Of course the threat is stated indirectly in these verses—using the interrogative—because the speakers are addressing a far more powerful hearer.

The speakers in these passages do not claim that their praise has any unique quality, any special eloquence or insight or musicianship (though a case of this special pleading arises in Psalm 71, discussed later in this

12. In a similar analysis of several of this chapter's examples in her book, *Language, Power, and Identity in the Lament Psalms of the Individual* (New York: T. & T. Clark, 2008), Amy C. Cottrill argues that the relationship between God and the individual is one of patron and client. The client praises the patron to maintain the relationship, but turns to complaint/petition in times of trouble. The patron's reputation is at stake if the client is abandoned or treated shabbily. In addition to rhetorical theory, Cottrill draws on modern sociological studies. While I find her approach congenial to my own, Cottrill does not work out some of the limitations of the patron/client model, particularly the absence in Israelite culture of legitimate alternative patrons. She also tends to treat the psalms as a form of therapeutic 'role-playing' (p. 26), rather than as authentic discourse.

chapter). Rather, the speakers identify with all who perish. Perhaps claims for special eloquence were omitted because they would detract from the expected stance of humility. Perhaps they were excised in the reworking and reuse of a psalm. Or perhaps claims to eloquence didn't apply to a speaker who commissioned the psalm from a professional. In any case, the effect is a sense of egalitarianism; it is not that *this* speaker's praise is especially valuable to God but that the death of faithful Israelites in general is a loss, reducing the number of people capable of offering praise and thereby reducing the overall amount of praise.

Leveraging Praise as a quid pro quo
In addition to noting that the dead cannot praise, speakers also ask explicitly to be rescued in order to praise God, as in Pss. 51.16-17 and 9.14-15. Praise is the reason for God to act.

Ps. 51.16-17	Save me from bloodshed, O God, God of my rescue. Let my tongue sing out Your bounty. O Master, open my lips, that my mouth may tell Your praise.
Ps. 9.14-15	Grant me grace, O LORD, see my torment by my foes, You who raise me from the gates of death. So that I may tell all your praise in the gates of the Daughter of Zion. Let me exult in your rescue.

A bargain is also evident apart from references to death. The characteristic final promise of praise at the end of a lament 'always carries the inference of conditionality' as Ellen Davis notes in her analysis of Psalm 22.[13] Speakers also refer to praise as the repayment of a debt or fulfillment of a נדר ('vow'), as if praise was part of the price for God's protection or rescue. The terms of repayment are most blatant in Psalm 116, where the speaker at first seems to take God's response for granted because of how regularly God has responded to his call.

Ps. 116.1-2	I love the LORD for He has heard my voice, my supplications. For He has inclined His ear to me when in my days I called.
Ps. 116.12-14	What can I give back to the LORD for all He requited to me? The cup of rescue I lift and in the name of the LORD I call. My vows to the LORD I shall pay in the sight of all His people.
Ps. 116.17-19	To You I shall offer a thanksgiving sacrifice and in the name of the LORD I shall call. My vows to the LORD I shall pay in the sight of all His people, in the courts of the house of the LORD, in the midst of Jerusalem. Hallelujah.

---

13. Ellen F. Davis, 'Exploding the Limits: Form and Function in Psalm 22', *JSOT* 53 (1992), pp. 93-105 (100).

The speaker in Psalm 116 makes no great case for his innocence, righteousness or faithfulness as do other speakers (see Chapter 4). God's rescue, in other words, is not contingent on the speaker's special worthiness for rescue, but rather on a habitual system of give and take.[14]

Psalm 30.10 is especially daring in suggesting that God benefits in some material way from praise. The speaker asks מה בצע בדמי ('what profit') there is to God in the speaker's death. In the Hebrew Bible, the word בצע ('profit' or 'material gain') consistently has a negative connotation, associated with greed and covetousness. In Gen. 37.26, Judah asks his brothers the same question in order to convince them to sell Joseph to the Ishmaelites instead of killing him: מה בצע כי נהרג את אחינו ('what do we gain by killing our brother?') By analogy, in Ps. 30.10, God is urged to spare the innocent Joseph-like speaker and to top the behavior of Joseph's crass brothers who profited only in dollars-and-cents terms. As in other laments, the speaker appeals to God's better nature, calling on God to be worthy of the praise. In complex situations, where the merits of the speaker are not perfectly clear, the challenge to God's championship of justice becomes ever more explicit.

It would be a mistake to think of this quid pro quo as a primitive form of thinking. It is clear that the psalmists were not expecting God to respond in the form of a voice or lightning bolt from the heavens. Rather, Israelites interpreted God's response from subsequent events: those who see events turn in their favor go on to offer psalms of thanksgiving to God, while those whose troubles persist have the option to go on petitioning and lamenting, seeking even more persuasive ways to move God to respond. The important social and cultural element is crediting God for their success or failure rather than themselves or other human agents.

Contending with Other Israelites and Non-Believers
The corollary to the notion that God is deprived by the absence of praise is that God suffers from the opposite of praise: taunting and disbelief. Thus when the wicked taunt the afflicted Israelite, asking 'where is your God?' the insult serves multiple purposes. It documents the faithfulness of the speaker who persists in calling on God and it raises the stakes for God. If the wicked vanquish the speaker, his or her praise is stifled, replaced by an arrogant victor who is unlikely to provide any praise and it leaves unchallenged the taunt that God is faithless or tolerates injustice.

Ps. 13.4-5	Regard, answer me, LORD, my God. Light up my eyes, lest I sleep death, lest my enemy say, 'I've prevailed over him', lest my foes exult when I stumble.

14. I point to some ways in which this rather presumptuous speaker is taken down a peg or two in Charney, 'Performativity and Persuasion', pp. 247-68.

Ps. 42.11	With murder in my bones, my enemies revile me when they say to me all day long, 'Where is your God?'
Ps. 57.4	He will send from the heavens and rescue me—he who tramples me reviled me—God will send his steadfast kindness.[15]

Opponents appear often in the psalms. But our only knowledge of them comes through the lens of a far from disinterested speaker, who represents the situation to God as a simple exchange of praise for rescue of the only innocent and faithful person involved. But a much more interesting picture emerges from allowing for the very plausible situation that the speaker is locked in a dispute with other ordinary Israelites who might themselves have praise to offer. Rather than a hero and a villain, both sides may have some right on their side, both may have contributed to the trouble. Few scholars have recognized that the characters of both speaker and opponents remain arguable, preferring to see the opponents as aliens or as irredeemably wicked apostates. The psalms themselves do not highlight the competitive nature of the situation; only in a few cases, such as Psalms 35 and 55, does the opponent's status as an Israelite emerge clearly.

Speakers competing with other Israelites are apt, not surprisingly, to characterize opponents as incapable of true praise. The wicked do not simply do evil things; they are abhorrent because they reject God's values and their speech discredits God. They are arrogant, believing themselves to be self-sufficient, rock-steady and beyond God's reach; those who take responsibility for their own successes or failures have no reason to praise God.

Ps. 5.9-10	Guide me, O LORD, in your righteousness. On account of my foes, make my way straight before me. For there is nothing right in their mouths, within them—falsehood. An open grave their throat, their tongue, smooth-talking.
Ps. 10.3-7	For the wicked did vaunt in his very lust, grasping for gain—cursed, blasphemed the LORD. The wicked sought not in his towering wrath—'There is no God' is all his schemes. His ways are uncertain in every hour, Your judgments are high above him. All his foes he enflames. He said in his heart, 'I will not stumble, for all time I will not come to harm'. His mouth is full of oaths, beneath his tongue are guile and deceit, mischief, and misdeed.
Ps. 28.3	Do not pull me down with the wicked and with the wrongdoers who speak peace to their fellows with foulness in their hearts.
Ps. 54.5	For strangers have risen against me, and oppressors have sought my life. They did not set God before them.

---

15. Paul Raabe notes concerning this verse that the direct object of 'revile' is unstated, leaving it ambiguous whether it is the speaker or God whom the enemy is reviling. See Raabe's 'Deliberate Ambiguity in the Psalter', *JBL* 110 (1991), pp. 213-27 (220).

The opponents' words are not to be trusted; they lie in giving false reports of the speaker or speak fair words aloud but foul words in their hearts. In characterizing their opponents in these terms, the speakers seek to narrow God's options. Only rescue of the speaker insures praise.

Psalm 71: Extending the Supply of Praise

All Israelites of course are mortal and therefore the eventual silencing of each individual Israelite is inevitable. Insuring an endless supply of praise, therefore, requires the perpetuation of the people of Israel over time. Accordingly special potency accrues to promises to extend the number of praise-givers beyond the individual speaker, as in the closing section of Psalm 22.

> Ps. 22.23-24, 31-32 Let me tell Your name to my brothers, in the assembly let me praise You. Fearers of the LORD, O praise Him! All the seed of Jacob revere Him! ... My seed will serve Him. It will be told to generations to come. They will proclaim His bounty to a people aborning, for He has done.

Here the speaker moves from expressing his own praise to exhorting praise from his family, the larger tribe, the children of Jacob, other nations and generations to come.

The potency of extending praise to future generations comes to its fullest expression in Psalm 71. The speaker argues that he is worthy of rescue because of his life-long history as an exemplary praise-giver, a practice that he wants to continue to perpetuate to future generations.

PSALM 71[16]

1   In You, O LORD, I shelter. Let me never be shamed.
2   Through Your bounty save me and free me. Incline Your ear to me and rescue me.
3   Be for me a fortress-dwelling to come into always. You ordained to rescue me, for You are my rock and my bastion.
4   My God, free me from the hand of the wicked, from the grip of the wicked and the violent.
5   For You are my hope, Master, O LORD, my refuge since youth.
6   Upon You I relied from birth. From my mother's womb You brought me out. To You is my praise always.
7   An example I was to the many, and You are my sheltering strength.
8   May my mouth be filled with Your praise, all day long Your glory.

---

16. Robert Alter, *The Book of Psalms: A Translation and Commentary* (New York: W.W. Norton, 2010), pp. 244-47.

9   Do not fling me away in old age, as my strength fails, do not forsake me.
10 For my enemies said of me, who stalk me counseled together,
11 saying, 'God has forsaken him. Pursue and catch him, for no one will save him'.
12 God, do not keep far from me. My God, hasten to my help!
13 May my accusers be shamed, may they perish [my life's opponents]—may they be clothed with shame and reproach who seek my harm.
14 As for me, I shall always hope and add to all Your praise.
15 My mouth will recount Your bounty, all day long Your rescue, for I know not numbers.
16 I shall come in the power of the Master, the Lord. I shall call to mind Your bounty—You only.
17 God, You have taught me since my youth and till now I have told Your wonders.
18 And even in hoary old age, O God, do not forsake me. Till I tell of your mighty arm to the next generation, to all those who will come, Your power,
19 and Your bounty, O God, to the heights, as You have done great things, O God, who is like You?
20 As you surfeited me with great and dire distress, You will once more give me life, and from the earth's depths once more bring me up.
21 You will multiply my greatness and turn round and comfort me.
22 And so I shall acclaim You with the lute.—Your truth, my God. Let me hymn You with the lyre, Israel's Holy One.
23 My lips will sing glad song when I hymn to You, and my being that You ransomed.
24 My tongue, too, all day long will murmur Your bounty. For they are shamed, for they are disgraced, those who sought my harm.

Psalm 71 has been relatively neglected by scholars; some downgrade its originality, pointing to the numerous passages that echo or are echoed in other psalms.[17] However, when seen as part of an overall strategy to leverage the availability of praise, these repetitions actually strengthen the persuasiveness of the psalm.

The structure of the psalm, as shown in Figure 1.1, consists of six sections of about four verses each. As in most petitionary psalms, the speaker's first task is to address the hearer, God, in terms that will capture attention and foster a positive attitude. In this case, the address in vv. 1-4 encapsulates the main argument: the speaker's past reliance on God as a refuge supports his worthiness for current and future rescue.

---

17. Hans-Joachim Kraus tries to present this intertextual aspect of Psalm 71 in a positive light, yet he persists in taking it as a kind of 'prayer formulary with which a definite type of oppressed person was able to bring his distress and petition before Yahweh'. See H.-J. Kraus, *Psalms 60–150* (trans. H.C. Oswald; Minneapolis: Augsburg Fortress, 1989), p. 72.

1-4	*Address:* Plea to God for attention and rescue
5-9	*Past praise:* Reminder of reliance on and praise of God, from birth to old age
10-13	Denunciation of opponents
14-16	*Future praise:* Promise of constant, exclusive faith and public praise in own life
17-19	Future praise in days to come: Promise to train next generation to praise
20-24	*Current praise*: Promise to sing praise now in response to rescue and humiliation of opponents.

Figure 1.1. *Structure of Psalm 71*

As the structure suggests, all but one of the sections after the address catalog the stages of life during which the speaker has praised, does praise and will praise God. This lifetime of experience is of value to God both because the speaker has extended praise to others in his own circle during his lifetime and because the speaker promises to raise new generations of praise-givers. The centrality of praise is underscored by the progression of different verb forms for the act of praising that plays out across the sections.

In the second section, vv. 5-9, the speaker reminds God that their relationship began at the moment of the speaker's birth and that, since then, he has stood out for his praise of God. The speaker's praise תהילתי ('my praise') has only been directed to God in v. 6. In v. 7, the speaker characterizes himself as a good influence on others in describing himself as מופת ('an example') to many. The term מופת is usually used in the context of God's miraculous 'signs and wonders'. The only other people to whom it is applied are the prophets Isaiah and Ezekiel.[18] In the context of Psalm 71, then, the speaker claims to be modeling the type of relationship of protection and praise that the whole nation should emulate. He prays or predicts that his mouth will always be filled with תהילתך ('your praise') and תפארתך ('your glory') in v. 8.

The only obstacles are the speaker's old age (v. 9) and the looming threat from opponents, described in the third section, vv. 10-13. As usual, the opponents are depicted as mortal enemies taunting the speaker. The public standing of these antagonists is a zero-sum game: either the speaker or the opponents must remain shamed and reviled or die.

The fourth section, vv. 14-16, uses a new set of praise terms to signal that the speaker's response to rescue from the current threat will surpass his previous efforts. The speaker promises in succession הוספתי את כל תהילתך ('add to all your praise') to elaborate or extend the amount of praise (v. 14), יספר צדקתך ('recount your bounty') to list out or enumerate your bounty to

18. Isa. 8.18, 20.3 and Ezek. 12.6, 12.11, 24.24, 24.27. The term מופת is sometimes taken negatively as a 'portent' to reflect the speaker's history of troubles from opponents. For example, Kraus (*Psalms 60–150*, p. 72). See also Bill Blackburn, 'Psalm 71', *RevExp* 88 (1991), pp. 241-45.

others (v. 15), and אזכיר צדקתך ('call to mind your bounty'), to cause oneself or more likely others to remember your bounty or justice.

The fifth section, vv. 17-19, spells out the promise to train future generations to praise God in the same lifelong way from birth to old age, using praise terms that connote declaring, publishing or making known. The speaker has אגיד נפלאותיך ('told of your wonders') and asks for his life to be extended in order to אגיד זרועך לדור ('tell of your mighty arm to the next generation') and לכל יבוא גבורתך ('your power to all who will come').

Finally, the sixth section, vv. 20-24, shows off the speaker's musical powers, promising to thank God for rescue from the current crisis with songs of thanks, אודך בכלי נבל ('acclaim you with the lute') and לך בכנור אזמרה ('hymn you with the lyre') (v. 22), to use lips and tongue in song, תרננה שפתי ('my lips will sing glad songs') (v. 23) and כל היום תהגה צדקתך לשוני ('my tongue, too, all day long will murmur Your bounty'). The progression of types of praise reaches its crescendo at the conclusion, leading to the downfall of the foes. In the end, the speaker aggrandizes his own abilities as a singer of praise in order to convince God that it is worthwhile to preserve his life.[19]

Psalm 71, then, takes praise as both its subject and as its most persuasive tactic. As Susan Stewart notes of all poems of praise, praise is a gift that adds glory to its subject by its very incapacity to exhaust the possibilities of praise: 'Praise is affirmative—it reveals, augments, and at the same time creates surpluses in excess of what it discloses.'[20] A poem of praise, like Psalm 71, fulfills its promise as it continues to be published and performed and as it resonates with representations of other texts, old and new. As Stewart puts it, 'the ode gathers an accumulating knowledge in time; it makes absent things present by recalling them rather than by manifesting them'. In this way, the reuse of verses from other psalms adds to rather than detracts from the power of Psalm 71.

Ancient Israelites use the provision of praise to position themselves in advantageous ways relative to God whom they assume to be shaping a dynamic ongoing relationship with their community. At stake in most first-person psalms is an individual's personal relationship with God, on whom the individual relies for health, security and happiness. As suggested

---

19. The lack of specific identifying information about either the author or the speaker in the psalms (leaving aside the superscriptions) is a stark contrast to the attribution of texts in ancient Greece where, as David Carr notes, 'the authority of cultural texts often seems to reside in the authorial personages themselves: Homer, Hesiod, Aeschylus, and other key poets'. See David Carr, *Writing on the Tablet of the Heart: Origins of Scripture and Literature* (Oxford: Oxford University Press, 2005), p. 107.

20. Susan Stewart, 'What Praise Poems are For', *PMLA* 120 (2005), pp. 235-45 (236).

thus far, the relationship can be viewed in some sense as the exchange of protection for praise.

The psalms thus have all the characteristics of epideictic discourse. They are performed in public settings, they reinforce and transmit key cultural values, they center on praise (of God) and blame (of opponents), and they aim to change the hearers' judgments of the current worthiness of the speaker. However the audience is more complicated than that of ancient Greek epideictic. The psalms are directly addressed to God, to whom is attributed the ultimate power to judge, help or ignore the speaker. But they are performed before human spectators, who have the practical power to shun or support the speaker. Public praise from a speaker therefore serves notice to assorted listeners (probably including opponents)—'I'm not finished. You'd better hedge your bets, don't give up on me yet. God hasn't.' The relationships between individual Israelites and God are complex, depending on the individual's personal circumstances and standing in the community. Both the human and divine audiences, in this non-judicial setting, may be persuaded to reserve, pass or reconsider their judgments.

Praise as a Charged Current

One of the most significant ways in which the psalms enrich the rhetorical notion of epideictic discourse is in stretching out the concept of the present or the current moment. In Aristotle's conception of the forums for rhetoric, forensic (judicial) and deliberative (policy) discourse were bounded in episodes that led to an immediate decision or judgment: determining whether a crime was committed by a defendant in court or deciding what military actions to take in the near future toward a foreign power. In contrast, epideictic discourse—outside the context of a speaking contest—did not lead to a decision or action by the audience. The hearers might reflect on the speaker's eloquence; they might decide to give a response. But the occasion did not demand resolution or action. For this reason, epideictic discourse came to be seen as merely ceremonial and lacking in social import.

The Israelite timeframe in the psalms is not bounded into discrete episodes. Praise keeps the current flowing in the continual present. Praising God keeps the relationship current across an individual's lifespan and along the lifespan of the community and, with it, the cultural and ethical values that it explicitly celebrates. The positive value is not all on one side. It is because God needs praise that God needs to be praiseworthy—and must not tolerate injustice, allow loyal innocents to be persecuted or abandon the nation to utter destruction. The threats to the relationship are legion, from temptations to assimilate to neighboring cultures to the daily disappointments of inevitable suffering and loss. Praise must be continual because, as Chaïm Perelman and Lucie Olbrechts-Tyteca describe the epideictic speaker in *The New Rhetoric*: 'the one who by speaking wishes to strengthen established values may be likened to the guardian of dikes under constant assault by the ocean'.[21]

Unlike dikes, however, Israelites were expected to have some resilience and capacity for adaptation. The psalms discussed in the remainder of this chapter suggest that the most desirable quality in a speaker is not fixity but changeability, not complacency but openness to refinement, not imperviousness to temptation but recalibration back to the right path.

Psalm 16: Balancing with God's Guidance

Psalm 16 depicts what might be considered the paradigm case of epideictic discourse, a case of an ordinary person using a psalm to keep up good relations with God. The speaker affirms God as the source of all the good that has come his way and requests God to keep him securely on the right path. A closer look, however, reveals the speaker's awareness of the play of chance.

PSALM 16[22]

A David *michtam*

1 Guard me, O God, for I shelter in You.
2 I said to the LORD, 'My Master You are. My good is only through You'.
3 As to holy ones in the land and the mighty who were all my desire,
4 let their sorrows abound—another did they betroth. I will not pour their libations of blood, I will not bear their names on my lips.
5 The LORD is my portion and lot, it is You Who sustain[s] my fate.
6 An inheritance fell to me with delight, my estate too, is lovely to me.
7 I shall bless the LORD Who gave me counsel through the nights that my conscience would lash me.
8 I set the LORD always before me, on my right hand, that I not stumble.
9 So my heart rejoices and my pulse beats with joy, my whole body abides secure.
10 For You will not forsake my life to Sheol, You won't let your faithful one see the Pit.
11 Make me know the path of life. Joys overflow in Your presence, delights in Your right hand forever.

To support his worthiness for this response, the speaker immediately identifies himself with God in vv. 1-2 in three ways: first, in v. 1, by declaring that he trusts God: 'I shelter in You'; then in v. 2, by making a performative statement of allegiance that invokes God's name; and, third, by denying that he receives good from anywhere else. Developing and supporting this latter claim—that God is the speaker's only source of goodness—occupies the rest of the psalm.

---

21. Perelman and Olbrechts-Tyteca, *The New Rhetoric*, pp. 54-55.
22. Alter, *The Book of Psalms*, pp. 45-47.

In vv. 3-4, the speaker describes the alternative sources of good that he has rejected, those stemming from powerful inhabitants of the land on whom the speaker had previously set his desires.[23] Perhaps the speaker lives in a region with many nearby pagan communities and was tempted to ally himself with them. But because they espouse alien gods, the speaker now wishes their sorrows to multiply. The speaker declines even to name their gods, let alone to make blood libations to them. While this choice is described in definite and even absolute terms, what emerges from the rest of the psalm is a sense of the chanciness and uncertainty of any decision or aspect of life.

In vv. 5-6, the speaker affirms that it is God who controls whatever chance befalls him and describes the good that has come to him in his inheritance and heritage. The chanciness of such bequests is emphasized by words related to casting lots: the nouns חלקי וכוסי ('my portion and lot'), or more literally 'my portion and my cup', the noun גורלי ('my fate'), and the verb נפלו ('fell'). According to Anne Marie Kitz, the Near Eastern root in גורלי ('my fate') refers to stones and וכוסי ('my cup') may refer to the receptacle from which they were cast.[24] In her study of practices across the Near East and Greece, Kitz distinguishes between drawing lots and casting lots to decide how to allocate property: 'Lot casting, it appears, was executed when the deity, who was the actual or implied owner of the items, had the right to determine which person was to receive a particular parcel.'[25] In Ps. 16.6, the speaker says חבלים נפלו לי ('an inheritance fell to me'), with a phrase that literally describes how the ropes that mark the boundaries of a land-holding happened to fall.[26] Of course, the terms for inheritance and heritage refer both to physical property and metaphorically to the speaker's role within Israelite tradition. The speaker emphasizes in v. 6 the pleasant and desirable qualities of what has befallen him.

The image of chance also pervades the next verses, vv. 7-8, which are perhaps intended to explain how the speaker achieved his present favorable state. Having admitted some attraction to the mighty who hastened to other gods (v. 3), the speaker blesses God for counseling him through

---

23. While Alter and NJPS treat the 'holy ones' as idolators, other translators and commentators have tried to interpret them positively. For a review of the argument that supports the idolator reading, see Hendrick G.L. Peels, 'Sanctorum communio vel idolorum repudiatio? A Reconsideration of Psalm 16,3', *ZAW* 112 (2000), pp. 239-51.

24. Anne Marie Kitz, 'The Hebrew Terminology of Lot Casting and its Ancient Near Eastern Context', *CBQ* 62 (2000), pp. 207-14. For a similar view, see Walter Brueggemann and William H. Bellinger, Jr, *Psalms* (New York: Cambridge University Press, 2014), p. 87.

25. Kitz, 'Hebrew Terminology', p. 208.

26. The word חבלים (ropes) is used elsewhere in the same sense of land boundaries (Pss. 78.55; 105.11). But its other uses imply life's chanciness: it refers to life-threatening troubles in Pss. 18.5-6; 116.3; 119.61 and 140.6.

troubled thoughts (perhaps lingering temptation) during the night. In v. 7, the word כליותי ('conscience') literally refers to the speaker's kidneys, in Israelite psychology the seat of emotions and affections. Just as the stones in a cup are agitated for casting lots, the speaker's feelings are conflicted in the night; just as God made the lots fall the right way in the allocation of land, so God guides the speaker יעצני ('counseled me') at night to come down on the right side. The decision process involved here, however, is not random or devoid of reason. Rather the image is one of persuasion, with God serving as advisor or guide.

In addition to heeding God's guidance at night, in v. 8, the speaker relies on God as physical guide by day so that he will not stumble or be pulled off-course. The path the speaker is following is literally precarious: he could fall either way. So in v. 8 the speaker chooses to steer by God, setting God simultaneously לנגדי ('before me') and מימיני ('on my right') hand. Following that path leads to a sense of physical security expressed in vv. 9-11 that will preserve the speaker throughout a long life.

In Psalm 16, then, the speaker develops a detailed argument supporting his past, current and future commitment to following God's path as the only way to achieve what is good. The argument is epideictic in focusing on his or her current state of being, a state best characterized as a balancing act on a narrow bridge. The speaker is not arguing to change this state, recognizing that temptations, doubts and chances will always be present, whether from neighbors, unexpected bequests or desires surfacing at night in dreams. In all these circumstances, the speaker attests to seeking and following divine guidance. This is a psalm composed by or for a clear-eyed realist, not an unshakable pietist.

Psalm 26: Ongoing Refinement

Psalm 26 goes even further than Psalm 16 in challenging the notion that the psalms of trust express serenity and unmixed confidence. Rather, the speaker in Psalm 26 invites God to judge, test, try and purify him in an ongoing, life-long process.

PSALM 26[27]

1   For David. Judge me, O LORD. For I have walked in my wholeness, and the LORD I have trusted. I shall not stumble.
2   Test me, O LORD, and try me. Burn pure my conscience and my heart.
3   For Your kindness is before my eyes and I shall walk in Your truth.
4   I have not sat with lying folk nor with furtive men have dealt.
5   I despised the assembly of evildoers, nor with the wicked have I sat.

---

27. Alter, *The Book of Psalms*, pp. 88-90.

6   Let me wash my palms in cleanness and go round Your altar, LORD,
7   to utter aloud a thanksgiving and to recount all Your wonders.
8   LORD, I love the abode of Your house and the place where Your glory dwells.
9   Do not take my life's breath with offenders nor with blood-guilty men my life,
10 in whose hands there are plots, their right hand full of bribes.
11 But I shall walk in my wholeness. Redeem me, grant me grace.
12 My foot stands on level ground. In the chorus I bless the LORD.

Psalm 26 has stirred longstanding scholarly debate as to both structure and setting. Paul Mosca, who himself champions rhetorical analysis of the psalms, reviews the debate and proposes a five-part structure that I adopt in Figure 1.2 with my own description of each part.[28] This structure reveals an outer frame in which the speaker describes a state of unity with God, walking with wholeness or integrity, without stumbling (vv. 1-3) and on steady ground (vv. 11-12). Within the frame are two passages describing the speaker's relationship to evil-doers, deliberately avoiding them in vv. 4-5 and requesting God not to lump him in with them in vv. 9-10. Between these (vv. 6-8) comes a passage describing the actions the speaker takes at the Temple and his attitude toward God's house.

1-3	I request God's purification and wholeness
4-5	I reject temptations from others
6-8	I value the state of purity in God's proximity
9-10	I seek to avoid the fate of others
11-12	I request redemption, grace, and wholeness

Figure 1.2. *Structure of Psalm 26*

In Mosca's reading, the speaker of the psalm is a Kohen, a Levitical priest descended from Aaron with official duties at the Temple, who is privately praying for God to acknowledge both his physical and moral integrity.[29] Mosca bases his claim in vv. 6-8, where the speaker appears to have access to the inner court of the Temple and the copper laver in which priests are commanded to wash before carrying out a ritual. Physical integrity is as important as moral integrity because blemishes or handicaps would disqualify a priest from certain offices. The threat of death raised in vv. 9-10,

---

28. Paul G. Mosca, 'Psalm 26: Poetic Structure and the Form-Critical Task', *CBQ* 47 (1985), pp. 212-37.

29. Mosca's reading is compatible in most ways with Craig Broyles's reading of Psalm 26 as a ritual for establishing worthiness for a priest or pilgrim to enter the Temple vicinity on analogy with Psalm 15 and Psalm 24. See Broyles, 'Psalms Concerning Temple Entry', in Peter W. Flint and Patrick D. Miller (eds.), *Book of Psalms: Composition and Reception* (VTSup, 109; Leiden: Brill, 2005), pp. 248-87.

Mosca argues, comes from the risks associated with conducting sacrificial rites in proximity to the altar. Mosca acknowledges one difficulty for this reading. In v. 7, the speaker promises to לשמע בקול ('utter aloud a thanksgiving') and to ולספר ('recount') God's wonders. However, many scholars believe that it was only the non-priestly Levites who proclaimed and sang psalms, while the Kohanim conducted their rituals in silence.[30] To deal with this difficulty, Mosca proposes grammatical emendations to the two verbs to indicate that the speaker does not utter or recount himself but merely listens in to the proclamations of others while performing his work.

The first verse of the psalm, I argue, is not actually an assertion of the speaker's wholeness but rather part of a series of requests for God to try him and, in fact, to purify him. The term בתומי 'in my wholeness' in v. 1 conveys sincerity more than actual innocence.[31]

The possibility of sin is deepened by the three imperative verbs in Ps. 26.2: בחנני ('test me'), נסני ('try me') and צרופה ('burn pure'). All three derive from the context of metallurgy, where ore is tested for the presence of impurities or refined through smelting to separate out the impurities. The metallurgic connotation is explicit in other psalms, for example כסף צרוף ('silver purged') occurs in Ps. 12.7 and an explicit comparison between בחן ('try') and צרף ('refine') occurs in Ps. 66.10:

Ps. 12.7   The words of the LORD are pure words, silver purged in an earthen crucible, refined sevenfold.

Ps. 66.10   You have tried us, O God, refining us as one refines silver.

The use of these verbs suggests that the speaker is not asserting complete innocence or calling for vindication against false accusations, but rather volunteering for a process of purification and refinement. Part of the process of testing includes making fair judgments of the quality of some material. The theme of equity is also conveyed in v. 2 by the objects of the testing לבי ('my heart') which in Biblical Hebrew describes the seat of understanding and כליותי ('my kidneys') translated here (as in Ps. 16.7) as 'conscience'. Testing these two organs provides a way for God to decide how to give to each person his or her due, for example as reported by the prophet Jeremiah (see also Jer. 11.20 and 20.12):

Jer. 17.10 I the LORD probe the heart, search the mind—to repay every man according to his ways, with the proper fruit of his deeds.

---

30. See Israel Knohl, 'Between Voice and Silence: The Relationship between Prayer and Temple Cult', *JBL* 115 (1996), pp. 17-30.

31. The same term תם 'integrity' is used to protest a lack of evil intent or even awareness of sinning in Gen. 20.5-6, 2 Sam. 15.11 and 1 Kgs 22.34.

NJPS translates כליות ('kidneys') here as 'mind'. The key implication is that the process of refinement can be long and difficult. When elements are mixed together, the outcome of the test at any given time is uncertain; any given material does not simply pass or fail the test. Rather it is rated along some scale of purity. On the millesimal fineness scale for silver, even sterling silver contains 75 parts per thousand of copper or other metals. Across a human lifetime, it is unavoidable for those who act in innocence to become impure or contaminated, even unknowingly.

In light of this reading, the speaker's effort to dissociate himself from evil-doers takes on special meaning. The speaker needs to persuade God to continue the refinement process—or perhaps to set the quality standard with mercy and graciousness—because otherwise God is liable to reject him and count him among the wicked. In vv. 4-5, the speaker describes efforts to avoid contamination by staying away from the wicked. The force of vv. 6-8 may simply be an affirmation of the kinds of speech and actions that contrast most with those of the evil-doers, namely offering sacrifices and praising God. In vv. 9-10, the speaker pleads with God to treat him differently from the wicked, using the imperative אל תאסף ('do not take'), or more literally 'do not gather', his life's breath with that of the wicked.

The final section vv. 11-12 continues the theme of evaluation, with the speaker, walking in his state of wholeness, asking to be redeemed and treated with graciousness. The test facing the speaker is the continual need to live in the midst of evil, with the knowledge of his own impurities and with the uncertainty of God's judgment. These ordinary conditions of life are even suggested by the positive and negative associations that the speaker gives to finding himself in assemblies or congregations. In v. 5, the speaker declares his hatred for קהל מרעים ('the assembly of evildoers'); yet in v. 12 the speaker situates himself among others במקהלים ('in the chorus'), engaged in blessing God. The speaker's declaration at the end of v. 1, לא אמעד ('I will not stumble'), seems a play on the word אעמד ('I will stand'), conveying the speaker's awareness of just how possible it is to slip.

In this alternative reading, the speaker of Psalm 26 is another realist aware of the unavoidable presence of evil or impurity, who seeks to persuade God to continue the ongoing process of purging and refinement that any faithful person must undergo.

Psalm 131: Bragging on Quietism

Any theory of epideictic discourse that situates the audience in judgment of the speaker leaves open the possibility of a negative judgment, even though evidence is scarce that such critiques were ever leveled in ancient Greece. However, one psalm of trust, Psalm 131, contrasts so strongly with the rest in its construction and values that I believe it represents a minority view that the psalmists did not favor.

PSALM 131[32]

1   A song of ascents for David. LORD, my heart has not been haughty, nor have my eyes looked too high, nor have I striven for great things too wondrous for me.

2   But I have calmed and contented myself like a weaned babe on its mother—like a weaned babe I am with myself.

3   Wait, O Israel, for the LORD, now and forevermore.

The speaker in Psalm 131 depicts himself in a state of complete harmony. In v. 1, he disavows arrogance, ambition and even curiosity, declaring that he stays away from גדלות ונפלאות ('great things too wondrous') for him and asserting the absence of these qualities from his לבי ('heart'), עיני ('eyes') and הלכתי ('walk'). In v. 2, the speaker uses positive terms to declare that he has actively sought the opposite qualities, calming and contenting his נפשי ('entire being'). The term שויתי ('calmed') conveys laying even or still; in addition to stillness, the term דוממתי ('contented') also conveys the sense of silencing or keeping mum. From a state of such stillness, it is fitting that this humble speaker can only advise other Israelites to wait as well in v. 3. The speaker takes on exactly those traits of 'un-self-sufficiency' that Moshe Greenberg described as 'the proper stance of man before God'.[33]

What is most striking about this brief psalm—among the briefest in the book of Psalms—is that it contains no thanksgivings, no petitions and no praise. Its positive and negative claims are expressed poetically with parallelism of sounds and syntax but they are not developed with either restatement or supporting observations and reasons. Lack of elaboration may be a sign of confidence in the audience's support and assent, a possibility that will be raised in Chapter 3 in the cases of Psalms 13 and 54. And in fact this positive view is the one most scholars have taken toward Psalm 131. Phil Botha lauds it, saying that it 'must certainly be one of the most beautiful poems ever written'.[34] Robert Alter agrees that the expression of humility is 'simple, concise, and affecting'.[35] Dave Bland conjectures that the speaker's 'childlike' trust is a return to innocence: after having been restless and proud, the psalmist achieves 'victory over frivolous ambition' and becomes calm, composed, content, submissive and silent.[36]

---

32. Alter, *The Book of Psalms*, p. 457.
33. Greenberg, 'On the Refinement', p. 90.
34. Phil J. Botha, 'To Honour Yahweh in the Face of Adversity: A Socio-Critical Analysis of Psalm 131', *Skrif En Kerk* 19 (1998), pp. 525-33 (525).
35. Alter, *The Book of Psalms*, p. 457.
36. Dave Bland, 'Exegesis of Psalm 62', *ResQ* 23 (1980), pp. 82-95 (86).

But a soul employing brevity is not always a wit; set against Psalms 16 and 26, the speaker in Psalm 131 seems an extraordinarily passive person with little to say for himself. In this case, perhaps the lack of elaboration signals deficiency. This is a speaker who currently has a quiet unchanging life and wants to keep it that way. Certainly the quest to attain knowledge can be dangerously agitating. But avoiding great and wondrous things is not necessarily a good thing; it may even imply staying apart from the divine. The source of the 'great' (גדל) and the 'wondrous' (נפלא) is God, as the speaker declares in Ps. 86.10.

Ps. 86.10   For You are great and work wonders. You alone are God.

The reluctance of the speaker in Psalm 131 to attain knowledge is not echoed in other psalms. For example, the speaker in Ps. 139.6 describes God's scope of knowledge as beyond him but does not denigrate the effort to attain it; he goes on in Ps. 139.14 to acknowledge himself, as a creature of humanity, as one of these works.

Ps. 139.6   Knowledge is too wondrous for me, high above—I cannot attain it.
Ps. 139.14   I acclaim You, for awesomely I am set apart, wondrous are Your acts, and my being deeply knows it.
Ps. 111.2   Great are the deeds of the LORD, discovered by all who desire them.

In the same vein, Ps. 111.2 emphasizes that those who delight in God's great deeds actively seek or inquire into them.

Additional grounds for a critical or at least ambivalent stance toward the speaker of Psalm 131 derives from the use of the verb דוממתי ('I contented myself') in v. 2 without any elaboration of the context. In the Hebrew Bible and especially in other psalms, the verb has both positive and negative connotations. The positive connotation of becoming contented, stilled or self-contained also occurs in three other psalms, Pss. 4.5, 62.5 and 37.7.

Ps. 4.5   Quake, and do not offend. Speak in your hearts on your beds, and be still.
Ps. 62.5   Only in God be quiet, my being, for from Him is my hope.
Ps. 37.7   Be still before the LORD and await Him. Do not be incensed by him who prospers, by the man who devises schemes.

In Psalm 4, those who stray from faithfulness are advised to fight temptation until they become still. In Psalm 62, the speaker who is faithful contrasts his own stillness with the shakiness of those who stray.[37] In Ps. 37.7, still-

---

37. Psalms 4 and 62 are treated in more detail in Chapter 2.

ness as a sign of faithful patience is advised for those agitated by the injustice of the wicked.

At times, however, the state described as stillness is portrayed as inappropriate, particularly when it suppresses either praise of God or challenge of iniquity. In Ps. 30.12, the speaker promises לא ידם ('I will not be still') but instead will praise God. Similarly, to document his integrity, Job demands to know whether he was ever so scared that he ואדם ('ke[pt] silence') in the face of wickedness, especially his own.

Ps. 30.12   O, let my heart hymn You and be not still, LORD, my God, for all time I acclaim You.

Job 31.33-34   Did I hide my transgressions like Adam, bury my wrongdoing in my bosom, That I should [now] fear the great multitude, and am shattered by the contempt of families, so that I keep silent and do not step outdoors?

Seen from a critical standpoint, the speaker in Psalm 131 comes across as someone who can only rouse himself enough to deny any semblance of ambition and to celebrate the successful reduction of his soul to a state of helpless dependence. By risking nothing, he achieves no triumphs and avoids making enemies. As a result, he feels insufficient gratitude to explicitly praise or give thanks and feels insufficient grievance at injustice or danger to require a lament.

From a state of stillness, the speaker can only advise others in v. 3 to wait. The paucity of this advice is highlighted by the use of a nearly identical verse at the conclusion of the adjacent Psalm 130, which offers much more, an abundance of loving-kindness and redemption.

Ps. 130.7   Wait O Israel for the LORD, for with the LORD is steadfast kindness, and great redemption is with Him.

The strong implication of the contrast of similar and neighboring psalms is that asking for nothing much gains nothing much. It is not surprising that the Israelite population included those with a certain degree of passivity. But in its very brevity, Psalm 131 could be signaling that such passivity is far from normative or even ideal for Israelites.

Chapter 2

INSTRUCTIONS FOR KEEPING FAITH

In this chapter I bring together three psalms, Psalms 4, 62 and 82, that have not previously been seen as similar. The speakers in these psalms devote unusual attention to other people rather than God, a feature that has generated some debate about the setting of Psalm 4 but that has been generally overlooked in Psalm 62. In only five first-person psalms does a speaker directly address opponents at any length: Psalms 52 and 58, Psalms 4 and 62, and Psalm 82. In Psalms 52 and 58 the speaker's direct address takes the form of 'shock and awe': The opponents are rebuked, reminded of God's might and threatened with complete destruction. Psalms 4 and 62, however, move beyond rebukes to offering advice for returning to faithful or moral practice. Psalm 82 is unique not only because the speaker is God addressing an assembly of deities, but because God offers advice before threatening destruction. I will argue for viewing all three psalms as public efforts by confident speakers to persuade skeptical or immoral hearers to return to moral behavior.

Two Pieces of Rhetorical Theory:
Amplitude and Identification

In modern times, the scope of rhetorical theory has broadened beyond the classical venues of courts, legislatures, sanctuaries and civic ceremonials to all occasions for public or professional discourse. In order for a situation to be a rhetorical situation, a speaker must experience a sense of exigence or urgency that can be productively addressed with language.[1] The speaker fashions language into a spoken or written text and delivers it in such a way as to influence a set of hearers/readers who have some ability to affect the situation and perhaps ameliorate the urgency.

Much of rhetorical theory focuses on the challenges of addressing diverse audiences, a topic raised by two of the most important twentieth-century

---

1. For discussions of whether rhetorical situations simply arise or are constructed, see Lloyd Bitzer, 'The Rhetorical Situation', *Philosophy and Rhetoric* 1 (1968), pp. 1-14 and Scott Consigny, 'Rhetoric and its Situations', *Philosophy and Rhetoric* 7 (1974), pp. 175-86.

theorists, the Belgian Chaïm Perelman and the American Kenneth Burke.[2] Both recognized that agreement is a changeable matter of degrees, not absolutes.

In any public gathering, the assembled are likely to represent a wide spectrum of viewpoints. A few agree on most or all points with the speaker, some are opposed on one or two points, some are somewhat negatively disposed and a few are outright hostile. In any given crowd, all types of hearers will be present in greater or lesser proportions, so speakers adjust their strategies accordingly. To move the preponderance of a crowd in his or her direction, a speaker may well focus on winning over a swath of those opposed on just a few points rather than trying to convert the small group of altogether hostile listeners. By standing up to opponents in public, of course, the speaker also encourages those who already agree to remain steadfast.

One useful strategy for addressing diverse audiences is the allocation of material in a text, what Perelman calls 'amplitude' and Burke calls 'amplification'.[3] Perelman observes that a speaker seeking to persuade allocates time carefully: 'the length of each part of his speech will usually be in proportion to the importance he would like to see it occupy in the minds of his hearers'.[4] Perelman notes that repeating a point and elaborating on it increases its presence or salience in the hearers' minds. When addressing a mainly supportive crowd, a speaker may vividly rehearse points everyone agrees on and emphasize their urgency. But when seeking to change the hearers' beliefs, attitudes or behaviors, the speaker must also anticipate points of disagreement. Time and space may be devoted to an accumulation of support for a claim, because different hearers may be susceptible to different reasons and appeals.

Most theorists have discussed amplitude in terms of the patterns with which a point can be developed and elaborated, overlooking its usefulness as an important clue for rhetorical analysis. Looking for where writers have devoted the most space is an important clue to the point they consider most important or most controversial.[5] Gorgias, the ancient Greek sophist, rhetorical theorist, and teacher, did exactly this in his showpiece, the *Encomium*

---

2. Perelman and Olbrechts-Tyteca, *The New Rhetoric*; Kenneth Burke, *A Rhetoric of Motives* (Berkeley: University of California Press, 1969).

3. Perelman and Olbrechts-Tyteca, *The New Rhetoric*, p. 474; Burke, *A Rhetoric of Motives*, p. 69. For a discussion and history of amplification, see Jeanne Fahnestock, *Rhetorical Style: The Uses of Language in Persuasion* (New York: Oxford University Press, 2011), pp. 390-417.

4. Perelman and Olbrechts-Tyteca, *The New Rhetoric*, p. 143.

5. Writers of public policy arguments regularly allocate the greatest proportion of total textual space to the most important and controversial points, as illustrated in Davida Charney and Christine Neuwirth, *Having your Say: Reading and Writing Public Arguments* (New York: Pearson/Longman, 2006).

*of Helen.*⁶ Gorgias considers four causes for Helen's running off with Paris of Troy—the will of the gods, force, persuasion or love, but gives the greatest amplitude, fully one-third of the entire speech, to his métier, persuasion. Amplitude is just one of the means whereby Gorgias uses this speech to explain, illustrate and evoke the power of persuasion. Amplitude will be used in this chapter to help disambiguate the settings of Psalms 4 and 62.

A second important persuasive strategy for the speaker is to create psychological connections with the hearers, a strategy that Perelman calls 'association' and that Burke calls 'identification'. Identification, perhaps the central concept for Burke, can be positive or negative. In the positive form, a speaker emphasizes interests held in common with the hearers. In the negative form, a speaker emphasizes how a rival's interests conflict with those of the hearers. Burke calls this 'identification by antithesis' which creates 'union by some opposition shared in common'.⁷ Apart from explicitly criticizing rivals, a speaker may also create dissociation by challenging the meaning of a concept, distinguishing some aspect of it as true or good and disparaging the other. In some cases, as M.A. van Rees notes, the speaker uses definitional or value claims for dissociation, putting two seemingly similar concepts side by side, assigning positive value to one and negative value to the other.⁸

In the readings that follow, I will show the similar ways in which amplitude and identification are deployed in Psalms 4 and 62. In both cases, the strategies aim to turn strayers away from more extreme apostates and back toward faithful moral behavior.

Psalm 4: A Seven-Step Recovery Program

The setting for Psalm 4 has generated some debate: Has the speaker come to the Temple seeking vindication against the false accusations of assembled opponents? Or is the speaker primarily a Temple functionary giving a wisdom-like speech against apostasy?

---

6. D.M. MacDowell, *Gorgias: Encomium of Helen* (Bristol: Bristol Classical Press, 1982).

7. Kenneth Burke, 'The Rhetorical Situation', in Lee Thayer (ed.), *Communication: Ethical and Moral Issues* (New York: Routledge, 1973), pp. 263-74.

8. M.A. van Rees, 'Indicators of Dissociation', in Franz H. van Eemeren and Peter Houtlosser (eds.), *Argumentation in Practice* (Amsterdam: John Benjamins, 2005), pp. 53-67. The economist and commentator Paul Krugman created this kind of dissociation in an op-ed column, 'Boring Cruel Romantics', *New York Times* (20 November 2011), p. A29. Krugman, who considers himself a 'technocrat', challenges the application of this term to new leaders in Europe who are bent on implementing fiscal austerity. Krugman argues that these leaders 'are not technocrats. They are, instead, deeply impractical romantics.'

PSALM 4[9]

1   For the lead player, with stringed instruments, a David psalm.
2   When I call out, answer me, my righteous God. In the straits, You set me free. Have mercy upon me and hear my prayer.
3   Sons of man, how long will My glory be shamed? You love vain things and seek out lies. Selah
4   But know that the LORD set apart His faithful. The LORD will hear when I call to Him.
5   Quake, and do not offend. Speak in your hearts on your beds, and be still. Selah
6   Offer righteous sacrifices and trust in the LORD.
7   Many say, 'Who will show us good things?' Lift up the light of Your face to us, LORD.
8   You put joy in my heart, from the time their grain and their drink did abound.
9   In peace, all whole, let me lie down and sleep. For You, LORD, alone, do set me down safely.

The false-accusation reading is the standard, adopted by Hans-Joachim Kraus, Richard Clifford, and Brueggemann and Bellinger, among others.[10] Anti-apostasy readings have been offered by Steven Croft, Craig Broyles and John Goldingay.[11] In reviewing the debate, Rolf Jacobson shows that both readings plausibly account for some but not all the contentious points of translation and interpretation.[12] No one takes the two readings as mutually exclusive; as Jacobson argues, there is no 'altar of certitude' on which to decide among historical, theological and canonical readings. However, seeking evidence for competing interpretations often highlights important elements within and across psalms. In this case, scholars have thus far overlooked the similarity of Psalms 4 and 62.

Psalm 4 can be divided by addressee into three sections. The speaker addresses God in the frame v. 2 and vv. 8-9 but addresses opponents in the central section, as sketched below. Clearly, the preponderance of space is devoted to the opponents. As I show in Figure 2.1, even the final two verses can be read as a rejoinder to opponents.

    9. Alter, *The Book of Psalms*, pp. 10-11.
    10. Hans-Joachim Kraus, *Psalms 1–59* (trans. H.C. Oswald; Minneapolis: Augsburg Fortress, 1988); Richard Clifford, *Psalms 1–72* (AOTC; Nashville, TN: Abingdon Press, 2002), pp. 52-55; Brueggemann and Bellinger, *Psalms*, p. 40.
    11. Steven J.L. Croft, *The Identity of the Individual in the Psalms* (JSOTSup, 44; Sheffield: JSOT Press, 1987); Craig C. Broyles, *Psalms* (Peabody, MA: Hendrickson, 1999); John Goldingay, 'Psalm 4: Ambiguity and Resolution', *TynBul* 57 (2006), pp. 161-72.
    12. Rolf Jacobson, 'The Altar of Certitude', in R. Foster and D.M. Howard, Jr (eds.), *My Words are Lovely: Studies in the Rhetoric of the Psalms* (New York: T. & T. Clark, 2008), pp. 3-18.

2. *Instructions for Keeping Faith*

1 Superscription
2 Plea to God for attention
3 Rebuke to opponents for apostasy/false accusation
4 Advice to opponents
5 Advice to opponents
6 Advice to opponents
7 Citation of opponents' response/Expression of trust
8 Rejoinder/Expression of trust
9 Rejoinder/Expression of trust

Figure 2.1. *Structure of Psalm 4*

The opening verse, v. 2, is a fairly standard address, establishing the speaker as a faithful Israelite who calls on God in times of trouble and expects to be answered. In contrast to the opening of most laments, the speaker makes no additional calls for God's attention and gives no description of the current situation. So, while v. 2 may be setting up expectations of a charge of false accusation, it also sets up a dramatic reversal. The assembled hearers are led to expect a lament, but the speaker instead turns and rebukes them.

The rebuke that opens the lengthy central section (vv. 3-7) comes in the form of a rhetorical question: 'how long will my glory be shamed?' The interpretation of כבודי ('my glory') is crucial for deciding between the false accusation and anti-apostasy readings. False accusation readings of Psalm 4 seize on the phrase as a reference to the speaker's own honor or reputation because little else in the psalm refers to attacks on the speaker. Such attacks are quite explicit in other psalms assigned to the false accusation category.[13] In contrast, the anti-apostasy reading takes the speaker's glory to be God.[14] Glory is used in exactly this sense in two other contexts that refer to acts of apostasy, Ps. 106.19-20 which refers to the golden calf and Jer. 2.11 in which God refers to Israelites adopting other gods.

Ps. 106.19-20   They made a calf at Horeb and bowed to a molten image. And they exchanged their glory for the image of a grass-eating bull.
Jer. 2.11   Has any nation changed its gods even when they are no-gods? But My people has exchanged its glory for what can do no good.

---

13. For a close discussion of the criteria that should be applied to this category, see William H. Bellinger, Jr, 'Psalms of the Falsely Accused: A Reassessment', *SBL Seminar Papers* 25 (1986), pp. 463-69. Bellinger distinguishes between false-accusation psalms where the context of a judicial proceeding seems justified (Psalms 7, 17 and 27) from apparent cases where opponents seem merely to be engaging in malicious gossip (Psalms 31, 64 and 28). Only the former include uses of legal language and forms: self-imprecation, appeals for acquittal, and oaths; references to a 'just cause'; and verbs of testing and trying.
14. See references in nn. 10 and 11 for further discussion of these options.

Interpreting the opponents as apostates in v. 3 sets up a clear contrast between those who love worthless things and seek lies (i.e., loving and listening to gods that aren't real gods) and those in v. 4 who are faithful to God, in particular the speaker. Notably the verse omits any reference to injuries at the hands of the opponents, which might be expected in a false accusation psalm or lament.

The speaker follows the rebuke with an extended effort to persuade opponents to return to faithful observance and offers a specific process for doing so. The first step of this process, in v. 4, is reminiscent of contemporary self-help programs: asking hearers to admit that they have a problem in lacking God's favor. He urges them to דעו ('realize') which god it is who hears, God not the idols, and to know who it is that God will answer, namely the speaker and not the hearers. Six more steps are spelled out in vv. 5-6 with three pairs of imperative verbs set in a logical progression: quake and refrain, speak and be still, offer and trust. The first verb in each pair is an action and the second an inaction.

The first pair, 'tremble, sin no more', refers to getting out of the habit of apostasy. The verb רגזו ('quake') is found four other times in the psalms (Pss. 18.9; 77.17, 19; 99.1), all of which describe the physical world exhibiting awe of God—the hills, the water, the earth. If awe of God can inspire nature to quake, then apostates can find it in themselves to do the same. Paired with quaking is the inaction of not sinning; that is, the apostate is urged to intentionally refrain from inappropriate action. The first pair, then, refers to externally manifested behavior.

The next pair are psychological steps: speaking and becoming still in bed, where, as Michael Barré has noted, a person is most sincere.[15] The image of overcoming internal debate while in bed also occurs in Ps. 16.7 in which the speaker is helped by God's counsel after being lashed by his conscience (or kidneys). The speaker in Ps. 4.5 is instructed to engage in this internal struggle. Pairing this struggle with an effort to become still is far from contradictory. In fact, the sense of דומם ('stilling') as a recovery from agitation is also posited in Ps. 131.2 by Phil J. Botha and H. Stephen Shoemaker.[16] Achieving stillness after struggling against the lures of materialism and other gods would be quite an accomplishment for apostates.

The final pair of imperative verbs, in Ps. 4.6, is 'offer and trust'. After feeling awe, refraining from sin, struggling with temptation and achieving stillness, the strayer is ready to make a positive action to serve God. The

---

15. Michael Barré reviews biblical images of conscience-stricken insomnia in 'Hearts, Beds, and Repentance in Psalm 4,5 and Hosea 7,14', *Bib* 76 (1995), pp. 53-62.

16. Botha, 'To Honour Yahweh'; H. Stephen Shoemaker, 'Psalm 131', *RevExp* 85.1 (1988), pp. 89-94. In contrast, Barré ('Hearts, Beds', pp. 58-60) translates this pair of verbs as 'quake' and 'wail'. Raabe ('Deliberate Ambiguity', p. 215) gives a helpful suggestion that the resonance of stilling and wailing enriches the effect.

2. *Instructions for Keeping Faith*

emphasis on making 'righteous' sacrifices may be needed for people who are partially assimilated; apostates may well have been combining practices appropriate for YHWH with those distinctly associated with foreign gods. Only purely appropriate sacrifice can lead to a final state of trust in God. The ordering of sacrifice before trust implies that practice may precede belief, a positioning that echoes Exod. 24.7, 'we will do and we will hear'.

Thus the greatest amplitude in Psalm 4, the bulk of the space, is devoted to addressing opponents with a rebuke followed by a persuasive and poetic sequence of steps that strayers can follow to return to faithfulness. While it is still possible to view the speaker as a troubled petitioner, his attention is almost exclusively devoted to the future behavior of the opponents, rather than to securing rescue or vindication.

Returning to faithfulness is also promoted through the strategy of identification. The speaker uses positive identification in the framing sections by modeling appropriate behavior and referring to first-hand experiences. While v. 2 is addressed to God, it also establishes the speaker as someone בצר ('in dire straits'), who has suffered 'distress' and who calls out to God. This is not someone whose life has gone altogether smoothly—a history that hearers of all degrees of faithfulness are likely to share. While the speaker may have been unusually successful when he has called to God (vv. 2 and 4), being answered or relieved in times of trouble is a shared goal that they all aspire to. More shared goals are set out in vv. 8-9. The speaker is able to sleep soundly and quietly at night, in contrast to the quaking hearers in v. 5, and achieves joy in his relationship with God, a joy that may match or exceed 'the good' that the hearers are seeking in v. 7. These positive forms of identification set up the speaker as someone who is enough like the hearers that they may feel motivated to reconnect with God. Thus the frame of the psalm strengthens the force of the process for returning in the central verses.

The most powerful strategy in Psalm 4, however, is the use of disidentification in vv. 7-9 where the speaker pulls receptive opponents away from extremists who are characterized as greedy and irreverent. The dissociation is accomplished in part by a change in voice. Up until now, in vv. 4-6, the speaker has addressed the opponents directly using the second person. He has accused all those assembled of seeking vain things and lies. But in v. 7, the voice shifts. In v. 7, the speaker figuratively points at רבים (the 'many') who are asking, in essence, which god will provide 'the good(s)', namely, material rewards. The speaker is like a school principal at an assembly announcing 'students have been sassing teachers and writing graffiti on the walls'. The culprits are present and well-known to the crowd, as if the principal had said 'and you all know very well who they are'. By referring to the worst culprits in the third person, the speaker is inviting the lesser offenders to distance themselves from the habitual or extreme offenders. Then the speaker reports what the offenders are saying.

The direct quote from this group is confined to the question 'Who will show us good things?' in Alter's translation as well as in the NJPS. However, I believe that the quote should be read as extending to the end of v. 7, 'Many say, "Who will show us good things? Lift up the light of Your face to us LORD"', as in the RSV. The extremists are not seriously asking for the favor of God's face but are mockingly asserting that they don't need it; apparently, they are worshipping other gods because they have prospered materially by doing so. The indirect reference to the lifting of God's face from the Priestly Blessing (Num. 6.24-26) is then an especially cheeky bit of mockery.[17] The key to interpreting v. 7 is remembering that it is the speaker who is reporting the putative words of the offenders. The balder and more irreverent the words of the extremists, the better for the speaker's goals. Hearers who have not strayed quite so far may be shocked by the alleged mockery at the same moment as they are pushed by the pronouns to take sides, either to identify with the 'us' of the extremists or to see the extremists as 'them' along with the upright speaker.

In the concluding two verses, Ps. 4.8-9, the speaker returns to addressing God, providing the usual closing expression of praise and trust. Goldingay sees the speaker, having failed to reach people with a 'bad attitude', moving on to his or her own concerns, simply hoping 'that God may change these people'.[18]

But it is also possible to interpret vv. 8-9 as a rejoinder to the extremists' view. The speaker concedes in v. 8 that the apostates have gained material rewards: דגנם ותירושם ('their grain and their drink'). But the speaker trumps these rewards with the greater joy he receives from communing with God. Goldingay notes that the timing of the speaker's joy is ambiguous. On one hand, מעת may be translated as 'at the same time'. In this case, the speaker feels joy *even at the moment when* the opponents seem to be rewarded. But מעת may also be translated (as Jacobson does) as a comparative 'more than when', implying that the speaker's joy is greater than the joy coming from material rewards. Either way, the speaker is challenging the value of the apostates' goods.

The final verse, v. 9, with its reference to sleeping well and having peace, contrasts directly with the state prescribed for the strayers in v. 5. The reference to peace, Goldingay suggests, harkens back to the final part of the Priestly Blessing, which conveys a state of physical completeness or wellbeing. The speaker is not joyful in the face of deprivation, but in the expectation that God also provides sufficient material sustenance.

---

17. In addition to reading this phrase as mockery, Goldingay also admits a translation of it as an assertion of estrangement: 'the light of your face has fled from over us' ('Psalm 4', p. 167). In this, he follows John H. Eaton, 'Psalm 4:7', *Theology* 67 (1964), pp. 355-57.

18. Goldingay, 'Psalm 4', p. 170.

2. *Instructions for Keeping Faith* 47

In sum, the speaker's persuasive power derives from the considerable space devoted to addressing and referring to the strayers, the choice and sequence of imperative verbs used to address them, as well as the use of both positive and negative strategies of identification to draw the strayers toward the speaker and away from more extreme rivals.

Psalm 62: Restoring the Expletive

The setting for Psalm 62 has not seemed controversial; it is generally taken as a call from an individual for vindication or rescue. Kraus and Mandolfo see the speaker as an ordinary individual, one facing persecution and seeking judicial or divine protection at the sanctuary.[19] Croft and Dave Bland see the speaker as an embattled king seeking an oracle of safety when facing treachery or a military siege.[20] However, on closer examination, the case for seeing the speaker as a petitioner is actually quite weak.

PSALM 62[21]

1		For the lead player, on *jeduthun*, a David psalm.
2	אך	Only in God is my being quiet. From Him is my rescue.
3	אך	Only He is my rock and my rescue. I shall not stumble at all.
4	עד אנה	How long will you demolish a man—commit murder, each one of you—like a leaning wall, a shaky fence?
5	אך	Only from his high place they schemed to shake him. They took pleasure in lies. With their mouths they blessed and inwardly cursed. Selah
6	אך	Only in God be quiet, my being, for from Him is my hope.
7	אך	Only He is my rock and my rescue, my fortress—I shall not stumble.
8	על	From God is my rescue and glory, my strength's rock and my shelter in God.
9	בטחו	Trust in Him at all times, O people. Pour out your hearts before Him. God is our shelter. Selah
10	אך	Only breath—humankind, the sons of man are a lie. On the scales all together they weigh less than a breath.
11	אל	Do not trust in oppression and of theft have no illusions. Though it bear fruit of wealth, set your heart not upon it.
12	אחת	One thing God has spoken, two things have I heard: that strength is but God's,
13	ולך	and Yours, Master is kindness. For You requite a man by his deeds.

In the petitioner reading, a vulnerable speaker is seeking protection in a religious or judicial setting. It is the speaker who is the subject of the attacks

---

19. Carleen Mandolfo, *God in the Dock: Dialogic Tension in the Psalms of Lament* (JSOTSup, 357; London: Sheffield Academic Press, 2002), p. 18. Kraus, *Psalms 60–150*.
20. Croft, *The Identity of the Individual*, p. 127; Bland, 'Exegesis of Psalm 62'.
21. Alter, *The Book of Psalms*, pp. 213-15.

of the crowd, who at times feels safe in God's refuge and at times feels as weak as a tottering fence, who swings between complaining and expressing trust. Having reached safety by the end, the speaker can indulge in a hortatory impulse to advise the opponents to give up their bad ways.

But the case for seeing the speaker as a conflicted petitioner is quite weak. Yes, the plot in vv. 4-5 is similar to laments in which enemies try to trap or trip up a speaker using lies, wiles or violence (e.g., Psalms 35; 64; 140). But unlike these psalms, Psalm 62 makes no direct second-person plea to God for rescue. The speaker never asks God 'when will you rescue me?' In fact, the speaker never connects the threat to himself with any first-person reference. The speaker does not say '*I* am like a leaning wall' and does not ask 'when will you stop trying to murder *me*?' Instead the victim is consistently described in impersonal and non-specific terms, in the third person or as איש ('a man'). While it is possible for איש ('a man') to refer back to the speaker, the word is not used as a self-reference in that way in any of the 35 other psalms where it occurs. Thus the target of the opponents seems not to be the speaker but rather an unnamed third party, who may or may not be present.[22] The speaker's purpose then is not to protest on his own behalf but, like the speaker in Psalm 4, to rebuke a crowd of people for attacking another person or people. He is making a public effort to persuade hearers to return to faithful, moral behavior. Rather than oscillating between trust and doubt, the speaker is consistent in modeling a sense of security while trying to protect the weak-willed from the bad influence of the opponents. To support this reading, I will again examine both the amplitude of points and the use of identification.

Space in Psalm 62, as sketched below, is dominated by the speaker's expressions of trust in God as a personal refuge and rescuer at the opening, center and closing of the psalm. The repetition of the phrasing 'Only He is my rock and my rescue. I shall not stumble at all' from vv. 2-3 in vv. 6-8 turn these verses into a refrain bracketing the rebukes. Repetition is the classic form of amplitude; here it emphasizes and re-emphasizes the speaker's security and contrasts it to the doubts and weaknesses of the others.

The seven verses expressing security (vv. 2-3, 6-8 and 12-13) create a lattice-work to enclose the five verses addressed to opponents: a rebuke in vv. 4-5 and a sequence of prescriptions in vv. 9-11. The amplitude of the psalm thus projects stability.

As in Psalm 4, the rebuke in Ps. 62.4-5 opens with questions addressed to all the hearers challenging their misdeeds. Rather than worshipping other gods, however, these hearers seem to be attacking other members

---

22. Brueggemann and Bellinger also translate איש as 'a person', an unnamed victim (*Psalms*, p. 274).

1	Superscription
2	God as refuge
3	God as refuge
4	Direct rebuke
5	Indirect rebuke. Selah.
6	God as refuge
7	God as refuge
8	God as refuge
9	Process: Trust and pour out. Selah.
10	Human strength/value as illusory
11	Process: Reject violence; reject robbery; reject ill-gotten gains.
12	God's might
13	God's faithfulness; God's fairness.

Figure 2.2. *Structure of Psalm 62*

of the community and leading them astray. They seek to push the victim down from משאתו ('his elevation'), a less than challenging task given that the man is already as weak as כקיר נטוי ('a leaning wall') and גדר הדחויה ('a shaky fence'). As lofty and secure as the man may once have been, he is now literally a push-over. The speaker addresses the tempters, but by offering shelter to the weak, he also rails at those feeling pressured to give in to them.

As in Psalm 4, the prescribed actions for recovery in Ps. 62.9-11 follow a logical order. The first two steps, in v. 9, are for the opponents בטחו ('to trust') in God and שפכו לבבכם ('to pour out') their hearts to God. The series of imperatives is interrupted in v. 10 with a reminder that humans lack strength, endurance and value—the very qualities repeatedly attributed to God in the three-part frame. Gaining security from relying on God rather than humans enables the opponents to reorder their values. Accordingly, in v. 11, they are told to renounce robbery and ill-gotten gains. The renunciation, in three negative commands, is more cognitive than active: אל תבטחו ('don't trust'), אל תהבלו ('don't be deluded') and אל תשיתו לב ('don't set your heart'). The negative commands mirror the earlier positives: trust/ don't trust, pour/don't set. As in Psalm 4, the underlying motive for straying turns out to be greed, an attraction to material reward. So the wisdom-like pronouncements in the closing verses, vv. 12-13, serve as a rebuttal. In the greater scheme of things, material gain is immaterial because God balances the accounts.

Viewing the psalm as a public argument against greed-induced bad behavior changes the speaker from an aggrieved victim into moral agent. The speaker also comes across as a virtuoso performer, by virtue of the careful balance of space, the refrains and the sound pattern of the verses (discussed below). These qualities set the speaker apart from the crowd, as someone to be admired. The speaker makes some of the same gestures of positive identification as the speaker in Psalm 4. The repeated declarations of security show the speaker to be successful in calling on God in times of trouble. In v. 2, the speaker alludes to previous struggles from which דומיה נפשי ('is my being quiet') he has achieved stillness and been rescued. He even qualifies his stability in v. 3, לא אמוט רבה ('I shall not stumble at all'). But it is only at the key moment of prescribing steps for returning to faithfulness in v. 9 that the speaker invites the hearers into a shared space by referring to the hearers as עם ('nation') and referring to God as מחסה לנו ('our refuge') rather than 'my refuge'.

That this speaker is more showman than shepherd is also evident in his use of disidentification. The initial rebuke in v. 4 is hyperbolic, asking when the entire crowd כלכם ('all of you') will stop destroying and murdering a weak-willed victim. He's asking the classic loaded question: 'When will you stop beating your wife?' Everyone and no one is singled out. Then, as in Psalm 4, the speaker shifts to talking about the offenders in the third person. In v. 5, he accuses 'them' of scheming, lying and hypocrisy. At this point, hearers may well shift mentally away from others around them, especially if the unnamed victim, rather than representing a general type, is a specific person who has been dallying with the wrong crowd. Anyone who has committed minor offenses feels singled out for rebuke—but can still feel superior to others in the crowd who may be guilty of worse. The advice for recovering stability and moral values in vv. 9-11 is useful for everyone, waverers and tempters alike.

The most potent persuasive device in Psalm 62 is the sound pattern of the verse-initial Hebrew words. The initial words of all but one verse begin with vowels (א, ע, ו), as shown in Figure 2.3, with the exclamation *ach* (אך) at the head of six verses. While biblical scholars have often noted the pattern, it has generally gone unrepresented in translation.[23] Alter tries to capture part of the effect by using 'only' wherever *ach* (אך) appears. But even he misses the rest of the alliteration and the important role of *ach* (אך) as a stand-alone exclamation. Rendering the word *ach* (אך) as 'indeed' or 'surely' is in many ways less effective than simply writing 'Ahhh'.

The opening alliteration across all the verses must have been quite striking in oral performance. A skillful speaker may draw out or cut short such

---

23. Bland, 'Exegesis of Psalm 62' is one of the few commentators who notes the alliteration of the vowel-initial words in the first half of the psalm as well as the adversative meaning of אך. Jin H. Han in his recent talk 'Lists with Wit in Proverbs' at the SBL meeting in Chicago (17 November 2012) noted similar aural uses of wit outside the psalms.

		Alter	NJPS	KJV	RSV
1					
2	אך	Only	Truly	Truly	For
3	אך	Only	Truly	He only	He only
4	עד אנה	How	How	How	How
5	אך	Only	They	They only	They only
6	אך	Only	Truly	My soul	For God
7	אך	Only	He	He only	He only
8	על	From	I	In God	On God
9	בטחו	Trust	Trust	Trust	Trust
10	אך	Only	Men	Surely	Men
11	אל	Do not	Do not	Trust not	Put
12	אחת	One	One	God	Once
13	ולך	And you	And	Also unto	And

Figure 2.3. *Verse-Initial Words in Psalm 62*

sonorous open vowels in attention-getting ways, playing with drama or humor. In particular, after hearing a pattern of six verses with אך, hearers may well have expected a canonical seventh in v. 12, when what they got instead of *ach* (אך) was *akhat* (אחת) 'one'. The break in pattern emphasizes the 'one' word from God. More importantly, the pattern of alliteration itself breaks in only one place and at the most important moment. Verse 9 opens with the word *bit-khu* (בטחו) 'trust', replacing a sonorant with a voiced stop or plosive consonant. The pattern breaks at the very point where the speaker commands the hearers to return to faithful behavior, with the first step being to trust in God.

Finally, the sense of *ach* (אך) adds to the effect that the speaker is engaging with the crowd. Norman Snaith argues that the *ach* (אך) always carries a restrictive or adversative meaning.[24] He translates it as 'yes but on the contrary' or 'despite' or 'whatever may be said to the contrary'. So, while the speaker of Psalm 62 is less explicit than the speaker in Psalm 4 in anticipating and responding to the opponents' objections, he may skillfully use the repetitions of *ach* (אך) to suggest that he sees his claims as sufficient response to whatever they might say. The translation offered below conveys some of these effects.

---

24. Norman Henry Snaith, 'The Meaning of the Hebrew "אך"', *VT* 14 (1964), pp. 221-25.

PSALM 62: Alternative Translation

1		For the leader, on *jeduthun*, a David psalm.
2	אך	Ach! In God does my being find quiet. From Him comes my rescue.
3	אך	Ach! He is my rock, my rescue. I hardly stumble at all.
4	עד אנה	Until when will you batter a man—commiting murder, each of you—like a leaning wall, a tottering fence?
5	אך	Ach! From his perch they schemed to shake him. They enjoyed their lies. Outwardly their mouths blessed and inwardly they cursed. Selah
6	אך	Ach! In God find quiet, my being, for from him comes my hope.
7	אך	Ach! He is my rock, my rescue, my fortress—I barely stumble.
8	על	In God I find rescue and glory, rock-hard strength, and shelter in God.
9	בטחו	Bank on him at all times, O people. Pour your hearts out before him. God is our shelter. Selah
10	אך	Ach! A mere breath—humanity, the sons of man are a lie. All together on the scales, they amount to less than a breath.
11	אל	Avoid banking on coercion and of theft disabuse yourself. Though it produce wealth, do not set your heart on it.
12	אחת	A catchphrase of God is told, a by-word have I heard: that strength is none but God's,
13	ולך	and yours, Master is kindness. For you requite a man according to his deeds.

Overall, taking the speaker of Psalm 62 as a confident and secure individual aiming to persuade an unruly crowd produces a coherent reading that accounts for the careful balancing of space between expressing security and addressing opponents, the contrast between God's power and human instability and evanescence, and the carefully designed sound pattern that heightens attention to the command to 'trust in God'. The psalm presents a unified and striking statement of communal values. As Jeffrey Walker notes in his analysis of oral poetic argument in archaic Greece, 'the successful poem will offer its audience an elegant, memorable, aesthetically satisfying representation of situations and attitudes with which they more or less identify already: the audience sees itself, or its values, reflected strikingly'.[25]

Psalm 82: Persuading Gods

The rhetorical situation employed in Psalm 4 and Psalm 62 involves a speaker offering himself and his ongoing experiences as a living example to the audience. Hearers who are already in close alignment with the speaker's values see them as validated, while those opposed in some way are rebuked

---

25. Walker, *Rhetoric and Poetics*, p. 268.

but also invited to take specific steps toward the speaker and away from more extreme opponents.

PSALM 82[26]

1   An Asaph psalm. God takes His stand in the divine assembly, in the midst of the gods He renders judgment.
2   'How long will you judge dishonestly, and show favor to the wicked? Selah
3   Do justice to the poor and the orphan. Vindicate the lowly and the wretched.
4   Free the poor and the needy, from the hand of the wicked save them.
5   They do not know and do not grasp, in darkness they walk about. All the earth's foundations totter.
6   As for Me, I had thought you were gods, and the sons of the Most High were you all.
7   Yet indeed like humans you shall die, and like one of the princes, fall'.
8   Arise O God, judge the earth, for You hold in estate all the nations.

This rhetorical situation arguably applies in one additional psalm, Psalm 82. In this case, of course, the speaker addressing a straying audience is not an ordinary person but God, and the opponents are other gods. The unique opening verse sets the context from an otherworldly observer's standpoint. Yet Psalm 82 shares many features with the other two psalms. The preponderance of space is devoted to direct address of the opponents from a first-person speaker, the rebuke takes the form of a question, and a process for returning to the right path is laid out in a series of imperatives (see Figure 2.4).

1   Context
2   Direct rebuke
3   Process
4   Process
5   Indirect rebuke
6   Direct rebuke
7   Direct rebuke
8   Appeal to God

Figure 2.4. *Structure of Psalm 82*

In light of the other two psalms, what seems most striking about Psalm 82 is its lack of persuasive strategies. The setting of the divine assembly portrays God among a set of peers. Without any first-person self-references in vv. 1-2, however, there is little effort at positive identification. Rather than a sequence of self-help actions, the imperatives in vv. 3-4, שפטו ('judge'),

26. Alter, *The Book of Psalms*, pp. 291-93.

הצדיקו ('vindicate'), פלטו ('rescue') and הצילו ('save'), all refer to actions the gods should take toward others, the lowly and the poor. These directives do allow for the possibility that some gods might reform.[27] The shift from second to third person in v. 5 allows for a dissociative reading, castigating some of the gods as worse than others. However, the speaker's final statements return to addressing and condemning כלכם ('all of you') in the audience. On the whole, the absence of persuasive strategies indicates that the speaker is using the barest possible framework of claims with the intention more to condemn than to move the hearers.[28]

Yet the similarities between Psalm 82 and the more persuasive Psalms 4 and 62 are enough to cause a productive resonance. The similarity of the rebukes in both form (questions) and content (favoring material success) underscore the moral force of the human speakers: no matter how powerful the human opponents, they can never hope to escape judgment any more than can foreign gods. Yet, from the perspective of Psalm 82, the human speakers in the other two psalms seem even more approachable to their peers. In their self-references, the human speakers do not make themselves out to be God-like; they admit to the need for safety and security. As a result, the actions that the speakers prescribe end up seeming more achievable. The more formal setting of the assembly and the language of judgment in Psalm 82 bespeak a final resolution for the wayward gods. The human opponents, by contrast, seem to be afforded much more opportunity to change their ways, rejoin the community of loyal Israelites, and live.

Conclusion: Bait and Switch?

In this chapter, I have promoted anti-apostasy readings of Psalms 4 and 62. In both cases, the speakers deploy an array of persuasive strategies to persuade strayers to return to faithful behavior, a mission that the speaker in Ps. 51.15 also subscribes to: 'I will teach transgressors Your ways that sinners may return to You'. But if the strayers are the intended hearers and the targets of the speakers' persuasive strategies, why do Psalms 4 and 62 look so much like other individual psalms, whether psalms of lament, thanksgiving or trust, where both the underlying and ostensible addressee is God? Psalm 4 both opens and closes by calling on God's protection, as in many laments.

---

27. David Frankel considers and rejects this possibility in 'El as the Speaking Voice in Psalm 82:6-8', *Journal of Hebrew Scriptures* 10 (2010), pp. 2-24.

28. The final verse turns God's actions in the divine assembly into a precedent for applying the same remedy to corrupt judges and rulers on earth. Rolf Jacobson (*Many are Saying: The Function of Direct Discourse in the Hebrew Psalter* [New York: T. & T. Clark, 2004], pp. 113-14) raises the possibility that the final verse was added to a previously existing text to turn it into a persuasive petition to God. My reading of God's speech does not require such an assumption.

Psalm 62 opens by expressing trust in God and closes by declaring God's power, as in many psalms of trust. If we assume that many first-person psalms were performed in public places by talented poets and musicians, then they may have attracted hearers of many stripes. It is possible that the speakers of these psalms used the usual setting as bait to attract crowds that included many strayers who expected to hear an ordinary lament or thanksgiving, but then switched tack to address the strayers directly.

In supporting the anti-apostasy readings, I'm not intending to offer them up on the altar of certainty that Rolf Jacobson has rightly rejected. Every psalm can support a variety of readings, even those that seem mutually exclusive. My goal here rather has been to raise attention to the value of contemporary rhetorical theory for recognizing additional aspects of a psalm that should be considered when weighing the plausibility of alternative readings.

Chapter 3

THE LAMENT AS PROPOSAL

The speakers of lament psalms are in trouble now or have been in trouble recently, trouble that they have not been able to resolve by ordinary means. Their goal is to persuade God to intervene to relieve their illnesses, save their lives, disarm their assailants or vindicate them in the face of their accusers. The speakers attribute their troubles to God's absence or refusal to hear them, so their first task is to gain or regain God's attention. For faithful Israelites who assume that God's sense of justice entails protecting the innocent, only God's absence can explain their finding themselves in trouble in the first place.

The speakers' next task is to describe their situation in urgent terms. In many laments, an opponent is mistreating, attacking or making false accusations against the speaker. The opponent is often described as arrogant, deceitful, impious or unjust. The opponent's attack is חנים ('baseless') and comes despite the speaker's own previous kindness to the opponent. The speaker asks God to take sides. And even though God is omniscient, the speakers generally go to some lengths to build a persuasive case for their own innocence and/or their opponents' guilt. God must intervene, the speaker argues, to restore justice or to uphold cultural values, such as rescuing the poor and weak.

The speakers ask God for rescue and vindication, meaning that the opponents are destroyed or defeated or at least brought low and humiliated, giving the speaker the opportunity to rejoice in public at their expense.

As a text that appeals for the hearer's attention, lays out a significant problem and proposes steps for the hearer to take to address the problem, a lament bears many important similarities to a modern public policy argument or proposal. In today's society, policy arguments address a wide array of issues of public concern, such as education, health care or the environment and may take many forms: op-ed columns, research grant proposals, political speeches.

As in ancient times, policy arguments occur in what Aristotle referred to as the deliberative forum, dealing with proposals for action—what to do about an issue. As Christian Kock notes, arguments about what to do are qualitatively different from arguments about what has happened in the past.[1] Proposals urge action or inaction based on future consequences that can only be surmised; proposals come down to value arguments about what action is best, easiest, most effective, least harmful. Should the country go to war? Adopt a new health care system? Reduce climate-changing emissions? The parties may disagree over the need to act, the criteria for judging available actions, the degree to which any proposal satisfies the criteria and even the timing and manner of decision-making. An individual who feels that the situation is dire may have no power other than persuasion to influence the outcome.

The speaker/writer often begins with an effort to gain the attention of the hearers/readers, trying to make them see some aspect of the issue in a new way, perhaps with vivid narration or an unexpected twist in a long-standing situation. Next, the author focuses on the nature of a problem brought to the fore by this new perspective on the issue. Claims may be made about the existence and nature of the problem, its significance, causes and ripeness for action. Finally, the author proposes and evaluates one or more solutions, specifying actions that the hearer may take to mitigate the causes of the problem as the author has defined it. Claims may be offered about the relative feasibility of various solutions, their costs and benefits, side effects and implementation. As in any type of argument, these claims may be supported by appealing to *ethos* (or authority), to *pathos* (emotion) or to *logos* (reason and observation).

These basic parts map fairly neatly onto well-recognized sections of first-person psalms. The address attempts the first task of the psalmist: to gain or regain God's attention. An address to a more powerful interlocutor inevitably includes a request for audience. However, for Israelites who consider themselves innocent and who assume that God is just, only God's absence or inattention can explain their finding themselves in trouble in the first place.

The 'complaint' (or 'problem') section describes the crisis situation in vivid terms: the direr the straits, the more God's help is needed.

The petition (or 'proposal for divine action') sets out the actions that God should take to relieve the crisis, usually with a sequence of imperatives. This section corresponds to the solution section of a deliberative public policy argument which is also marked by the use of imperative language.

The final section, the shift to praise, is often described as a confession of faith and interpreted as an emotional breakthrough. A better term may be 'proposal for reciprocal action'. Rhetorically, these verses might

---

1. Christian Kock, 'Constructive Controversy: Rhetoric as Dissensus-Oriented Discourse', *Cogency* 1 (2009), pp. 89-111.

serve as proffers of the speaker's contribution to a proposed agreement with God. The speaker is promising (and in some cases actually delivering) public declarations of praise and thanksgiving in exchange for divine intervention on his or her behalf whenever it eventually occurs. In contemporary public policy arguments, it is usual for an author to begin using inclusive language ('we', 'our') in the solution section, thereby accepting a share of responsibility. Perhaps this move in a psalm reflects the reciprocal nature of the covenant; the speaker must act as God's partner in resolving the crisis.

In this chapter, Psalm 54 and Psalm 13 will be used to illustrate how the basic shape of a lament corresponds to a policy argument.

Psalm 54: Invoking Action

In Psalm 54, the speaker lays out a sequence of points that is very standard for biblical laments, beginning by addressing God, describing a problem that often involves external enemies, proposing a recuperative course of action and ending by describing the desired outcome of restored good relations between the speaker and God.

PSALM 54[2]

1 For the lead player on stringed instruments, a David *mas-kil*,
2 when the Ziphites came and said to Saul, 'Is not David hiding out among us?'
3 God, through Your name rescue me and through Your might take up my cause.
4 God, O hear my prayer, hearken to my mouth's utterances.
5 For strangers have risen against me, and oppressors have sought my life. They did not set God before them. Selah
6 Look, God is about to help me, my Master—among those who support me.
7 Let Him pay back evil to my assailants. Demolish them through Your truth!
8 With a freewill offering let me sacrifice to You. Let me acclaim Your name, LORD, for it is good.
9 For from every strait He saved me, and my eyes see my enemies' defeat.

The speaker in Psalm 54 immediately implores God to act and to hear (vv. 3-4). As shown in the structural diagram in Figure 3.1, the central verse of Psalm 54, v. 5, narrates the crisis: the appearance of strangers who do not respect God. The following verses (vv. 6-7) anticipate and propose the solution to the problem: God intervenes on the speaker's behalf and destroys the enemy. Alter's translation of הנה אלהים עזר לי ('Look, God is about to help me') in v. 6 suggests that God is already in action. The psalm closes (vv. 8-9) with the speaker's vow to repay God for the rescue with sacrifice and public praise.

2. Alter, *The Book of Psalms*, pp. 189-90.

3. *The Lament as Proposal* 59

	1	Title
	2	Ascription to 1 Kgs
	3	Plea for a hearing
	4	Plea for a hearing
	5	Threat and denunciation
	6	*Divine Action*: vision of God acting
	7	Retribution, destruction
	8	*Reciprocal Action*: speaker sacrifices
	9	Speaker praises

Figure 3.1. *Structure of Psalm 54*

Psalm 13: Questioning Absence

Like Psalm 54, Psalm 13 makes a very basic argument from a speaker in trouble. Psalm 13 is so typical that Hermann Gunkel called it 'a parade example' of the individual lament.[3]

PSALM 13[4]

1   To the lead player, a David psalm.
2   How long, O LORD, will You forget me always? How long hide Your face from me?
3   How long shall I cast about for counsel, sorrow in my heart all day? How long will my enemy loom over me?
4   Regard, answer me, LORD, my God. Light up my eyes, lest I sleep death,
5   lest my enemy say, 'I've prevailed over him', lest my foes exult when I stumble.
6   But I in Your kindness do trust, my heart exults in your rescue. Let me sing to the LORD for He requited me.

The description of the problem in Psalm 13 is far less explicit than in Psalm 54; apart from vaguely describing a looming enemy, the speaker focuses more on his inner state than an external situation. As shown in Figure 3.2, Psalm 13 opens by addressing God with a series of four rhetorical questions (vv. 2-3) which make clear that the issue is God's silence. As directed to God, the sequence of questions can itself be seen as persuasive: the questions seek to move God from forgetting the speaker entirely, to a slightly improved state of being aware but in hiding, to actively considering the speaker's agitated internal state, to considering the speaker's dangerous external circumstances, with an enemy looming.

---

3.   Hermann Gunkel and Joachim Begrich, *Introduction to Psalms: The Genres of the Religious Lyric of Israel* (trans. James Nogalski; Macon, GA: Mercer University Press, 1998).
4.   Alter, *The Book of Psalms*, pp. 38-39.

Title	1	Title
Address	2	Question: Plea for a hearing
	3	Question: Plea for a hearing
	4	Plea; threat
Complaint	5	Threat
Proposal	6	*Reciprocal Action*: Speaker trusts, praises

Figure 3.2. *Structure of Psalm 13*

According to Stephen Dolson-Andrew, the phrase אשית עצות בנפשי ('cast about for counsel') in v. 3 has concerned a few commentators who would prefer to translate 'counsel' as 'troubles' in order to create a more precise parallel to יגון ('sorrow') in the second half of the verse.[5] However counsel is a better echo of the imagery of sleepless indecision depicted in Pss. 16.7 and 4.5, discussed by Michael Barré.[6]

Ps. 16.7	I shall bless the LORD Who gave me counsel through the nights that my conscience would lash me.
Ps. 4.5	Quake, and do not offend. Speak in your hearts on your beds, and be still. Selah

When an Israelite enjoys a close relationship with God, as in Ps. 16.7, he is able to settle the internal turmoil or 'lashing' of his conscience at night because God יעצני ('gave me counsel'). The root for counsel in Ps. 16.7 is the same as עצות ('counsel') in Ps. 13.3. But when an Israelite has strayed and is urged to return, as in Ps. 4.5, part of the process is to initiate some internal speech in his לבב ('heart' or 'mind') in bed at night before he can become still.

If this theme is applied to Ps. 13.3, it becomes clear that the speaker is bemoaning the absence of God's 'counsel' at night when, presumably like the speaker in Psalm 16, his conscience is lashing him. The next phrase of Ps. 13.3 indicates that the speaker's days are likewise troubled because his heart is full of sorrow. Verse 3 thus provides an embodied image of unending trouble by tacitly balancing disturbance from a lashing conscience at night, a sorrowful heart by day, not to mention a looming enemy.

The series of questions in Ps. 13.2-3 suggests that what the speaker wants most is a response. Any response. Presumably, the speaker would be satisfied even if a voice from heaven took 'how long?' literally and answered with a time period, like 'seven lean years'. Even that would resolve some of the anxiety! In fact, however, in v. 4, the speaker shapes the form of the

---

5. Stephen L. Dolson-Andrew, 'An Exegesis of Psalm 13', *Chafer Theological Seminary Journal* 10 (2004), pp. 49-71.

6. Barré, 'Hearts, Beds'.

requested response, pleading for a sequence of actions that like the earlier questions become progressively greater in interactivity: הביטה ('look', give a sign of awareness); עֲנֵנִי ('answer me', give some kind of word or gesture); and האירה עיני ('light up my eyes', cause a change in the speaker's physical condition).

In the second part of v. 4 and in v. 5, the speaker goes on to outline the evil consequences of continued neglect: the speaker may die (v. 4) and the presumably unworthy enemy will exult over his fall (v. 5).

The psalm ends as the speaker affirms his trust that God will act (v. 6) and promises to offer public praise following the desired rescue. Some commentators, such as Staton, take v. 6 itself as the offering of praise, believing that expressing the psalm is so therapeutic that the speaker is enabled to end by affirming trust: 'Commentators have often expressed amazement at the transition from lament to praise found in this and similar psalms... Psalm 13 suggests that honest prayer may bring aid and hope to the desperate pray-er.'[7] However, it is also possible to see v. 6 as a sort of promissory note for the praise and thanksgiving that the speaker will offer after rescue has been achieved.

Absence of Amplitude

Psalm 54 and Psalm 13 follow the proposal structure fairly clearly without elaborating on either the problem or the solution. In Psalm 54, the address consists of vv. 3-4, in which the speaker pleads to God for rescue. The problem, described in v. 5, states clearly that 'strangers have risen against me'. The solution, in vv. 6-7, calls on God to appear and demolish the strangers. The reciprocal action in vv. 8-9 clearly promises a formal sacrifice with a preview of the praise to be offered at that time. In Psalm 13, the address in vv. 2-3 is laid out more feelingly than in Psalm 54 with the series of questions, but the problem is not described explicitly on its own terms. God's part of the solution appears in vv. 4-5: regard, answer, light up my eyes (i.e., make me happy to see you). The speaker's reciprocal action is conveyed in v. 6 by an affirmation of trust and promise to sing praises.

In comparison to most psalms, Psalm 54 and Psalm 13 develop their arguments very sparely, without providing many specifics of the address, problem or solution and without offering much in the way of appeals to the classical sources of support: ethos (or authority), pathos (emotion) or logos (reason and observation). Before turning to more fully developed psalms, it is worth considering whether the spareness of Psalms 54 and 13 should be considered a defect. Are these the 'bargain basement' variety of psalm, available to sponsors with few resources? Were they composed for people

---

7. Staton, 'How Long', p. 65.

who were uncommunicative or reluctant to air the particulars of their situation in public, even before God? Are they the product of beginning psalmists who lack the skill to develop each point? Are they meant as skeletal models upon which psalmists can build more beautiful and elaborate poems?[8]

All these explanations are plausible. But I will advance another possibility, that these psalms reflect appropriate choices for speakers who believe so firmly in their innocence, in the justice of their claim or in God's omniscience, that they considered additional elaboration unnecessary. From a rhetorical perspective, the degree of elaboration or 'amplification' in a text signals the degree of controversy that the speaker expects; a relative lack of development reflects the degree to which the speaker expects the topics to be familiar and matters of agreement.

In the realm of policy arguments, arguments about addresses, problems and solutions are developed following a sequence of claims known as *stases*, consisting of claims concerning existence, definition, value, cause and action.[9] The stases were developed in classical rhetorical theory in antiquity to guide arguments in a courtroom dispute. The parties to a legal dispute proceeded from establishing that an incident happened, through defining the event as a particular type of crime, estimating its value or seriousness, tracing its causes and repercussions and finally proposing the action to be taken by the judge or jury.

The stases follow a plausible sequence: a speaker does not advance to argue claims at a higher *stasis* until agreement has been secured or can be presumed on the earlier ones. That is, it makes little sense to argue whether a neighbor's possession of the plaintiff's ox should be defined as a theft, a gift or a rescue without first establishing that the ox in question exists, is currently in the neighbor's possession and previously belonged to the plaintiff. In a modern courtroom, attorneys can officially lay out, or stipulate, the points on which they agree. In antiquity, the proceedings may have actually paused—reached a point of stasis—to see whether the opposing party would object before one side continued, as suggested by Troy Martin.[10] A pause is also available to a speaker in a conversation or to an instructor in a classroom who can ask whether the hearers understand and agree (at least provisionally) before continuing. In most situations, however, people who are planning an argument, especially one to be delivered as a public lecture or in writing, do not wait to get an answer. Instead,

---

8. This possibility was raised most recently by Schuele, 'Call on me', p. 323.

9. For discussion see Charney and Neuwirth, *Having your Say*. For a general discussion, see Michael Carter, 'Stasis and Kairos: Principles of Social Construction in Classical Rhetoric', *Rhetoric Review* 7 (1988), pp. 97-112.

10. Troy Martin, 'Apostasy to Paganism: The Rhetorical Stasis of the Galatian Controversy', *JBL* 114 (1995), pp. 437-61.

the speaker tries to anticipate which points will spark disagreement in the current circumstances and elaborate those points with more explanations, reasons and evidence. The degree of elaboration in a text—the amount of what might be called 'page real-estate'—signals the degree of controversy that the speaker expects.

The most obvious claims, the ones for which there is immediate agreement, do not need to be stated at all. Stating the obvious wastes the hearer's valuable time and attention—in the terms of philosophers of language, it violates philosopher Paul Grice's maxim of quantity for conversational aptness.[11] Belaboring arguments on which there is already agreement may backfire, reducing good-will or even irritating the hearer. To the contrary, Aristotle believed hearers are more likely to be persuaded when they are left to draw the unstated inferences needed to complete a logical-seeming argument or 'enthymeme'. As Perelman and Olbrechts-Tyteca emphasize, the only reason to state the obvious is to increase the claim's presence or salience for hearers whose attention has been elsewhere or for hearers who need to be revved up, as at a political convention.

It is possible, then, that the arguments in Psalms 54 and 13 are so spare because these speakers considered additional development unnecessary. As shown in Figure 3.1, Psalm 54 divides the space rather evenly among the address, the complaint, the proposed divine action, and the proposed reciprocal action. As shown in Figure 3.2, the amplitude in Psalm 13, what there is of it, occurs in the address section. The repeated plaintive questions that open Psalm 13 can be seen as underscoring just how inexplicable the speaker finds it that God has not responded before now. The speaker's only explicit proposal is the plea to resolve God's inattention in v. 4. The actions that God should take to deal with the opponent are treated as too obvious even to state. So, unlike the corresponding section in Psalm 54, the proposal in Psalm 13 only includes the speaker's reciprocal proposal to offer praise when rescued. The speakers in Psalms 54 and 13 may have believed so firmly in their innocence, in the justice of their claim or in God's omniscience, that even the starkest expression of lament should suffice.

A major theme of this book, that public poetry can be a forum for individual argument, grows out of the observation of the wealth of variations in elaboration of this basic structure, available because so many psalms address similar situations, such as laments or thanksgivings. The analyses throughout the rest of this book reflect the standing rhetorical hypothesis that the extent of elaboration betokens the speaker's assessment of controversy. Conciseness betokens what is generally agreed; elaboration and

---

11. Paul Grice, 'Logic and Conversation', in Heimir Geirsson and Michael Losonsky (eds.), *Readings in Language and Mind* (Cambridge, MA: Blackwell, 1996), pp. 121-33.

restatement betoken a point that, from the speaker's point of view, requires the most emphasis, development and support.

The remaining psalms in the book make more developed arguments, including explicit evidence of the speaker's worthiness. As such, these speakers see their innocence as arguable. Arguments for worthiness are so basic to the laments that they often occur at the outset, in the section corresponding to the address of a policy argument. However, as will become evident, many rhetorical options are available throughout a psalm to cast the speaker's character or ethos in a good light.

Chapter 4

Songs of Innocence

A pervasive approach adopted by speakers in the psalms is to assume the mantle of innocence. In contrast to the Mesopotamians who readily confessed faults in their prayers, 'the general stance of the psalmist is that of an innocent sufferer'.[1] In the three psalms in this chapter, the argument for the speaker's worthiness is especially powerful, dominating the content and expression. These speakers treat their innocence not as obvious but as a point in need of articulation and support. Innocence is not a simple quality; these speakers are not as similar to each other as newborn babes. They start from different standpoints relative to God and aim for distinct goals. The speaker in Psalm 44 dramatically accuses God of turning against faithful and innocent followers. The speaker in Psalm 22 makes an elaborate case to re-establish innocence and become God's public champion, while the speaker in Psalm 17 uses claims of innocence to seek apotheosis.

Psalm 44: God's Breach of Covenant

Psalm 44 is a bold challenge to God in the face of military defeat from a speaker who speaks both for himself personally and as a representative of the community. Just as the speaker attributes Israel's previous successes to God rather than to human prowess, so God is fingered as the cause of the community's current failure and humiliation. The speaker's main goal is to persuade God that the community has upheld its end of the covenant through faithful service and righteous behavior even during its current trials and is therefore deserving of rescue. The psalm also aims to persuade the public to maintain their adherence to God.

Psalm 44[2]

1 For the lead player, for the Korahites, a *maskil*.
2 God, with our own ears we have heard, our fathers recounted to us a deed that You did in their days, in days of yore.
3 You, Your hand dispossessed nations—and You planted them. You smashed peoples and sent them away.

---

1. Patrick and Diable, 'Persuading the One and Only God to Intervene', p. 21.
2. Alter, *The Book of Psalms*, pp. 154-57.

4	For not by their sword they took hold of the land, and it was not their arm that made them victorious but Your right hand and Your arm, and the light of Your face when you favored them.
5	You are my king, O God. Ordain the victories of Jacob.
6	Through You we gore our foes, through Your name we trample those against us.
7	For not in my bow do I trust, and my sword will not make me victorious.
8	For You rescued us from our foes, and our enemies You put to shame.
9	God we praise all day long, and Your name we acclaim for all time. Selah
10	Yet You neglected and disgraced us and did not sally forth in our ranks.
11	You turned us back from the foe and our enemies took their plunder.
12	You made us like sheep to be eaten and scattered us through the nations.
13	You sold Your people for no wealth and set no high price upon them.
14	You made us a shame to our neighbors, derision and mockery to those round us.
15	You made us a byword to the nations, an object of scorn among peoples.
16	All day long my disgrace is before me, and shame has covered my face,
17	from the sound of revilers and cursers, from the enemy and the avenger.
18	All this befell us, yet we did not forget You, and we did not betray Your pact.
19	Our heart has not failed, nor have our footsteps strayed from Your path,
20	though You thrust us down to the sea monster's place and with death's darkness covered us over.
21	Had we forgotten the name of God and spread out our palms to an alien god,
22	would not God have fathomed it? For He knows the heart's secrets.
23	For Your sake we are killed all day long, we are counted as sheep for slaughter.
24	Awake, why sleep, O Master! Rouse up, neglect not forever.
25	Why do You hide Your face, forget our affliction, our oppression?
26	For our neck is bowed to the dust, and our belly clings to the ground.
27	Rise as a help to us and redeem us for the sake of your kindness.

Psalm 44 clearly fits the three-part lament structure described in the previous chapter, with an address that establishes the previous relationship between God and the speaker, a lengthy complaint section and a brief proposal for divine action that notably lacks a promise of reciprocal action (see Figure 4.1).

The address (vv. 2-9) lays out the terms of the covenant in quasi-syllogistic form. In the past, the ancestors conquered and possessed the land through God's might, not their own; they deserved continued possession of the land because of their proper humility and attribution to God of due thanks and praise. Now in the present, the speaker, a direct descendant of Jacob, shows the same humility and readiness to thank and praise in the face of renewed military action. If the speaker is a member of the same class as the ancestors and has acted as faithfully as they did to uphold the covenant, then he is justified in fully expecting God to ordain victory in the current situation. But the expectation is not fulfilled.

4. *Songs of Innocence*

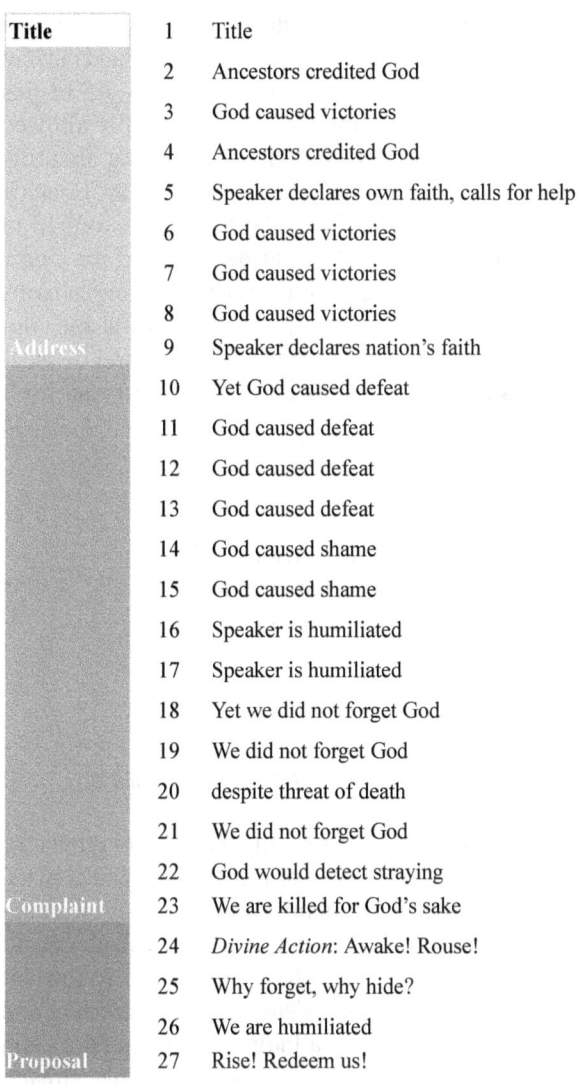

Figure 4.1. *Structure of Psalm 44*

To the contrary. The complaint (vv. 10-17) vividly describes God acting not as defender but as assailant, causing defeat and humiliation. This kind of clash between expectation and reality is the essence of a problem, an urgent rhetorical situation that initiates inquiry and deliberation.[3] The

---

3. As defined in Charney and Neuwirth (*Having your Say*, ch. 10), a problem involves the thwarting of a goal, expectation or theory. In addition to reality clashing with expectation (or an observed outcome clashing with an hypothesis), a problem may

complaint, which is half again as long as the address, uses diction, syntax and allusion to heighten the vivid contrast between past victory and current failure. As Loren Crow points out, each verse from v. 10 to v. 15 begins with a second-person singular verb showing God has not simply allowed other nations to defeat Israel, but 'has actively sought to bring about its end'.[4] As Martin Kessler observes, the phrase כל היום ('all day'), which first designates a period spent in praise of God (v. 9), is transformed to time spent contemplating humiliation (v. 16) and being killed for God's sake (v. 23).[5] And Dalit Rom-Shiloni notes that the complaint reuses terms referring to Israel and its opponents from the address in a chiastic and concentric order, showing that God has changed from smashing and displacing other nations for Israel's sake to smashing and displacing Israel itself (see Figure 4.2).[6]

A	v. 3	אומים 'nations', גוים 'peoples'
B	v. 5	יעקב 'Jacob'
C	v. 6	צרינו 'our foes', קמינו 'those against us'
D	v. 8	צרינו 'our foes', שנאינו 'our enemies'
D'	v. 11	צר 'foe', שנאינו 'our enemies'
C'	v. 12	גוים 'the nations'
B'	v. 13	עמך 'Your people'
A'	v. 15	אומים 'nations', גוים 'peoples'

Figure 4.2. *Chiastic Structure of References in Address and Complaint in Psalm 44*

A striking aspect of the complaint is how forthrightly the speaker rebuts the possibility that the failure is due to the people's or leader's own faults in vv. 18-23. A fair and persuasive rebuttal must identify the source of the claim being disputed, state the claim in a way that source would consider accurate, and provide counter-claims and/or counter-evidence. In Psalm 44, the claim being disputed is no less than the existence of the covenant and its continuation in force by both parties. By alluding to the ancestors and claiming a direct line of transmission from them, the speaker has already established that the covenant exists and has been in force until now.

---

arise from adopting multiple goals that seemingly cannot be realized simultaneously (such as cheap energy and a clean environment) or from a seemingly intractable obstacle that prevents a goal from being achieved.

4. Loren D. Crow, 'The Rhetoric of Psalm 44', *ZAW* 104.3 (1992), pp. 394-401 (397).

5. Martin Kessler, 'Psalm 44', in Janet W. Dyk *et al.* (eds.), *Unless Someone Guide Me...* (Festschrift Karel A. Deurloo; Maastricht: Shaker, 2001), pp. 193-204 (202).

6. Dalit Rom-Shiloni, 'Psalm 44: The Powers of Protest', *CBQ* 70 (2008), pp. 683-98 (687).

4. *Songs of Innocence*

The complaint clearly identifies God as the one whose actions violate the terms of the deal. The rebuttal in vv. 18-23 counters a possible warrant for God's actions, that the people broke the covenant first by forgetting God. As Rom-Shiloni notes, an accusation is not stated directly in the psalm itself, but the use of the verb שכח ('forget') in vv. 18 and 21 alludes to biblical and prophetic accusations of forgetting in Deuteronomy and Jeremiah that would warrant divine wrath.[7] In Psalm 44, forgetting is denied in a series of four sweeping counterclaims in vv. 18-20: 'yet we did not forget you', 'our heart has not failed', 'we did not betray your pact', 'nor have our feet strayed from your path'. The sequence moves from internalized attitudes to externally observable actions, suggesting the completeness of the people's faith as well as the ease of verifying the claims.

The accusation of forgetting is also denied counterfactually in vv. 21-22, the most dramatic and riskiest appeal of the psalm as a whole. The speaker argues that if the people had forgotten God (אם שכחנו 'Had we forgotten the name of God'), had the people begun worshipping a foreign deity, then God would surely have known about it. Raising a counterfactual possibility is always risky because it allows that the condition could be true. In the current instance, if God had detected apostasy, then all the punishments described so vividly in the complaint would be justified and the speaker's whole premise is undermined. But the speaker does not admit fault. Instead, the point of the counterfactual may be that if God had detected apostasy, he would have *said* something about it. In other words, the speaker may be implying that no prophet and no oracle gave warning that God was displeased with the people's conduct. Coming on top of the outright denials of fault, the counterfactual may force God to admit that the people have in fact been faithful and that no breach of covenant justified their defeat in battle or their current suffering. Instead, as v. 23 emphasizes, faithful Israelites have been and are being slaughtered in God's name.

The appeal for divine action in vv. 24-27 calls for God to undertake a dramatic change in role and revert to being a redeemer. As Kessler has noted, the verses use four imperative verbs of engagement (עורה 'awake' and הקיצה 'rouse' in v. 24; קומה 'rise' and פדנו 'redeem' in v. 27) to bracket, mirror and undo four verbs of withdrawal (תישן 'sleep' and תזנח 'neglect' in v. 24; תשכח 'forget' and תסתיר 'hide' in v. 25). As Loren Crow notes, the withdrawal verbs themselves represent a significant softening of action, considering that until this point God has been hostile rather than dormant.[8]

---

7. Rom-Shiloni also notes several allusions between Psalm 44 and Psalm 37 (such as a bodily connection between true hearts and steady feet) that add to the persuasiveness.

8. Kessler, 'Psalm 44', p. 200; Crow, 'The Rhetoric of Psalm 44'.

This section, in effect, presents two options or two stages, either of which is to be preferred to God's present enmity: God may withdraw to a state of benign neglect or arise in a more merciful and faithful mood. The absence of reciprocal action is entirely fitting for this psalm; promising praise would imply that it was not currently being supplied, undercutting the central thrust of the argument.

Interestingly, Adele Berlin offers a different reading of Psalm 44 in which the speaker argues only for present faithfulness and does not argue that God's initial assault was unjustified.[9] She groups Psalm 44 along with Psalms 137, 69 and 78 as psalms concerned with the Babylonian exile. While she notes that the lack of references to Jerusalem make it harder to tie this psalm to the exile than the others, she sees Psalm 44 as an effort from Babylon to convince God to bring the exiles home. The main difference between her reading and the one offered here is the interpretation of vv. 18-23. Berlin rightly notes that this section establishes that the community is exhibiting faithfulness in the present, even after suffering at God's hand. She is also right that the section sets up a rationale for God's rescue and redemption that the concluding section explicitly requests. However, Berlin excludes reading it as denial of past failings. She reads the opening of v. 18 כל זאת באתנו ('all this befell us') as turning the topic completely to the present, reading ולא שכחנוך as 'yet we do not forget you', translations also used by the *New English Bible* and the *Revised English Bible*.[10] In short, Berlin's reading assumes that the speaker is ready to concede that God's punishment was justified or at least is not contesting the point. She reads the counterfactual in vv. 21-22 as noting how easily the exiles might have turned to other gods while demonstrating their awareness that God's power extends even to Babylon.

Certainly the psalm permits both readings. However, more of the literary and rhetorical elements in the psalm support the reading in which faithfulness extends back to the past as well as forward to the present. The speaker had opportunities to admit fault before asking for rescue—an opportunity taken up in other psalms, such as those treated below in Chapter 6. But the speaker in Psalm 44 made no such move in the address, instead taking steps to heighten the reversal of expectation and to dwell on God's harshness. Similarly, the counterfactual phrasing seems unnecessary if the current situation is simply part of an extended justified punishment. In short, if Psalm 44 does refer to the exile, then the speaker went to great lengths both to hint at and conceal anger at God's actions.

---

9. Adele Berlin, 'Psalms and the Literature of Exile: Psalms 137, 44, 69, and 78', in Peter W. Flint and Patrick D. Miller (eds.), *Book of Psalms: Composition and Reception* (VTSup, 109; Leiden: Brill, 2005), pp. 65-86.

10. Berlin, 'Psalms', p. 72.

4. *Songs of Innocence*

Psalm 22: From Worm to Champion

As in Psalm 44, the speaker in Psalm 22 takes head-on the challenge of convincing God of his innocence and worthiness for rescue. In this case, however, the speaker's debilitation and despair convince him that God doesn't even recognize him as human, let alone as a partner in the covenant. Thus the speaker must recover this standing with God before the current problem can be broached and a solution proposed.

Accordingly, Psalm 22 can be divided into three sections: the Address (vv. 2-12), Petition (vv. 13-22) and Proposed Action (vv. 23-32) as shown schematically in Figure 4.3.[11] In terms of amplitude, the longest sections are the address (11 verses) and the proposal (13 verses) with the complaint taking only seven verses. Though vivid and pathos-laden, the complaint is not the site of the real persuasive work.

PSALM 22[12]

1   To the lead player, on *ayeleth hashahar*, a David psalm.
2   My God, my God, why have You forsaken me? Far from my rescue are the words that I roar.
3   My God, I cry out by day and You do not answer, by night—no stillness for me.
4   And You, the Holy One—enthroned in Israel's praise.
5   In You did our fathers trust, they trusted and You set them free.
6   To you they cried out, and escaped, in You they trusted and were not put to shame.
7   But I am a worm, and no man, a disgrace among men, by the people reviled.
8   All who see me do mock me—they curl their lips, they shake their head.
9   Who turns to the LORD, He will set him free. He will save him, for He delights in him.
10 For You drew me out from the womb, made me safe at my mother's breasts.
11 Upon You I was cast from birth; from my mother's belly You were my God.
12 Do not be far from me, for distress is near, for there is none to help.
13 Brawny bulls surrounded me, the mighty of Bashan encompassed me.
14 They gaped with their mouths against me—a ravening roaring lion.
15 Like water I spilled out, all my limbs fell apart. My heart was like wax, melting within my chest.
16 My palate turned dry as a shard and my tongue was annealed to my jaw; and to death's dust did You thrust me.

---

11. The sectioning follows that of John S. Kselman, '"Why have you abandoned me": A Rhetorical Study of Psalm 22', in David Clines, David M. Gunn and Alan J. Hauser (eds.), *Art and Meaning* (Sheffield: JSOT Press, 1982), pp. 172-98. Earlier versions of my analysis appeared in Charney, 'Performativity and Persuasion', pp. 247-68 and Charney, 'Maintaining Innocence before a Divine Hearer: Deliberative Rhetoric in Ps. 22, Ps. 17, and Ps. 7', *BibInt* 21 (2013), pp. 33-63.

12. Alter, *The Book of Psalms*, pp. 71-77.

17 For the curs came all around me, a pack of the evil encircled me, they bound my hands and my feet.
18 They counted out all my bones. It is they who looked, who stared at me.
19 They shared out my garments among them and cast lots for my clothes.
20 But you, O Lord, be not far. My strength, to my aid O hasten.
21 Save from the sword my life; from the cur's power my person.
22 Rescue me from the lion's mouth. And from the horns of the ram You answered me.
23 Let me tell Your name to my brothers, in the assembly let me praise You.
24 Fearers of the Lord, O praise Him! All the seed of Jacob revere Him! And be afraid of Him, all Israel's seed!
25 For He has not spurned nor has despised the affliction of the lowly, and has not hidden His face from him; when he cried to Him, He heard.
26 For You—my praise in the great assembly. My vows I fulfill before those who fear Him.
27 The lowly shall eat and be sated. Those who seek Him will praise the Lord. May you be of good cheer for ever!
28 All the far ends of earth will remember and return to the Lord. All the clans of the nations will bow down before You.
29 For the Lord's is the kingship—and He rules over the nations.
30 Yes to Him will bow down all the netherworld's sleepers. Before Him will kneel all who go down to the dust whose life is undone.
31 My seed will serve Him. It will be told to generations to come.
32 They will proclaim His bounty to a people aborning, for He has done.

The speaker takes on a two-fold task in the address, anticipating God's reasons for withholding aid and refuting those reasons. The section is bounded by pleas for a hearing both at its opening (vv. 2-3) and at its closing (v. 12). Thus, the dramatic questions that open the psalm are not in this case a standard rhetorical ploy and do not simply express deep emotion. The question 'Why have you abandoned me?' in fact initiates an inquiry into God's possible doubts, doubts that must be fully dispelled before going on to the complaint.

First, in vv. 4-6, the speaker reminds God of the ancestors who trusted, called in times of trouble and were answered. Although the speaker refers to ancestors as אבותינו (literally 'our fathers'), the speaker does not at this point make an explicit claim to share their faith. Rather, citing the ancestors in this way serves both to remind God of the covenant that should govern their relationship and to anticipate the possible grounds for God's silence. Perhaps God doubts that the speaker is bred from the same stuff as the ancestors.

The speaker accentuates the doubt even further in vv. 7-9 by referring to himself as 'a worm and no man' and as an object of public scorn. As an expression of the speaker's psychological state, the power of this move

4. *Songs of Innocence* 73

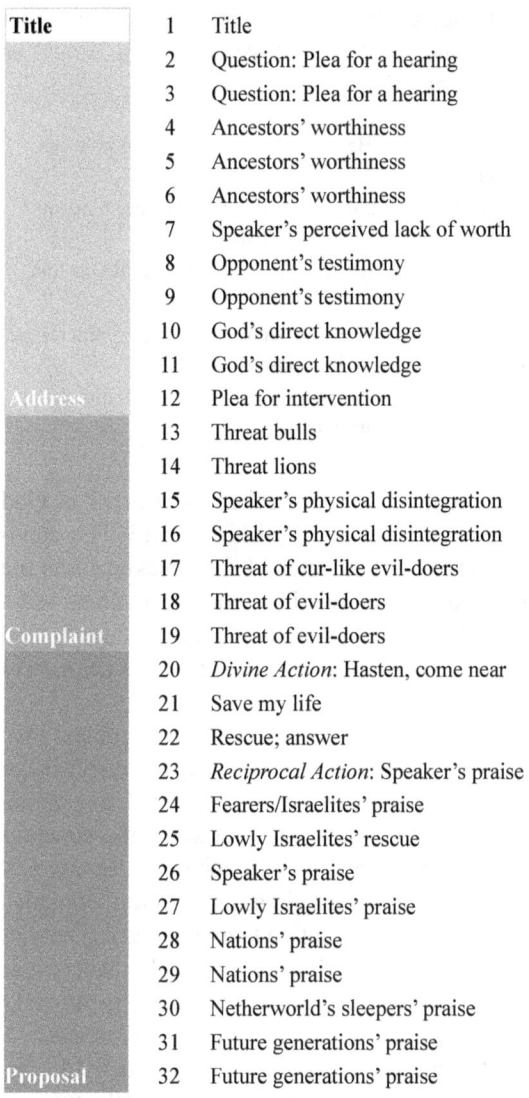

Title	1	Title
	2	Question: Plea for a hearing
	3	Question: Plea for a hearing
	4	Ancestors' worthiness
	5	Ancestors' worthiness
	6	Ancestors' worthiness
	7	Speaker's perceived lack of worth
	8	Opponent's testimony
	9	Opponent's testimony
	10	God's direct knowledge
	11	God's direct knowledge
Address	12	Plea for intervention
	13	Threat bulls
	14	Threat lions
	15	Speaker's physical disintegration
	16	Speaker's physical disintegration
	17	Threat of cur-like evil-doers
	18	Threat of evil-doers
Complaint	19	Threat of evil-doers
	20	*Divine Action*: Hasten, come near
	21	Save my life
	22	Rescue; answer
	23	*Reciprocal Action*: Speaker's praise
	24	Fearers/Israelites' praise
	25	Lowly Israelites' rescue
	26	Speaker's praise
	27	Lowly Israelites' praise
	28	Nations' praise
	29	Nations' praise
	30	Netherworld's sleepers' praise
	31	Future generations' praise
Proposal	32	Future generations' praise

Figure 4.3. *Structure of Psalm 22*

is obvious: while the ancestors were spared humiliation, the speaker feels dehumanized. But by overstating the case so dramatically, the speaker also begins to oppose the doubts, inviting God to concede that worms are not prone to psalmistry. Similarly, the opponents' taunting in vv. 8-9 serves simultaneously to express and to undermine the image of unworthiness. The taunt—under certain translations—conveys the sting of humiliation at the same time that it documents the speaker's faith in God through the testimony of external witnesses. This is the effect of the translations by

Kselman, Kraus and the RSV (among others) who treat Ps. 22.9 as a direct quote of the taunters and who take 'גל אל ה' ('trust/commit to God') as describing the speaker's prior actions.

Ps. 22.9	Alter	Who turns to the LORD, He will set him free. He will save him, for He delights in him.
	NJPS	'Let him commit himself to the LORD; let Him rescue him, let Him save him, for He is pleased with him'.
	Kselman	'He lived for Yahweh—let him deliver him; let him rescue him, if he delights in him'.[13]
	Kraus	He put it in the hands of Yahweh, let him free him, let him rescue him, for he is obviously well disposed to him![14]
	RSV	'He committed his cause to the LORD; let him deliver him, let him rescue him, for he delights in him!'

On this reading, the taunting proves that the speaker has trusted in God openly—so openly that his opponents make fun of him for it.[15] The opponents unwittingly validate the ethos or character of the speaker; he is the type of person to whom God should respond. The mockery even serves a third purpose, raising the threat that God's own reputation is at stake: If God does not reply, if the speaker is not rescued, then God may also be open to the mockery of non-believers.

This reading seems more plausible and coherent within the context than the translations by Alter and the NJPS. Alter treats v. 9 not as a direct quote but as an expression of hope from the speaker. One problem with this option is its sudden impersonality, having the speaker now refer to faithful Israelites in the abstract as 'him'. A second problem is lack of cohesion, leaving v. 9 with no clear relation to the surrounding verses, either forward to v. 10 which describes the speaker's birth or back to the point on taunters in v. 8. The NJPS does treat v. 9 as a direct quote from by-standers but curiously renders it as friendly advice rather than a taunt, even though many descriptions of mocking opponents in the psalms are followed by direct quotes of their taunts.

In the third step, vv. 10-11, the speaker describes his birth, finally declaring his faith explicitly in a way that also thoroughly erases the dehumanization. The vivid image of the speaker's birth re-establishes him as a human being and not a worm. He was literally born and bred as an Israelite, not only connected to the ancestors but also serving God in life-long dedication.

13. Kselman, 'Why have you', p. 173.
14. Kraus, *Psalms 1–59*, p. 291.
15. In 'Persuading the One and Only God to Intervene', Patrick and Diable interpret reports of taunting this way. After citing Pss. 3.3, 22.9 and 42.4, 11, they comment that 'the citation of the enemies' taunts regarding reliance on YHWH is just one of a number of ways the supplicant makes his reliance known to YHWH' (p. 26).

The description of God acting as mid-wife invites God to recall observing the speaker's birth first-hand and knowing of his dedication. The reference to the mother's רחם ('womb') also appeals metaphorically to God's רחמים, the womanly quality of mercy. It is only after elaborating this argument that the speaker closes the section by repeating the plea for response in v. 12.

In this analysis, then, the entire address of Psalm 22 consists of an extended argument about the speaker's worthiness, with both logical and emotional appeals to God's own past behavior, eye-witness testimony from the speaker's mocking opponents and reminders to God of having directly observed the speaker's birth.

The complaint, the second and briefest section of the psalm in vv. 13-19, describes the speaker's untenable situation, threatened by opponents that seem alien both in species and nationality. The problem is developed as a narrative with the presence of the threatening forms of bulls, dogs and a lion. In face of the threat, the speaker's physical integrity dissolves and congeals, deteriorating to the point of death in vv. 14-16. His weakness allows the enemies to get close enough to count his bones, bind him and divide up his possessions (vv. 17-19). Whether the opponents are native or foreign, the nature of the crisis in Psalm 22 involves isolation and deprivation, physical threat from people and animals, bondage and closeness to death.

The longest section, the proposal, devotes little of its space to spelling out the actions for God to take. The four actions in vv. 20-22 counteract respectively the kinds of harms spelled out in the complaint, isolation, physical debilitation and the threats from human and inhuman enemies. God is asked to אל תרחק ('be not far'), חושה ('hasten' in bringing back physical strength), הצילה ('save') and הושיעני ('deliver' the speaker). The quick succession of imperative verbs amounts to a staccato call for action, which is answered in v. 22.

The weightiest part of the proposal is the speaker's reciprocal action in vv. 23-32. Ellen Davis, who calls this section the 'confession of faith', notes that the 'chief formal peculiarity' of Psalm 22 is that 'nearly a third of the poem stands at the antipodes to lament—the last ten verses of this lament are an extravagant portrayal of the circles of those who offer praise to Israel's God'.[16] In addition to declaring his own praises of God, the speaker directs/predicts praise from widening circles of others, from his immediate family (the 'brothers' in v. 23), to the 'great assembly' (vv. 23-26), to other nations (vv. 28-29), to all mortal creatures and generations yet unborn (vv. 30-32).

The amplitude of this section underscores the speaker's worthiness—more than compensating for the initial doubt and dehumanization in the address. Now the speaker is empowered to persuade others to remain as dedicated to God as he was even in times of despair. The speaker becomes

---

16. Davis, 'Exploding the Limits', p. 96.

God's champion relative to all three types of people described in the address: the ancestors who were answered when they called, the mockers who must return to faith, and the children who are and will be born into the faith. The covenant continues for as long as God responds to loyal followers; those deserving of response are those who carry on with praising, calling and reasserting their claims to be heard.

Psalm 17: Assertions of Godliness

Whereas the speaker in Psalm 22 gradually builds a case for rescue by virtue of God's covenant with Israel, the speaker in Psalm 17 asserts his righteousness from the outset. The occasion is far less dire: this speaker is hemmed in by his rivals, not sunk in degradation; his object is loftier than mere physical well-being. Ultimately, the speaker in Psalm 17 seeks through vindication to raise himself far above his rivals, let alone the common mass of humanity. Rather than inspiring other Israelites, nations and future generations to praise God, his goal is to achieve his own intimate rapport with the divine.

Psalm 17[17]

1. A David Prayer. Hear, O Lord, a just thing. Listen well to my song. Hearken to my guileless prayer.
2. From before You my judgment will come, Your eyes behold rightness.
3. You have probed my heart, come upon me by night, You have tried me, and found no wrong in me. I barred my mouth to let nothing pass.
4. As for human acts—by the word of Your lips! I have kept from the tracks of the brute.
5. Set firm my steps on your pathways, so my feet will not stumble.
6. I called You, for You will answer me, God. Incline Your ear, O hear my utterance.
7. Make Your mercies abound, O rescuer of those who shelter from foes at Your right hand.
8. Guard me like the apple of the eye, in the shadow of Your wings conceal me
9. from the wicked who have despoiled me, my deadly enemies drawn round me.
10. Their fat has covered their heart. With their dewlaps they speak haughty words.
11. My steps they now hem in, their eyes they cast over the land
12. He is like a lion longing for prey, like the king of beasts lying in wait.
13. Rise, Lord, head him off, bring him down, save my life from the wicked with Your sword,
14. from men, by Your hand [Lord], from men, from those fleeting of portion in life. And Your protected ones—fill their bellies, let their sons be sated, and let them leave what is left for their young.
15. As for me, in justice I behold Your face, I take my fill, wide awake, of Your image.

---

17. Alter, *The Book of Psalms*, pp. 48-51.

Figure 4.4 shows schematically how Psalm 17 can be divided into three sections: the Address (vv. 1-8); the Complaint (vv. 9-12); and Proposals, for Divine Action (vv. 13-14) and Reciprocal Action (v. 15). The address clearly dominates the psalm taking up fully half the verses, in contrast to Psalm 22 in which the address was balanced by the proposal.

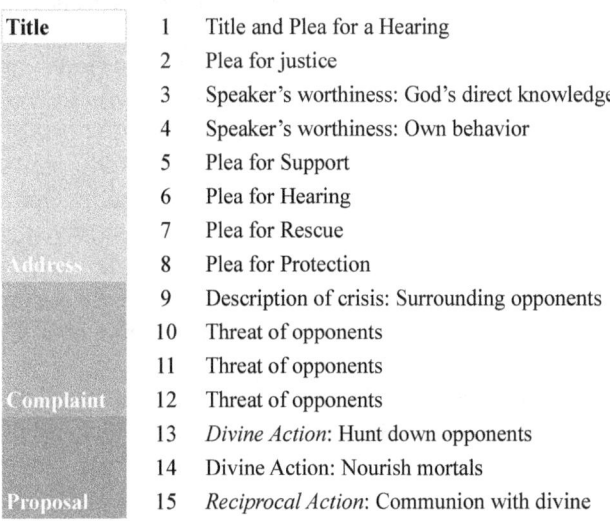

Figure 4.4. *Structure of Psalm 17 as Deliberative Argument*

As in Ps. 22.2-12, the address is an extended claim concerning the speaker's worthiness. In Ps. 17.1-8, however, the speaker stands at a much better starting point. Far from being neglected or dehumanized, the speaker in Psalm 17 combines the call for attention with an immediate explicit claim to innocence and uprightness. The speaker has a message to deliver, characterizes it as 'a just thing' and emphasizes that it will be transmitted through 'lips that are without guile'.[18] Accordingly, in v. 2, the speaker already anticipates winning God's approval, because God perceives what is right.

The speaker's claim to being innocent and righteous is supported in two ways in Ps. 17.3-4. First, in v. 3, the speaker reminds God of having found nothing wrong in a previous test of the speaker's mettle.[19] In v. 4, the speaker describes his own behavior, claiming to avoid the ways of evil people. Robert Alter gives v. 4 the form of a public oath: 'As for human acts—by the word of Your lips! I have kept from the tracks of the brute.'

---

18. In his translation of Ps. 17.3, Alter opts, rightly I believe, to treat the message as what is 'just' rather than God, as some other translators claim.

19. Gert Kwaakel treats this test as hypothetical: 'if you examine', 'if you investigate', in his *'According to my Righteousness': Upright Behaviour as Grounds for Deliverance in Psalms 7, 17, 18, 26, and 44* (Leiden: Brill, 2006), p. 70.

Oaths are especially powerful means of support because of their obvious underlying warrant: God condemns all false swearing and particularly swearing by God's name. By combining a reference to the results of a previous test and a public oath of having avoided evil, the address attempts to convey certainty about the speaker's innocence. Yet this is not the end of the section. The address continues with an unusually lengthy plea for response in vv. 5-8.

The plea for response is notable for its repeated references to God as an embodied figure with lips (v. 4), ears (v. 6), hands (v. 7), eyes and wings (v. 8). Even the phrase 'set firm my steps' in v. 5 uses a verb תמך ('grasp') that connotes using hands. Further, in each verse, the speaker's physical features are made to interact with God's: feet being grasped by God's hands, words being heard by God's inclined ear, body being sheltered at God's right hand, concealed by God's wings and guarded like the apple of God's eye. The imagery continually reinforces an identification between the speaker and God—an identification that remains important throughout the rest of the psalm.

The speaker's problem is laid out briefly in vv. 9-12. The first complaint is that the opponents 'despoiled me'. However, unlike Psalm 22, no vivid narrative of damage or deprivation is provided in Psalm 17; this speaker is not portraying himself as weak, deteriorating and suffering. Instead, the problem seems to be that the opponents are a continuing, looming threat.

The most striking aspect of vv. 9-12 is the speaker's description of the opponents as physically gross. First the speaker says חלבמו סגרו ('their fat has covered [their heart]'). As Alter remarks about this translation, the heart as the locus of the fat is only implied in v. 10: 'fat over the heart (presumably a token of the offensive prosperity of the wicked) insulates it from perception and feeling'.[20] In Alter's translation, the physical grossness carries over into the next verset ('with their dewlaps they speak haughty words'). Alter notes that פימו is

> a grammatically archaic form meaning 'their mouth'. Because of the prominent fat image in the first verset, this translation emends that word to *pimatam* (or, in an undeclined form, simply *pimah*), a term that refers to folds of fat under the chin.

Next, in v. 12, the enemies are represented in beastly form: 'he is like a lion longing for prey' (דמינו כאריה יכסוף לטרוף) or more literally, 'his form is like a lion...'. This section certainly does describe a threat but the main effect is to depict a stark physical contrast between the enemy and the presumably more attractive human features attributed both to God and to the speaker in the preceding section.

---

20. A similar reading is provided by Kraus, *Psalms 1–59*, p. 244.

4. *Songs of Innocence*

The solution that the speaker proposes for God to carry out is laid out in vv. 13-14. In v. 13, God is urged to go on the hunt, armed with a sword, to head off and bring down the beast, leading to the speaker's rescue. Psalm 17.14 seems to open by specifying from whom the speaker is to be rescued with the repeated phrase ממתים ('from mortals'). But surprisingly, the speaker goes on to exhort God to three additional actions toward these mortals: 'fill their bellies', 'let their sons be sated' and 'let them leave what is left for their young'. The extensive critical controversy on this verse centers on the identity of the referents. Does 'they' still refer to the enemies mentioned in v. 13? Or is there a shift in v. 14 to refer to a completely different group, perhaps those faithful to God, who have hitherto been absent from the psalm? Both possibilities have attracted scholarly adherents.[21]

Ps 17.14	Kwakkel	from men, by your hand, O Y<small>HWH</small>, from men without duration of life; you may fill their belly with their portion among the living and with what you have stored up (for them); may the sons be satisfied, and leave their residue to their children![22]
	Kraus	May a cruel death at your hand, O Yahweh, a cruel death put an end to their portion in life! What you have put in store for them—(with that) fill their belly, so that their sons may (still) have their fill and bequeath a remainder to their children![23]
	Alter	from men, by Your hand [L<small>ORD</small>], from men, from those fleeting of portion in life. And Your protected ones—fill their bellies, let their sons be sated, and let them leave what is left for their young.
	NJPS	from men, O L<small>ORD</small>, from men whose share in life is fleeting. But as to Your treasured ones, fill their bellies. Their sons too shall be satisfied, and have something to leave over for their young.

Joel LeMon has recently reviewed the possibilities and ends up siding with those such as Kwakkel and Kraus who construe all the referents in the verse as the enemies.[24] Translated this way, then, the speaker might seem surprisingly generous, allowing the remnant of the enemies to live and be well. As LeMon notes, however, it is also possible to give an ominous cast to the calls to fill their bellies with צפינך ('what you have in store for them') and

---

21. A third approach to the verse is offered by Jacob Leveen who substantially emends the text to make the entirety of verse 14 refer to faithful Israelites: 'They that are perfect in thy ways will praise thee, O Lord: As for the perfect of this world, their portion is in this life; and for thy saints, thou wilt fill their belly, they will be satisfied with children, and shall leave their substance to their offspring.' See 'Textual Problems of Psalm 17', *VT* 11 (1961), pp. 48-54 (52).
22. Kwakkel, *According to my Righteousness*, pp. 80, 95.
23. Kraus, *Psalms 1–59*, p. 244.
24. Joel LeMon, *Yahweh's Winged Form in the Psalms: Exploring Congruent Iconography and Texts* (Fribourg: Academic Press, 2010), pp. 62-67.

portray both God and the psalmist in a somewhat vindictive light. Not only are the enemies destroyed but their future generations are also in for it.

The second approach to Ps. 17.14, that provided by Alter and the NJPS, is also shared by Peter Craigie and John Eaton.[25] These scholars divide v. 14, with the first part referring to the wicked, and the second to a group of faithful allies who are introduced by translating צפינך as 'As for Your protected ones' or 'But your treasured ones'. The translation of this key term is uncertain because it is found nowhere else in the Hebrew Bible.[26] In the split-verse approach, it is possible to read the first use of ממתים ('from men') as referring back to the enemies and the second as referring forward to the faithful allies. The enjambment inevitably leaves hearers pondering the curious proximity of the wicked and the protected faithful ones. Both eat, both have fleeting lives. But the wicked act violently like wild beasts to satisfy their needs, while the faithful Israelites do not. When God acts, the wicked are swept away (at least for the time being) and God's followers go on in life and through future generations.

Regardless of whether the referents are taken to be friends or foes, Ps. 17.14 ends up with an unsavory aroma clinging to the image of God filling up someone's belly immediately after hunting down a beastly prey. The aroma is especially pungent if the ones to be fed are the wicked, those described earlier as lions, themselves longing for prey and depicted in v. 10 as grossly over-fed but still ravenous. Having a belly filled can only be a nauseating punishment, as was stuffing the Israelites with quail in Num. 11.1-34. But even if it is the 'protected ones' who are being fed, the juxtaposition of friends and freshly killed foes makes the outcome of having material needs satisfied into an anti-climax rather than a joyous affirmation.

The ineradicable ambiguity of reference suits the vagueness of the problem laid out in vv. 9-12. The speaker has enemies whom he would like to defeat, but as compared to Psalm 22, the situation is not an urgent life-or-death crisis. What the speaker hungers for is justice, not food, not health, not vindication, not children and not material means to support himself. Accordingly, the way is prepared for the stark contrast of the speaker's renunciation of material reward in v. 15, the concluding verse of the psalm.

Unlike speakers in many other psalms, the speaker does not conclude by promising to praise or sing, to sacrifice or to feast. Instead, with the

---

25. Peter C. Craigie, *Psalms 1–50* (Nashville, TN: Thomas Nelson, 2nd edn, 2005); John H. Eaton, *Psalms: A Historical and Spiritual Commentary* (New York: Continuum International, 2005).

26. The same root does appear however in another prominent but much later Judaic context. In the Passover Seder, the word צפן is used to refer to a morsel of matzah (the bread of affliction) set aside for dessert. Its use here then retains the paradoxical joining of affliction and reward.

appositive אני ('as for me'), the speaker moves apart from everyone else, whether friend or foe, and abjures material reward: 'As for me, in justice I behold Your face, I take my fill, wide awake, of Your image'. Alter's choice of 'I take my fill' for אשבעה ('I will be satisfied') contrasts especially nicely with the filled bellies in v. 14. For the speaker, sustenance comes from a relationship with God; the verse imagines God and the speaker as close together as intimates and on, as it were, equal footing. All the earlier bodily images culminate here. The speaker's desire is twofold: first, a visible manifestation of justice on the current occasion—which can only confirm the speaker's likeness to God—and second, the promise of an ongoing shared regard with God in the everyday world.

Conclusion

The speakers of the three psalms discussed in this chapter share a common persuasive goal—not to initiate a process of growth or change in themselves, but to instigate a change in God's attitudes and behaviors towards them, and, by extension, towards their communities. The crux of the argument, in each case, is the speaker's character, his or her claim to innocence, or at least worthiness, for God's regard and rescue.

In Aristotle's classical formulation, appeals to the speaker's character or *ethos* are one of the three means of proof for a claim—in addition to *logos*, appealing to rationality and *pathos*, appealing to emotion. In any public forum, the audience constructs a representation of the speaker's character from a variety of clues that the speaker supplies intentionally or unintentionally: physical appearance, explicit self-references, gestures of identification and good will, signs of wisdom, knowledge and practical skill. In Psalms 44, 22 and 17, the speakers make abundant appeals to their personal histories, their relations to the Israelite people, their unbroken faith and good will towards God, and their humility and ethical integrity. Yet it is not these appeals that set these three psalms apart from other first-person psalms. Rather, it is the centrality of the claim of worthiness itself.

A claim of worthiness is an argument at the stasis of value. Is the speaker qualified to receive God's attention or rescue? As outlined in the previous chapter, speakers following the sequence of stases do not argue about whether a thing is good or bad without having first established whether it exists and what kind of thing it is. That is, before assessing the quality of two apples, one first has to acknowledge the presence of two objects and classify both of them as apples rather than an apple and an orange or other round objects. In rhetorical situations, a powerful interlocutor can forestall all efforts at persuasion by simply refusing to acknowledge a speaker's presence. Psalm 8.5 celebrates God's willingness to attend to humanity at all: 'what is man that You should note him, and the human creature that You pay him heed?' The first-person psalms are premised on an even greater degree of openness—God's willingness to take note of individuals—a premise that must be considered so basic a condition of life that it usually goes unstated.

In the psalms, the basic claims that Israelites have on God are both definitional and value-based: first, that they belong to the people with whom God established a covenant and second that their actions merit good treatment. In both Psalms 44 and 22, the speakers accomplish the first task by identifying themselves explicitly with the ancestors whose claims God honored, with the speaker in Psalm 44 dwelling on this point at length. The speaker in Psalm 17 is confident enough of his standing with God that he by-passes the point altogether, moving immediately to the justice—the value—of his case. In all three psalms, establishing membership in the 'protected class' of Israelites is hardly sufficient.

Value claims build on definition claims because the quality of an item is assessed against others in the same class—apples are compared to apples, not oranges. Value judgments are intrinsically relative, not absolute. The psalms in the next chapter deal with speakers arguing that they are more worthy than their opponents by attempting to raise their own standing and lower their opponents'. In contrast, the speakers in Psalms 44, 22 and 17 argue that they meet or exceed some quality standard, that they are sufficiently worthy for rescue. In Psalm 44, after identifying with the ancestors, the speaker takes pains to argue that the community's current behavior is up to snuff—even after ill-use, they have not forgotten, betrayed or neglected God. In Psalm 22, the speaker brings in several forms of evidence of his own faithfulness to God—the testimony of opponents and God's own witnessing of his commitment since birth. In Psalm 17, the speaker declares himself a spokesman of justice and dares to set his own value far above that of his fellows, even approaching that of God.

Chapter 5

THE KAIROS OF CURSES

The persuasive power of the psalms in Chapter 4 turned on the character of the speaker, specifically on his claim to be sufficiently worthy for God to rescue. Most first-person psalms, however, also devote considerable attention to the characters of the speaker's opponents. The speakers in these psalms seek both rescue and vindication—the destruction of the opponents or at least their downfall and humiliation, which in turn allows the speaker to rejoice in public at their defeat. The arguments in these psalms turn on the notion of equity, asking God to weigh the interactions of two parties. Are they generous towards each other? Do they trade tit for tat? Does one party deal meanly with the other for no reason or—even worse—return evil for good? Ultimately, it is up to God to tip the balance in favor of merit and justice.

In most of these oppositional psalms, the two sides are depicted in absolute terms. Speakers depict themselves favorably and their opponents as devoid of merit and even humanity. Outside the uncertain attributions of a few superscriptions, opponents are never described in specific terms. Some opponents are described as alien nationals (e.g., Psalms 22 and 44) and some as Israelites who have rejected God (e.g., in Psalms 28 and 59.6, opponents are characterized as בגדי און ['wrong-doing traitors']). In several psalms, though, the opponent is clearly a fellow Israelite with some standing in the community, even a former friend (e.g., Pss. 35.13-14, 41.7 and especially 55.13-15). Hidden behind the absolute characterizations, however, is the fact that real-world disputes are rarely so clear-cut. All parties to a dispute are likely to believe themselves in the right, at least to some extent. If the disputants are all Israelites, it is even possible to imagine them all making sacrifices and offering psalms, each one appealing to God for justice against the other. It is this contest—not simply aggrieved innocence—that is reflected in the persuasive strategies.

A few speakers go so far as to curse their opponents, asking God to enact violent and horrific punishments on them, raining hot coals on their heads, binding their kings in fetters, smashing their infants against rocks. As Patrick D. Miller notes, the power of curses in the psalms is magnified because 'this is *poetry* in all its *power and evocative possibility*'.[1] Historically, Christian theologians have struggled with these so-called imprecatory psalms, psalms in which a 'major element or leading feature' is a plea for an opponent to suffer a terrible fate.[2] The theological problem has been spelled out by Joel LeMon: If prayer shapes belief and if belief, in turn, shapes action, then a liturgy that includes imprecation will surely debilitate a community's moral beliefs and lead to degenerate behavior.[3] This reasoning led many Christian theologians to excise these psalms from the liturgy or to hold them up as excuses for excoriating the primitive character of Israelite (and/or Jewish) beliefs. Recently, however, some scholars have sought to salvage the imprecatory psalms.[4] They note that imprecation cannot be so easily isolated and effaced; it occurs throughout the Psalter, and in the Christian as well as the Hebrew Bible. Further, they point out that imprecations can serve important psychological functions for victims who may gain therapeutic benefits from expressing outrage and calling for vengeance. Even the community might benefit; hearing imprecations could jolt congregants into considering their own toleration—or even perpetuation—of violence and injustice.

Rather than psychologizing the victims or even the hearers, my approach will be to consider how imprecations are used to craft persuasive arguments to God demanding justice. A curse is particularly explicit in challenging God to choose between the two parties and implicating God in the (in)justice of the outcome. While curses were common throughout the ancient world, according to Jan Assmann, curses in the ancient Near East—including ancient Israel—were far more explicit than Egyptian or Greek curses in implicating the deities directly in determining the truth and effecting punishment.[5]

---

1. Patrick D. Miller, 'The Hermeneutics of Imprecation', in Wallace M. Allston, Jr (ed.), *Theology in the Service of the Church: Essays in Honor of Thomas Gillespie* (Grand Rapids, MI: Eerdmans, 2000), pp. 153-63 (159); emphasis original.

2. J. Carl Laney, 'A Fresh Look at the Imprecatory Psalms', *BSac* 138 (1981), pp. 35-45 (36). He includes nine such psalms: Psalms 7, 35, 58, 59, 69, 83, 109, 137 and 139. Strict categorization is difficult, however, because speakers in many other psalms wish opponents ill.

3. Joel LeMon, 'Saying Amen to Violent Psalms', in Rolf Jacobson (ed.), *Soundings in the Theology of the Psalms: Perspectives and Methods in Contemporary Scholarship* (Minneapolis: Fortress Press, 2011), pp. 93-109.

4. In addition to LeMon, see Nancy deClaissé-Walford, 'The Theology of the Imprecatory Psalms', in Rolf Jacobson (ed.), *Soundings in the Theology of the Psalms: Perspectives and Methods in Contemporary Scholarship* (Minneapolis: Fortress Press, 2011), pp. 77-92.

5. Jan Assmann, 'When Justice Fails: Jurisdiction and Imprecation in Ancient Egypt and the Near East', *JEA* 78 (1992), pp. 149-62. See also Christopher Faraone, 'Molten Wax, Spilt Wine and Mutilated Animals: Sympathetic Magic in Near Eastern and Early Greek Oath Ceremonies', *JHS* 113 (1993), pp. 60-80.

5. *The Kairos of Curses*

Historically, the legal systems of the ancient Near East were underpinned by ritualized oaths and curses that depended on the people's belief in divine retribution. Curses were especially rife in cultures where the law was weak. As Assmann puts it, 'the law protects the social order, the curse protects the law'.[6] Assmann argues that the prevalence of oaths and curses was inversely related to the stability of local legal institutions: 'Disbelief in metaphysical agents will cause a decline in the tradition of cursing, disbelief in the functioning of socio-political institutions will have the opposite effect.'[7] Curses work, in part, because they inspire fear. But they also provide a way to cope with otherwise insoluble problems, cases in which the wrong-doing is undetectable or impossible to prove or cases that run up against limitations in the legal system itself.[8] Accordingly, the appearance of curses in the psalms may signal that the case is a particularly difficult one for the judicial system to handle.

For rhetorical scholars, the use of oaths and curses in the psalms may be particularly interesting because of their relative absence in Greek theories of rhetoric. In *The Rhetoric*, Aristotle treats oaths, trial by combat and sworn testimony as 'inartistic' proofs. Clearly Aristotle was not discouraging orators from using these forms of evidence; rather, he considered them less important to discuss at the outset because they are obvious, ready for use and simple to apply, not requiring much exercising of a rhetor's art of inventing, remembering or finding things to say. Michael Gagarin emphasizes that Aristotle regarded 'proofs' of either the artistic or inartistic variety as evidentiary material available for the rhetor to choose from, rather than as clinching moves that halt rational deliberation.[9] In an oath challenge, one party is asked to make a conditional self-curse, bringing down the wrath of the gods if he is lying or fails to carry out the vow. A speaker's willingness to swear a particular formulation of oath is open to rhetorical strategizing; the same holds true in US courts today concerning the decision of the accused to testify under oath in his or her own defense. Strikingly, Greek legal texts describe few cases in which oath challenges are offered and none in which one is accepted.[10]

---

6. Assmann, 'When Justice Fails', p. 149.
7. Assmann, 'When Justice Fails', p. 151.
8. For a fuller discussion, see Jeff S. Anderson, 'The Social Function of Curses in the Hebrew Bible', *ZAW* 110 (1998), pp. 223-37.
9. Michael Gagarin, 'The Nature of Proofs in Antiphon', *Classical Philology* 85 (1990), pp. 22-32.
10. For this reason, David Cyrus Mirhady disagrees with Gagarin, arguing that oath challenges were trumping moves that, if accepted, would end a proceeding. See Mirhady, 'The Oath-Challenge in Athens', *ClQ* 44 (1991), pp. 78-83. For a comparison of Greek and Near Eastern oath challenges, see Faraone, 'Molten Wax'.

In this chapter, I describe how the speakers in Psalms 7, 35 and 109 use curses as evidence of their own innocence (Psalm 7), as a contrast with an opponent's behavior (Psalm 35) and as a denunciation (Psalm 109). While the speakers depict pure good pitted against pure evil, their motives and actions are much more complex. Perhaps both parties are at fault to some extent. Perhaps, rather than being a pious and innocent victim, the speaker is unwilling to admit to his or her fault in public or is seeking to conceal it. As I will argue, a neglected dimension of the artistry of these psalms is how skillfully the scales representing the speaker and the opponent are kept in balance. In all three cases, the psalms subtly undermine the speaker's case. The psalms create a persuasive case indeed, aimed not only at God, but at the public and at the speakers themselves. With the righteousness of the speaker in doubt, these psalms leave it to God to sort it out and give each party what he or she deserves.

Psalm 7: Measured Innocence

In Psalm 7, the speaker's innocence is at issue, just as in the psalms in Chapter 4. This speaker is in peril from enemies who accuse him of some sort of betrayal and are out for blood. The speaker denies the accusation and seeks vindication. Several commentators (including Kraus, Kwaakel and Bellinger) read the situation as a Temple-based judicial ceremony in which a speaker claiming to have been falsely accused seeks a ritual vindication.[11] Psalm 7 seems to fall under the 'oath challenge' procedure envisioned in Solomon's plea to God in 1 Kgs 8.31-32:

> Whenever one man commits an offense against another, and the latter utters an imprecation to bring a curse upon him, and comes with his imprecation before Your altar in this House, oh, hear in heaven and take action to judge your servant, condemning him who is in the wrong and bringing down the punishment of his conduct on his head, vindicating him who is in the right by rewarding him according to his righteousness.

Most commentators view the speaker as entirely certain of his own innocence and of God's eventual vindication of him.[12] However, in this kind of head-to-head dispute between opponents, at least one party must be

---

11. See Kraus (*Psalms 1–59*, p. 167); Kwakkel (*According to my Righteousness*, p. 37); Bellinger, 'Psalms of the Falsely Accused', pp. 463-69. Bellinger limits false-accusation to contexts where a judicial proceeding seems justified (Psalms 7, 17 and 27) in contrast to cases where opponents seem merely to be engaging in malicious gossip (Psalms 31, 64 and 28). Only the former include uses of legal language and forms: self-imprecation, appeals for acquittal and oaths; references to a 'just cause'; and verbs of testing and trying.

12. Kraus, *Psalms 1–59*, p. 176; Breuggemann and Bellinger, *Psalms*, pp. 54-55.

dissembling; either the opponent's accusations are false or the speaker is false in denying them. In a similar case, two mothers both claimed the same child (1 Kgs 3.16-28) but Solomon's test revealed the false claimant by her willingness to let the child die. In the case described in 1 Kgs 8.31-32, however, the false party cannot be detected, so only God can determine who is in the right.

Psalm 7[13]

1 A David *shi-gay-on,* which he sang to the Lord regarding Cush the Benjaminite.
2 Lord, my God, in You I sheltered. Rescue me from all my pursuers and save me.
3 Lest like a lion they tear up my life—rend me, with no one to save me.
4 Lord, my God, if I have done this, if there be any wrongdoing in my hands.
5 If I paid back my ally with evil, if I oppressed my foes without reason—
6 may the enemy pursue and overtake me and trample to earth my life and make my glory dwell in the dust. Selah
7 Rise up, O Lord, in your anger. Loom high against the wrath of my enemies. Rouse for me the justice You ordained.
8 A band of nations surrounds You, and above it to the heights return.
9 The Lord will judge peoples. Grant me justice, Lord, as befits my righteousness and as befits my innocence that is in me.
10 May evil put an end to the wicked; and make the righteous stay unshaken. He searches hearts and conscience. God is righteous.
11 My shield—upon God, rescuing the upright.
12 God exacts justice for the righteous and El utters doom each day.
13 If a man repent not, He sharpens His sword, He pulls back his bow and aims it.
14 And for him, He readies the tools of death, lets fly His arrows at the fleers.
15 Look, one spawns wrongdoing, grows big with mischief, gives birth to lies.
16 A pit he delved, and dug it, and he fell in the trap he made.
17 His mischief comes down on his head, on his skull outrage descends.
18 I acclaim the Lord for His righteousness, let me hymn the Lord's name, Most High.

In rhetorical terms, the dispute is a matter of fact (at the stasis of 'existence'), a question of what really happened between the opponents. But Solomon's plea also raises questions at the stasis of quality or value, the significance or degree of harm. In judicial settings, determining the truth of the matter is not always sufficient for achieving justice—perhaps both parties share some portion of the blame or perhaps the degree of harm was slight, as in civil cases where the plaintiff wins but is awarded only a pittance in damages. The question of value is introduced in the key comparative particle –כ ('as' or 'like') from 1 Kgs 8.32 that also recurs repeatedly

---

13. Alter, *The Book of Psalms*, pp. 18-21.

in Psalm 7: '*according* to his/my innocence/righteousness': God is to assess gradations of righteousness.

Taking a public real-time judicial confrontation as the immediate rhetorical situation of Psalm 7 helps explain its shape and language. As shown in Figure 5.1, the address and complaint are highly truncated. The speaker's situation must be so obvious and so well-understood by everyone that details of the case and even the standard opening moves are reduced to shorthand. The accusation is referred to obliquely in v. 4: אם עשיתי זאת ('if I have done this'). To supply the missing antecedent of 'this', Hans-Joachim Kraus posits that the specific accusation was read immediately before the recitation of the psalm.[14]

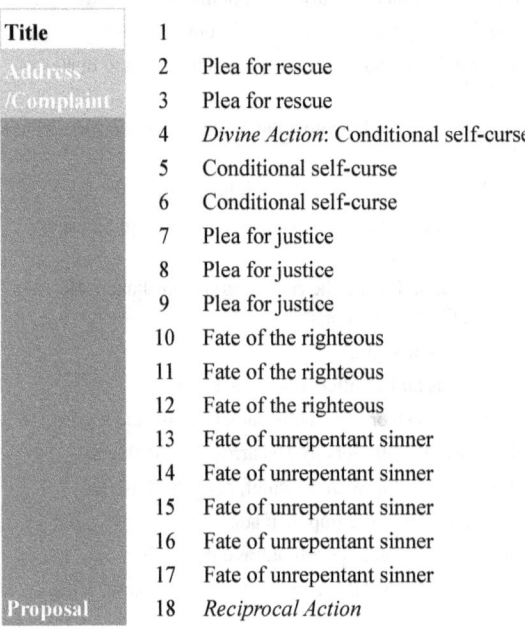

Figure 5.1. *Structure of Psalm 7*

While this assumption about the context permits these shortcuts, the fact remains that, compared to most laments, the condensed address and complaint in vv. 2-3 are most striking for what they leave out. Only one short phrase in v. 2 expresses the speaker's prior reliance on God and the remainder describes the life-and-death nature of the threat. Unlike the speakers in Psalms 22 and 17, the speaker does not support his innocence by associating himself with righteous ancestors, bringing in the testimony of witnesses or even evidence of prior righteous behavior. He does not appeal for sympathy

---

14. Kraus, *Psalms 1–59*, p. 167.

through a vivid description of suffering. Nor does he impugn the character of his opponent or lay out an alternative view of the case, as do speakers in other psalms. Were this text not labeled a psalm, readers might well view the speaker as impetuous and over-confident. These impressions are plausible even with the judicial setting in mind. From among the available means of persuasion, the speaker has chosen to rely on one and only one means to prove his innocence: his willingness to avow it in public.

Accordingly, the speaker in vv. 4-6 proposes conducting a test right then and there, calling on God to allow the enemy to trample and slay him if he has done what he is accused of doing. Following Kraus, Kwakkel identifies the oath as a conditional self-curse; if he is guilty of any of the 'if' conditions, the speaker submits to punishment at the hands of the opponent.[15] The speaker's phrasing in v. 3 ('lest like a lion they tear up my life') and v. 6 ('may the enemy pursue and overtake me') suggests that a physical ordeal is about to ensue, with God ensuring the victory of the righteous party. But it is not at all clear that actual combat is anticipated. Pronouncing the conditional self-curse may itself forestall combat, with the speaker and opponent both agreeing to let God settle the dispute. As a way to avoid adjudication, an oath may paradoxically foster doubts about the oath-taker's character rather than eliminating them. Oath-takers in Aristophanes' plays were even mocked for the extravagance of what they would swear to. Unless Israelites were unnaturally pious, they must likewise have been capable of swearing false oaths even in the awe-inspiring vicinity of the Temple. Certainly the Ten Commandments need not have prohibited false testimony and vain oaths if they were a rare occurrence.[16]

The proposal takes up the rest of the psalm, vv. 7-18. In vv. 7-11, the speaker connects God's action to his own situation: God, as a righteous judge, should vindicate the speaker, an innocent person. However, the speaker's self-references are muted, generally tucked away into possessive particles: צוררי ('my enemies'), אלי ('for me'), צדקי ('my righteousness'), תמי ('my innocence'), מגני ('my shield'). Notably, the speaker also qualifies his status in requesting to be judged 'according to my righteousness' and 'according to my innocence'. On the other hand, the calls to God to execute justice are blaring. For Kwaakel, it is 'amazing' that the speaker dares to imagine God looming over the assembled nations to witness the proceedings in vv. 7-8.[17] Calling the nations as witnesses puts God even more firmly on the spot; God's international reputation is at stake if justice is not done.

---

15. Kraus, *Psalms 1–59*, p. 170; Kwakkel, *According to my Righteousness*, p. 37.

16. The possibility of false oaths was certainly clear to rabbis in Mishnaic times who were pragmatic enough to debate degrees of liability for violating oaths of different formulations. See Elizabeth Shanks Alexander, *Transmitting Mishnah: The Shaping Influence of Oral Tradition* (New York: Cambridge University Press, 2006).

17. Kwakkel, *According to my Righteousness*, pp. 41-42.

The fate of the guilty party is vividly described in vv. 12-17. The wicked one is to be pierced by a sharp sword or arrows, caught in a pit and clobbered over the head. Scholars have often noted that this section temporizes the moment when justice will be done and even the means by which it will come about. Kwakkel interprets the phrase אל זואם בכל יום ('El utters doom each day') in v. 12 as allowing for delayed repercussions: 'even if those actions fail to materialize for some time, God is indeed indignant about the behaviour of the wicked'.[18] The engineer of the evil-doer's fate is left open by the use of third-person singular pronouns in vv. 13-14. Is it God who sharpens the sword, pulls back the bow and readies the tools of death?[19] Or is it the enemy sharpening the sword and pointing it at 'himself'?[20] The psalm offers two routes by which evil may be defeated—by God's direct intervention in history and by a cosmic order in which evil deeds eventually bring commensurate consequences. J.R. John Samuel Raj, observing that commentators have recognized but have not resolved 'the tension that existed between these two "conflicting ideas"', concludes that it is possible to see in Psalm 7 'the fusion of and not the conflict between ideas'.[21]

What these commentators leave unremarked, however, is that the identity of the wicked one is not specified as the opponent who accused the speaker. If the speaker is swearing falsely, as allowed for in the conditional phrasing of the self-curse, then it could be the speaker himself who fails to return, repent or recant in the conditional phrasing of v. 13. The speaker is voicing the possible retribution that would fall on his own head. On this reading, these verses may be read as continuing the self-curse: if the enemy doesn't finish off the guilty speaker, then God will; if God doesn't, then the speaker's evil-doing itself will eventually undo him.

The psalm ends as usual with a promise of reciprocal action. In v. 18, the speaker thanks or promises to thank God: 'I acclaim the LORD according to His righteousness'. Qualifying the promise in this way continues the uncertainty characteristic of this psalm as a whole. At least one party in the dispute is guilty to some extent; the fate of the guilty party determines the extent of God's righteousness. The speaker's praise will be meted out according to what God deserves in the handling of this tricky case.

My reading of Psalm 7 leaves the speaker's disposition wide open. A truthful and pious speaker may be vindicated by God—or not; a brazen

---

18. Kwaakel, *According to my Righteousness*, p. 49.

19. This is the reading ultimately preferred both by Alter, and Kwaakel, *According to my Righteousness*, pp. 50-56.

20. This is the view ultimately preferred by Kraus, *Psalms 1–59*, p. 167, as well as NJPS. See also the analysis by Raabe, 'Deliberate Ambiguity'.

21. J.R. John Samuel Raj, 'Cosmic Judge or Overseer of the World-Order? The Role of Yahweh as Portrayed in Psalm 7', *Bangalore Theological Forum* 34 (2002), pp. 1-15 (8).

and lying speaker may be revealed as such by God—or not. It is here that the two routes to the defeat of evil (delayed divine intervention and self-defeating evil) become most useful for those promoting faithfulness. A righteous speaker who prevails and succeeds after the oath has been persuaded to remain steadfast in his or her faith; a righteous person who suffers prolonged defeat and humiliation may be persuaded to wait for the opponent to eventually be undone. Such a person may, perhaps, continue to offer laments and sacrifices to remind God of the unresolved crisis. A truly impious speaker who suffers an immediate upset may be lured into a grudging respect for God. Even if the impious speaker prevails in the short run, he may lie uneasy in his bed, persuaded to stay on the lookout for a future come-uppance. Then, when God does eventually smoke him out and deal him a setback, a falsely swearing speaker might just end up fulfilling the terms of his vow, acknowledging that God has indeed enacted justice.

Psalm 7 is stunning in the multiplicity of situations in which it serves. This very multiplicity, however, militates against equating the speaker with the psalmist. Perhaps voicing the psalm itself constituted a judicial ordeal. If so, it is in the psalmist's interest to make the psalm as frightening as possible to pronounce in order to discourage guilty speakers from taking an oath as an easy way out of a jam. This would account for the lack of other support for the speaker's innocence, apart from the conditional self-curse. Rather than *choosing* to limit his persuasive options, the speaker has agreed to follow a script that provides no other cover than the oath while provoking God in the strongest possible terms to enact justice.

While Mandolfo prefers to see the speaker as innocent, her dialogic analysis allows for this full range of possibilities. She identifies vv. 9-17 as the words of the didactic voice, seeing their purpose as reassuring the speaker. The didactic voice

> counters the supplicant's shaky faith in God's justice (or at least deity's current application of it) and insists that God delivers justice according to deserts. The two voices seem to respond to one another until the end, where the supplicant seems satisfied by the insistence on God's fairness.[22]

However, the didactic voice might as well be seeking to unsettle the speaker; for a speaker who is swearing falsely, the didactic voice would be heard as anything but reassuring.

Ultimately, through the didactic voice and through many other appeals, the psalmist makes the most persuasive possible case to God—the hearer to whose sense of justice the outcome will ultimately be attributed. Whatever the status of the speaker, the psalmist argues that it is God who must enact justice, however indirect the means and however long delayed.

---

22. Mandolfo, 'Dialogic Form Criticism', p. 75.

Psalm 35: Paying Back in Kind

Whereas Psalm 7 depicts a daring speaker offering a conditional self-curse to establish his innocence of betraying an opponent, Psalm 35 portrays a speaker cursing opponents who have betrayed him and left him vulnerable to attack. The speaker and opponents are well known to each other and both sides have had their ups and downs. However, while the speaker has shown compassion in the opponents' times of need, the opponents have not reciprocated. Instead the opponents are acting harshly toward the speaker and endangering his health, his freedom and perhaps his very life. Accordingly, the speaker asks God to bring down the opponents both physically (vv. 1-10) and socially (vv. 19-28).

Scholars attempting to establish the setting have tended to see it as a psalm of the falsely accused.[23] Croft notes that the imagery points in two opposite directions: to a battlefield or to a courtroom. He concludes that the military imagery in the opening of the psalm is 'metaphorical' and that a courtroom is the real or poetic setting in which a lowly individual responds to elite accusers. I consider the battlefield and courtroom settings equally unlikely. The speaker does not seem concerned with establishing innocence on a set of charges; rather he is intent on besmirching and gaining vengeance on opponents he sees as equals, perhaps for spiteful behavior that never amounts to criminal conduct.

PSALM 35[24]

1   For David. Take my part, LORD, against my contesters, fight those who fight against me.
2   Steady the shield and the buckler, and rise up to my help.
3   Unsheathe the spear to the haft against my pursuers, [say to my being, 'Your rescue, I am'.]
4   Let them be shamed and disgraced, who seek my life. Let them retreat, be abased, who plot harm against me.
5   Let them be like chaff before the wind, with the LORD's messenger driving.
6   May their way be darkness and slippery paths, with the LORD's messenger chasing them.
7   For unprovoked they set their net-trap for me, unprovoked they dug a pit for my life.
8   Let disaster come upon him unwitting and the net that he set entrap him. May he fall into it in disaster.

---

23. While Kraus joins Croft in seeing Psalm 35 as a psalm of the falsely accused, Bellinger does not include it in the set he defines with somewhat stricter standards. Croft, *The Identity of the Individual*, p. 42; Kraus, *Psalms 1–59*; Bellinger, 'Psalms of the Falsely Accused'.

24. Alter, *The Book of Psalms*, pp. 121-25.

5. *The Kairos of Curses*   93

9   But I shall exult in the LORD, shall be glad in His rescue.
10 All my bones say, 'LORD, who is like You? Saving the poor from one stronger than he and the poor and needy from his despoiler?'
11 Outrageous witnesses rose, of things I knew not they asked me.
12 They paid me back evil for good—bereavement for my very self.
13 And I, when they were ill, my garment was sackcloth, I afflicted myself with fasting. May my own prayer come back to my bosom.
14 As for a friend, for a brother, I went about as though mourning a mother, in gloom I was bent.
15 Yet when I limped, they rejoiced, and they gathered, they gathered against me, like strangers, and I did not know. Their mouths gaped and they were not still.
16 With contemptuous mocking chatter they gnashed their teeth against me.
17 O Master, how long will You see it? Bring back my life from their violence, from the lions, my very being.
18 I shall acclaim You in a great assembly, in a vast crowd I shall praise You.
19 Let not my unprovoked enemies rejoice over me, let my wanton foes not leer.
20 For they do not speak peace and against the earth's quiet ones plot words of deceit.
21 They open their mouths wide against me. They say, 'Hurrah! Hurrah! Our eyes have seen it'.
22 You, LORD, have seen, do not be mute. My Master, do not keep far from me.
23 Rouse Yourself, wake for my cause, my God and my Master, for my quarrel.
24 Judge me by Your justice, LORD my God, and let them not rejoice over me.
25 Let them not say in their heart, 'Hurrah for ourselves'. Let them not say, 'We devoured him'.
26 Let them be shamed and abased one and all, who rejoice in my harm. Let them don shame and disgrace, who vaunted over me.
27 May they sing glad and rejoice, who desire justice for me, and may they always say, 'Great is the LORD Who desires His servant's well-being'
28 and my tongue will murmur Your justice, all day long Your praise.

As shown in Figure 5.2, the psalm's structure departs from the pattern of address–complaint–proposal. Rather, it consists of three fairly equal sections, a central complaint framed by two proposals. The opening proposal (vv. 1-8) directs God to a long series of physical assaults against the opponents with references to weapons, traps and pursuit, while the closing (vv. 19-26) proposes ways to silence the opponents and demolish their social standing. The middle section (vv. 11-18) offers an extended rationale: rather than reciprocating the speaker's sympathetic actions, the opponents gloat at his troubles. Each section ends with reciprocal actions (vv. 9-10, 18 and 27-28) as the speaker promises praise for God.

The psalm opens dramatically with an immediate call for divine action. The first words of the psalm are the imperative ריבה ה' את יריבי ('take my part LORD against my contesters'). A lengthy list of actions follows. In vv. 1-3, God is directed to fight, don armor and rise; to wield weapons and to declare protectorship over the speaker. In vv. 4-8, the speaker calls on God to bring down an evil fate on the opponents: they are to be shamed, disgraced, abased, routed, dispersed, pursued across slippery terrain, netted and trapped. The speaker repeatedly characterizes the opponents by their actions against him, using genitive construct forms.[25] The opponents are termed: יריבי ('those who contest against me'), לחמי ('those who fight me'), רדפי ('my pursuers'), מבקשי נפשי ('those who seek my life'), חשבי רעתי ('those who plot evil of me'). Thus the conflict with others is the paramount feature of the speaker's situation. Remarkably, while these actions all have violent overtones, they are presented as descriptions rather than as justifications for God to act. The one explicit rationale, using the term כי ('for' or 'because'), comes in v. 7, describing the opponents' sneaky efforts to ensnare or trap the speaker. While the association of pits, nets and traps with treachery and deceit is common in Near Eastern literature, according to Murray Lichtenstein, the Hebrew Bible is notable for using entrapment images specifically to call for poetic justice, for entrapping the trapper.[26] Poetic justice of this sort is exactly what the speaker calls for in v. 8. While the other actions that God is called on to take are posed as equal and opposite to those attributed to the opponents, they actually have excess potency, signified by the winds and God's own avenging angel chasing after them.

With respect to his own standing, the speaker makes no effort in this first section to establish a connection with God, in contrast to the speaker in Ps. 7.1, who at least declared allegiance to God ('LORD, my God, in You I sheltered') before turning to the imperative voice. Nor does the opening to Psalm 35 make explicit claims of the speaker's innocence or righteousness. Only in v. 7 does the speaker make a claim of blamelessness, saying twice that the opponents' plots are חנם ('unprovoked'). Even when promising to praise God in v. 10 as the rescuer of the weak, the poor and the needy, the speaker does not explicitly apply these terms to himself, in contrast to speakers in many other psalms who emphasize their poverty or neediness (e.g., Pss. 25.16; 40.18; 69.30; 70.6; 86.1; 109.22). In the opening section, then, the speaker does more to lower his opponents' characters than to establish his own. Is the speaker supremely confident in his standing with God? Or are concerns with propitiating God swept away by impetuous rage?

---

25. In addition to noting that each characterization appears only once, Marianne Grohmann also notes the variety of body terms used to describe the opponents, in 'Jewish and Christian Approaches to Psalm 35', in Marianne Grohmann and Yair Zakovitch (eds.), *Jewish and Christian Approaches to Psalms* (Freiburg im Breisgau: Herder, 2009), pp. 13-29.

26. Murray H. Lichtenstein, 'The Poetry of Poetic Justice: A Comparative Study in Biblical Imagery', *JANES* 5 (1973), pp. 255-65 (259).

5. *The Kairos of Curses*

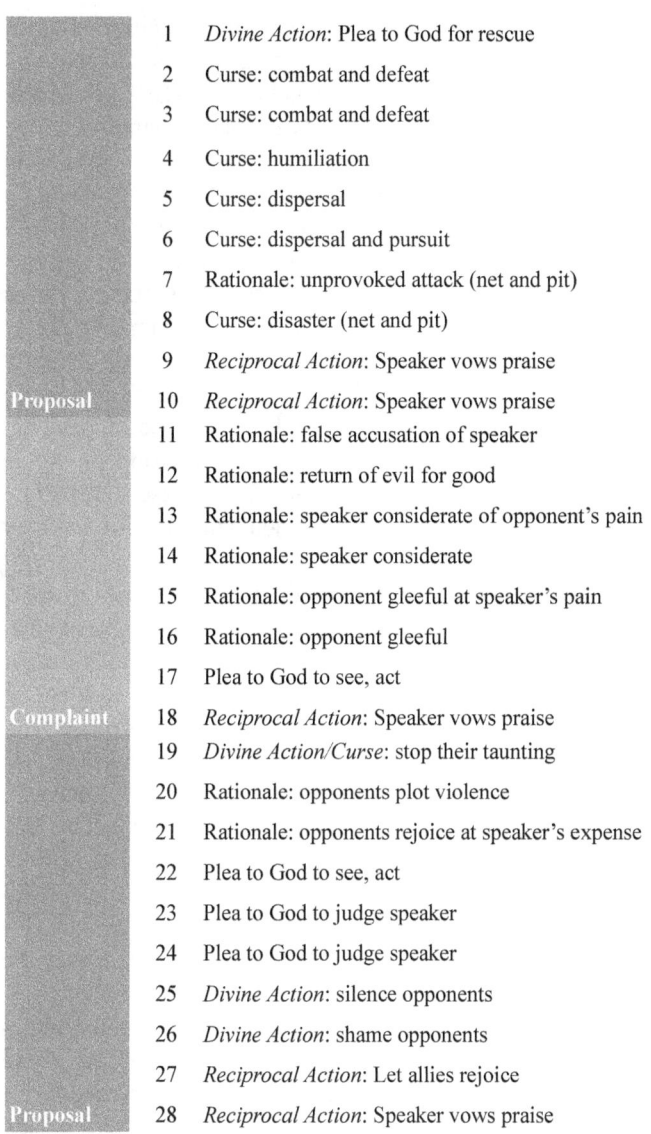

	1	*Divine Action*: Plea to God for rescue
	2	Curse: combat and defeat
	3	Curse: combat and defeat
	4	Curse: humiliation
	5	Curse: dispersal
	6	Curse: dispersal and pursuit
	7	Rationale: unprovoked attack (net and pit)
	8	Curse: disaster (net and pit)
	9	*Reciprocal Action*: Speaker vows praise
Proposal	10	*Reciprocal Action*: Speaker vows praise
	11	Rationale: false accusation of speaker
	12	Rationale: return of evil for good
	13	Rationale: speaker considerate of opponent's pain
	14	Rationale: speaker considerate
	15	Rationale: opponent gleeful at speaker's pain
	16	Rationale: opponent gleeful
	17	Plea to God to see, act
Complaint	18	*Reciprocal Action*: Speaker vows praise
	19	*Divine Action/Curse*: stop their taunting
	20	Rationale: opponents plot violence
	21	Rationale: opponents rejoice at speaker's expense
	22	Plea to God to see, act
	23	Plea to God to judge speaker
	24	Plea to God to judge speaker
	25	*Divine Action*: silence opponents
	26	*Divine Action*: shame opponents
	27	*Reciprocal Action*: Let allies rejoice
Proposal	28	*Reciprocal Action*: Speaker vows praise

Figure 5.2. *Structure of Psalm 35*

The central section (vv. 11-18) lays out the heart of the complaint. While the section opens in v. 11 with a reference to an interrogation by hostile witnesses—giving rise to the false accusation reading—the complaint does not identify the source of the speaker's troubles. Rather, what it boils down to is a lack of reciprocity. The speaker expects his peers to treat him as he has treated them, returning good for good and evil for evil. But, whereas the speaker showed solidarity with the opponents in their times of trouble, they shun him and gloat at his troubles behind his back. This return of evil for good is described at length and in vivid terms in vv. 12-16. The speaker mourned on their behalf during their trouble (vv. 13-14). Apparently, חלותם ('their illness') was presumed by the community to have resulted from sinful behavior and would have led to social ostracism, but the speaker took their part in public mourning activities as an effort to persuade God to spare them. But during the speaker's troubles, the opponents do not do the same. He mourned for them, but they rejoice (vv. 15-16); he treated them כרע ('as a fellow') and כאח ('as a brother') (v. 14), while they treat him כנכרים ('as strangers') (v. 15).[27] The parity of the two cases suggests that neither party was the source of the other's trouble or illness. The speaker's complaint stems not from the trouble or illness itself but from a sense of betrayal. Rather than showing public solidarity with the speaker, the opponents run down his reputation and take pleasure in his pain. The phrase לא ידעתי ('I didn't know') in v. 15 suggests that he had been deluded into thinking they were friends.

It is frustrating and humiliating to be denied support in times of trouble; the embarrassment is compounded if one has been fooled into extending oneself on behalf of a false friend. In an important sense, this kind of betrayal is not actionable. In itself, no blame seems to attach to gloating over another's downfall—or, at least, to rejoicing over the victory and vindication of one's own side. What amounts to gloating recurs constantly in the reciprocal actions of many psalms—in exchange for God's defeat of their opponents, speakers promise public and gleeful proclamations of the outcome. Circumstances permitting, either side would gloat. The crux of the matter for the speaker in Psalm 35 is that presumed friends are spreading news of, if not gloating at, his troubles.

Once a personal and public betrayal is recognized as the center of the complaint, the psalm's third section (vv. 19-28) becomes more intelligible. In this proposal, God is called on to silence and humiliate the opponents. The imperatives in this section are so much less violent than those in the opening section that the closing would seem anti-climactic if the speaker were in physical danger from the opponents. In active terms, God is to abase, shame and disgrace them (v. 26). But several of the imperatives are stated in negative form: God is to *prevent* the opponents from rejoicing or leering—אל ישמחו לי ('don't let them rejoice over me', v. 19)—and to *prevent* them from speaking gloatingly about him, even internally—אל יאמרו בלבם ('don't let them say in their hearts', v. 25). The void from the

---

27. Along with Kraus (*Psalms 1–59*, pp. 390-91), Alter here follows the Syriac text which has כנכרים ('as strangers') in place of the Masoretic term נכים which the NJPS translates as 'wretches'. Alter, *The Book of Psalms*, p. 123.

silencing of the opponents is now to be filled by speech on behalf of the speaker from God—who is urged אל תחרש ('do not be mute', v. 22)—and by public singing, rejoicing and speech from the speaker's well-wishers (v. 27). The theme of poetic justice is here refigured from physical entrapment to silenced humiliation. The relief that the speaker is asking for is not so much the annihilation of enemies as it is the replacement of disparaging speech with supportive speech. Lowering the opponents' standing simultaneously raises that of the speaker, reversing the scales and eventually restoring equity.

Poetic justice, then, appears to be the overriding goal of Psalm 35, restoring equity or reciprocity between peers who expect to be treated alike. Equity is a signal value in Israelite culture, from the positive injunction of Lev. 19.18, ואהבת לרעך כמוך ('love your fellow as yourself'), to constraints on penalties in the *lex talionis* of Exod. 22.23-25, 'life for life, eye for eye, tooth for tooth, hand for hand, foot for foot, burn for burn, wound for wound, bruise for bruise'. While many modern readers see talion as harsh, imposing severer punishments than we are used to, in ancient times its effect may have been the opposite, restraining the impulse to take a life for an eye. In situations where a judicial remedy is unavailable, the social equity imposed by revenge not only serves as a deterrent to civil injustice, but it also restores self-esteem through 'the balance of suffering', as psychologist Nico Frijda puts it.[28]

Achieving this goal is made possible for the speaker and his supporters in Psalm 35 by means of the curses of the opening section (vv. 1-10), precisely because of their seemingly over-wrought drama. Once it becomes clear that the speaker's complaint centers on speech rather than a physical attack, it becomes possible to assess the two proposal sections. Clearly, the equitable set of proposals comes in the third section, while the curses in the opening are revealed as both redundant and excessive. The proposals in the third section appears reasonable and persuasive not only because they match the specifics of the complaint but also because they appear in the normal position, following the complaint. In contrast, the curses in the first section now seem unreasonable in their violence and vividness, particularly the descriptions of the opponents threatening the speaker in physical terms. The speaker in the first section comes across as enraged—as it happens, the very emotion necessary to overcome shame.

As Jeffrey Walker has argued, a persuasive appeal to emotion depends on evoking a combination of attitudes and beliefs. The basis for all emotion is agitation, a diffuse physical arousal, which is given shape by specific beliefs

---

28. Nico H. Frijda, 'The Lex Talionis: On Vengeance', in Stephanie H.M. van Goozen, Nanne E. Van de Poll and Joseph A. Sergeant (eds.), *Emotions: Essays on Emotion Theory* (New York: Psychology Press, 1994), pp. 263-90.

about the situation and what can be done about it. As Walker reconstructs Aristotle's definition of anger in the *Rhetoric*, '"anger" is a *pained* feeling of *desire* for a *conspicuous revenge* for a *conspicuous insult*, accompanied by a *belief* that revenge is possible and the pleasurable anticipation of getting even (I.xi, 1370a; IIii, 1378a-b)'.[29] Walker shows how Cicero and Thomas Paine successfully incited their compatriots to war by deploying anger persuasively in their texts, reminding them of the painful insults they had borne. Both dwelt at length on the availability of the means of revenge in sections of the texts that seemed boring and unnecessary to later readers outside the heat of the moment. However, as Walker argues, these sections were crucial at the time. If revenge seems unavailable, then anger cannot be achieved and the agitation resolves into a less 'noble' feeling, such as shame.

The rhetorical situation of Psalm 35 is now clearer. The speaker is caught in a shameful situation, troubled not only by some kind of setback or illness but also by the exposure of his gullibility to false friends. His goal is to convert shame into rage and helplessness into revenge—both for himself and his true supporters. By opening with a dramatic and excessive set of curses, the speaker immediately grabs the attention of divine and human hearers and foregrounds the means for revenge. The speaker may lack power and recourse to the courts, but he can and does call on God whose capability to exact vengeance is unparalleled. No wonder he admits of no doubt that God will act. While admitting that the covenant does not explicitly oblige God to protect loyal followers from shame, Lyn Bechtel argues that such an expectation is supported by Deuteronomic theology and comparable obligations of other local deities.[30] Thus, in reminding God of these obligations in no uncertain terms, the speaker is not merely expressing anger but deploying it to change the beliefs, attitudes and actions of his hearers, who—if persuaded—will go on to grant the justice of the milder closing proposals. Yet the initial curse with all its excess remains immutable. God may well end up judging the speaker as over-reacting and the opponents as mean but not guilty enough to punish.

Psalm 109: Returning Curse for Curse

Psalm 109 contains the most extended and fearsome curses of the entire book of Psalms. Fifteen verses (vv. 6-19), fully half the length of the psalm, are

---

29. Jeffrey Walker, 'Enthymemes of Anger in Cicero and Thomas Paine', in Marie Secor and Davida Charney (eds.), *Constructing Rhetorical Education* (Carbondale, IL: Southern Illinois University Press, 1996), pp. 357-81 (359); original emphasis.

30. Lyn M. Bechtel, 'The Perception of Shame within the Divine-Human Relationship in Biblical Israel', in Henry Neil Richardson and Lewis M. Hopfe (eds.), *Uncovering Ancient Stones* (Winona Lake, IN: Eisenbrauns, 1994), pp. 79-92.

filled with chilling imprecations from turning the justice system against the target, destroying his home and family and finally completely obliterating his genetic line throughout eternity. Even more remarkably, however, the psalm leaves unclear who is pronouncing the curses, the speaker or his opponents. As such, this psalm supports many readings in which the merits of the speaker are posed against those of the opponents and God is left to sort things out.

Most scholars, including Brueggemann, Cottrill, Jacobson, Laney, Wright and the NJPS, believe that the speaker is the one doing the cursing.[31] Other scholars, such as Kitz, Kraus and Alter, treat the curse as reported speech; the speaker is quoting curses that the opponents have laid upon him.[32] None of these scholars has fully worked through the implications of these possibilities for the speaker's character and persuasiveness. Obviously, the speaker's rhetorical situation is completely different if he is taken as the pronouncer rather than as the target of the curses. Both readings will be entertained here; Figure 5.3 presents a structure for the speaker-as-curser reading and Figure 5.4 presents a structure for the opponent-as-curser reading.

The Speaker-as-Curser Reading

As shown in Figure 5.3, the speaker-as-curser reading has a four-part structure, with two complaints alternating with two proposals. In Ps. 109.1, the speaker declares his previous devotion to God through praise and calls for God to speak—or more precisely to end God's muteness. Speech, then, is quickly established as key to the psalm's kairos. The next four verses form a fairly standard complaint, giving the psalm a more conventional opening than Psalm 35.

PSALM 109[33]

1	For the lead player, a David psalm. God of my praise, do not be silent.
2	For the wicked's mouth, the mouth of deceit, has opened against me, they spoke to me with lying tongue.
3	And words of hatred swarmed round me—they battle me for no cause.
4	In return for my love they accuse me, though my prayer is for them.
5	And they offer me evil in return for good and hatred in return for my love:
6	'Appoint a wicked man over him, let an accuser stand at his right.
7	When he is judged, let him come out guilty, and his prayer be an offense.

---

31. Walter Brueggemann, 'Psalm 109: Three Times "Steadfast Love"', *WW* 5 (1985), pp. 144-54; Brueggemann and Bellinger, *Psalms*, pp. 473-74; Cottrill, *Language, Power*; Jacobson, *Many are Saying*; Laney, 'A Fresh Look', pp. 37-38; David P. Wright, 'Ritual Analogy in Psalm 109', *JBL* 113 (1994), pp. 385-404.

32. Anne Marie Kitz, 'Effective Simile and Effective Act: Psalm 109, Numbers 5, and KUB 26', *CBQ* 69 (2007), pp. 440-56. Kraus, *Psalms 60–150*, p. 338.

33. Alter, *The Book of Psalms*, pp. 391-95.

8   Let his days be few, may another man take his post.
9   May his children become orphans and his wife a widow.
10 May his children wander and beg, driven out from the ruins of their homes.
11 May the lender snare all that he has and may strangers plunder his wealth.
12 May no one extend to him kindness and no one pity his orphans.
13 May his offspring be cut off, in the next generation his name wiped out.
14 May the wrong of his fathers be recalled by the Lord, and his mother's offense not be wiped out.
15 Let these ever be before the Lord, that He cut off from the earth their name.
16 Because he did not remember to do kindness and pursued the poor and the needy, the heartsore, to put him to death.
17 He loved a curse, may it come upon him, he desired not blessing—may it stay far from him.
18 He donned a curse as his garb—may it enter his innards like water and like oil in his bones.
19 May it be like a garment he wraps round him and like a belt he girds at all times'.
20 This be the plight of my accusers from the Lord, and those who speak against my life.
21 And You, O Lord, Master, act on my behalf for the sake of Your name, for Your kindness is good. O save me!
22 For poor and needy am I, and my heart is pierced within me.
23 Like a lengthening shadow I go off, I am shaken away like the locust.
24 My knees falter from fasting and my flesh is stripped of fat.
25 As for me, I become a reproach to them. They see me, they shake their heads.
26 Help me, O Lord, my God rescue me as befits Your kindness,
27 that they may know that Your hand it is, it is You, O Lord, Who did it.
28 Let them curse, and You, You will bless. They will rise and be shamed, and Your servant will rejoice.
29 Let my accusers don disgrace, and let them wrap round like a robe their shame.
30 I highly acclaim the Lord with my mouth, and in the midst of the many I praise Him,
31 for He stands at the needy's right hand to rescue him from his condemner.

In v. 2, the speaker charges the opponent with duplicity and with making false and hateful accusations. Not only are these accusations חנם ('unprovoked') but the opponent has also failed to reciprocate the speaker's kindness, giving רעה תחת טובה ('evil in return for good') and שנאה תחת אהבתי ('hatred in return for my love', v. 5). Unlike the situation in Psalm 35, however, these exchanges are not spelled out in detail. So the betrayal from a false friend does not seem to be the crux of the speaker's discontent; rather it is the opponent's accusation itself that seems to be the direct source of the speaker's troubles. Yet the speaker does little to describe the legal or social predicament in which he finds himself.

5. *The Kairos of Curses*

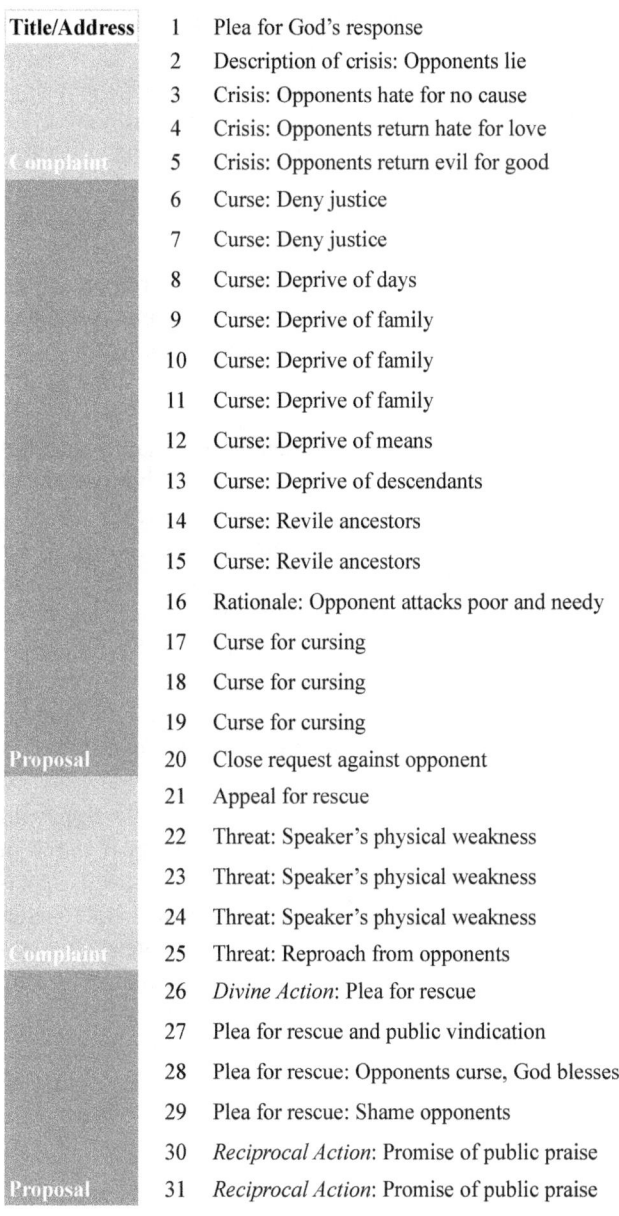

Title/Address	1	Plea for God's response
Complaint	2	Description of crisis: Opponents lie
	3	Crisis: Opponents hate for no cause
	4	Crisis: Opponents return hate for love
	5	Crisis: Opponents return evil for good
	6	Curse: Deny justice
	7	Curse: Deny justice
	8	Curse: Deprive of days
	9	Curse: Deprive of family
	10	Curse: Deprive of family
	11	Curse: Deprive of family
	12	Curse: Deprive of means
	13	Curse: Deprive of descendants
	14	Curse: Revile ancestors
	15	Curse: Revile ancestors
	16	Rationale: Opponent attacks poor and needy
	17	Curse for cursing
	18	Curse for cursing
	19	Curse for cursing
Proposal	20	Close request against opponent
	21	Appeal for rescue
	22	Threat: Speaker's physical weakness
	23	Threat: Speaker's physical weakness
	24	Threat: Speaker's physical weakness
Complaint	25	Threat: Reproach from opponents
	26	*Divine Action*: Plea for rescue
	27	Plea for rescue and public vindication
	28	Plea for rescue: Opponents curse, God blesses
	29	Plea for rescue: Shame opponents
	30	*Reciprocal Action*: Promise of public praise
Proposal	31	*Reciprocal Action*: Promise of public praise

Figure 5.3. *Structure of Psalm 109 for Speaker-as-Curser Reading*

Whereas the first complaint (vv. 1-5) lays out the opponent's treachery and false accusations, the second complaint, also five verses in length (vv. 21-25), lays out the physical consequences of the opponent's attack on the speaker. In v. 22, the speaker declares his low status עני ואביון אנכי ('poor and needy am I'). The speaker is alluding here to Deuteronomic law that emphasizes God's concern for the poor and needy and is, in effect, claiming 'protected status', akin to US 'hate crime' provisions for aggravating the degree of a crime if the victim was singled out for race, religion, gender identity and so on. Left unclear, though, is whether the speaker started out in such low circumstances or has now been reduced to them. The low status may result from his wasting away from fasting in response to the attack (vv. 23-24) and from his becoming an object of public scorn (v. 25). In neither complaint does the speaker explicitly present himself as innocent or righteous (even to the qualified degree used in Psalm 7); his merits are established only indirectly, with the protest that the attacks are unprovoked and that the opponent is a hateful liar. Accordingly, again in contrast to Psalm 7, God is never called on to restore צדק ('justice') but only to act out of חסד ('loving-kindness' or 'loyalty').[34]

The two proposals are of unequal length and neither one exactly matches the complaints. The first, 15 verses in length (vv. 6-20), is an vividly detailed set of curses against the opponent. Every aspect of the opponent's life is to be destroyed: having the cards stacked against him in court (v. 6), dying young, knowing that his orphaned children and widow will suffer, hearing his ancestors besmirched and his family name obliterated (v. 15). The curse is excessive when weighed against the first complaint (vv. 1-5). The reference to accusers at a court proceeding (v. 6) does echo the mention of accusations in the opening complaint (v. 4). But the brunt of the curse—a full seven verses—is the destruction of the opponent's family and heritage that does not correspond to any harms described in the complaints. It is only in v. 16 that the speaker sets out an additional rationale for the curse: the opponent has failed to show חסד ('kindness' or 'loyalty') and has pursued a victim in a 'protected class', איש עני ואביון ('a poor and needy man'), to death. Notably, the speaker is not using the first person, saying 'he pursued *me*'. Rather the phrase איש עני ואביון ('a poor and needy man') must be interpreted as a self-reference, though it is only afterward, in the second complaint, that the speaker declares himself to be poor, needy and wasting away (v. 22).[35]

Several aspects of the curse raise doubts about the speaker/curser's character. As compared to Psalm 35 or Psalm 7 where the judicial system may not have had occasion to act, Psalm 109 places the dispute directly in a

---

34. The term חסד ('loving-kindness' or 'loyalty') occurs four times in the psalm, once a curse against the target's children (v. 12), once in the rationale for the curse (v. 16) and twice as attributes of God (vv. 21 and 26). The term חסד seems to fall between unconditional favor רחמים ('compassion') and adherence to justice צדק ('righteousness'). For a discussion of the nuances of the term, see Sung-Hun Lee, 'Lament and the Joy of Salvation in the Lament Psalms', in Peter W. Flint and Patrick D. Miller (eds.), *Book of Psalms: Composition and Reception* (Leiden: Brill, 2005), pp. 224-47.

35. As noted in Chapter 2 with respect to Ps. 62.4, איש ('man') is not used anywhere in the psalms as a clear first-person self-reference.

courtroom. The curse (vv. 6-7) includes the terminology of assigning a case, הפקד עליו רשע ('appoint a wicked man'), locating the physical positions of the accused and accuser, שטן יעמד על ימינו ('let an accuser stand at his right'), and referring both to the judgment בהשפטו ('when he is judged') and to the verdict יצא רשע ('come out guilty'). But the curse simultaneously subverts justice by asking God to appoint a wicked official, an official who might condemn an innocent man or railroad a guilty one without sufficient proof. Why would an innocent person ask such a thing? Questions such as this have led some scholars to translate v. 6 in creative ways to square the speaker's intentions. Wright argues that appointing a wicked judge follows the principle of talion: just as the speaker is being accused by a wicked man, so should be the opponent, as if that is somehow more equitable than being condemned by an honest judge.[36] Brueggemann asserts that the descriptor רשע ('wicked man') actually refers to an honest judge who is known to be severe, that is 'a hanging judge'.[37] Kraus goes the furthest afield, reading the term רשע not as describing an official, but as quoting the judgment to be pronounced against ('appointed to') the accused at the end of the proceedings: 'Let "a wicked man" be appointed against him.'[38] None of these explanations seems completely satisfactory. Is the speaker committed to justice or not?

Another problematic passage is the remarkably potent curse against cursing (vv. 17-19), a plea that those who pronounce curses will end up being poisoned by them.[39] The passage is problematic for the speaker-as-curser reading because the speaker is the only one depicted engaging in cursing. Why would a speaker who has indulged himself at length in cursing an opponent into oblivion turn around and pronounce a curse on cursing? Is the speaker opposed to cursing or not? In another effort to square the speaker's character, Wright interprets the passage as explanatory, serving to clarify that the speaker's curse matches the opponent's own hateful speech in talion fashion. In Wright's view, this explanation is summed up in v. 20, which he translates as 'This is the recompense of my adversaries from Yhwh, and of those who speak evil against my soul.' The key term that Wright translates as 'recompense' is the noun פעולה which is more usually translated as 'work' or 'product'. The curse is recompense for curses or other hateful action the opponents have taken toward the speaker. Wright sees v. 20 as also having an emphatic purpose in which the anaphoric reference זאת ('this') 'gathers up all of the foregoing curses in a fist and delivers them in a single pugilistic stroke'.[40] The difficulty with this interpretation of vv. 17-20

36. Wright, 'Ritual Analogy', p. 395 n. 25.
37. Brueggemann, 'Psalm 109', p. 145.
38. Kraus, *Psalms 60–150*, p. 340.
39. See Kitz, 'Effective Simile', for a full discussion of this passage and its relationship to other ancient Near Eastern curses.
40. Wright, 'Ritual Analogy', p. 400.

is that up to this point in the psalm, the opponent has not been described as engaging in cursing; the opponent's speech is described as cursing only afterward in the final proposal (v. 28). Wright's explanation also requires inferring the extent of the opponent's actions and presupposing the ethical superiority of the speaker.

The final proposal, vv. 26-31, is more equitable than the initial proposal, as was the final proposal in Psalm 35. It recapitulates the speaker's plea to God for rescue and public vindication, which would cancel out the opponent's false accusations and the speaker's current humiliation. The opponents' hateful speech—referred to for the first time in v. 28 as cursing, יקללו ('let them curse')—is here countered with God's blessing, ואתה תברך ('You will bless') and God's bringing the enemies to shame. No reference is made to the opponent's family or heritage.

In his reciprocal action in vv. 30-31, the speaker promises to praise God for taking a public role, standing beside אביון ('the needy one') in court. The speaker, then, is imagining himself in a proceeding like the one invoked in the curse against the opponent (v. 6) but with God rather than an accuser at his side. The praise subtly incorporates a proposal for an extraordinary intervention by God in a human court, an intervention that can only result in the needy one prevailing. Thus this proposal, like the curse, ends up subverting justice. Deuteronomic injunctions regarding the needy call for them to be treated justly in court, not necessarily to prevail. In fact, Deuteronomy and Leviticus call for judges to be blind to the status of the defendant, saying לא תכיר פנים ('do not recognize faces'):

Lev. 19.15	You shall not render an unfair decision: do not favor the poor or show deference to the rich; judge your kinsman fairly.
Deut. 1.17	You shall not be partial in judgment: hear out low and high alike.

Overall, the speaker-as-curser reading is plausible but not especially coherent or persuasive. The curse is not fully justified by the complaints. The speaker leaves much of the case unstated, trusting hearers to draw a variety of inferences. Some elements that clarify the curse appear only afterward in the second complaint. While the second proposal is more equitable than the curse, it is only five verses in length, too short to fully balance out the curse. The speaker's character ends up questionable, given his excessive degree of cursing, willingness to subvert justice and inconsistent attitude toward cursing per se.

The Opponent-as-Curser Reading
As shown in Figure 5.4, the opponent-as-curser reading has a two-part structure, with one long complaint followed by a proposal. The long curse now serves as the crux of the complaint; the opponents have falsely accused and cursed the speaker, resulting in the speaker's physical deterioration and

5. *The Kairos of Curses* 105

isolation. The proposal is for God to counter the opponents' curse with a divine blessing, leading to the opponents' downfall and the speaker's rescue and vindication. The situation thus more directly matches the oath-challenge procedure in 1 Kgs 8.31-32: one man offends others who curse him for it; the dispute being undecidable by other means, the two parties come to the Temple and leave it to God to sort out who is right.

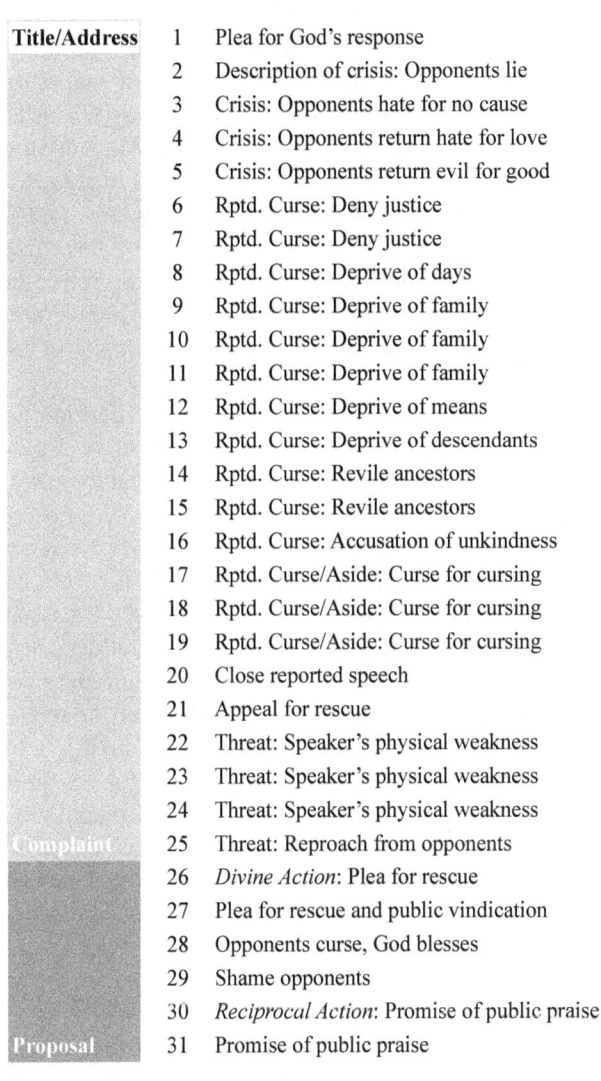

Figure 5.4. *Structure of Psalm 109 for Opponent-as-Curser Reading*

Scholars who support the opponent-as-curser reading point to several textual cues for treating vv. 6-19 as reported speech. Granted, the usual cue for a switch to reported speech, the gerundive לאמר ('saying'), is absent, though Wright concedes that it is not absolutely necessary. One cue is number. Whereas opponents in the preceding and following sections (vv. 1-5 and 20-31) are consistently referred to in the plural, the quoted section refers to a single person. Thus, in the opening verses, the speaker complains that plural opponents פתחו ('opened') the mouth of deceit and that they דברו ('spoke') the language of lies in v. 2; in v. 3, they סובבוני ('surrounded me') and they ילחמוני ('fought me'). In the closing section, the speaker again uses plural to refer to his accusers, שוטני ('my adversaries') (v. 29), anticipating that they will ידעו ('know') of God's rescue (v. 27) and that they will יבשו ('be ashamed') (v. 28). In contrast, the singular form is used throughout the section of reported speech: appoint עליו ('over him') a wicked man (v. 6), let ימיו ('his days') be few (v. 8), let אשתו ('his wife') be a widow (v. 9). If the many are the opponents, then it is they who pronounced the curse and it is the singular speaker who is the one being cursed. Those rejecting this reading—such as Wright—point to erratic shifts between singular and plural references in other contexts, including a switch to the singular in Ps. 35.8.

Another cue is evidence of a frame surrounding the quote. The framing elements preceding the curse include the references to speech in vv. 1-5— the opponents' פי מרמה ('mouth of deceit'), their לשון שקר ('lying tongue'), their דברי שנאה ('words of hatred'). These references pave the way for hearing what the opponents have said. The framing elements that close the quote appear in v. 20, which Alter translates as: 'This be the plight of my accusers from the LORD, and those who speak against my life.' The key term that Alter translates as 'plight' is again the noun פעולה ('work' or 'product') that Wright translates as 'recompense'. As part of a framing element, the pronoun זאת ('this') now can be seen to refer back to the whole of the opponent's accusation, exactly as it did in Ps. 7.4 אם עשיתי זאת ('if I did this'). In the case of Psalm 7, the opponent's accusation went unspoken (or was pronounced beforehand) and the speaker was forced to utter a conditional self-curse. In Psalm 109, in contrast, the speaker seems to be forced to repeat the opponent's curse. Each phrase gets more and more horrifying. One can imagine that an innocent party faced with this task would become more and more indignant at the injustice of having to enunciate such a curse, but someone who has a spotty record would refuse the ordeal or break down in the process.

This opponent-as-curser reading allows a different explanation of the mysterious curse against cursing (vv. 17-20). Rather than a continuation or explanation of the curse, it may actually be an interjection by the speaker to turn aside the curse that he has just repeated. In this case, the opponents' curse ends quite logically with the rationale in v. 16. Immediately afterward, the speaker interjects an aside, like taking a prophylactic, throwing the curse back on its originator. In a similar way, the speaker of Psalm 35 interrupted his account of his own good turn to his opponent in Ps. 35.13 with an aside wishing that his blessing, wasted on his false friends, return to his own bosom. In the case of Psalm 109, taking the curse against cursing as an interjection renders the disputants more consistent in attitude. The speaker's attitude toward cursing becomes consistently negative, while the opponents become clearly identified as ones who love to curse, with their talent at cursing documented by the vividness of the curse itself as well as by the speaker's description of them loving cursing and rejecting blessing both in v. 17 and in v. 28, 'Let them curse, and You, You will bless'. One weakness of this interjection explanation, however, is the continued use of the third-person singular—'he loved a curse'; one would expect the speaker to refer to the opponents in the plural throughout the psalm. However, it is possible that the interjection is a formula. Anne Marie Kitz[41] has demonstrated a close similarity between Ps. 109.17-20 and a Hittite oath ritual, both of which use metaphors of drinking, anointing and clothing. So this kind of curse against cursing may have been in common usage.

Unfortunately for the speaker, the opponent-as-curser reading does not leave him in the clear. Once it is seen as speech describing the speaker, the curse can now be mined for information about his status and character. The opponents' wish to deprive the speaker of job, home, financial resources, family and lineage indicates that the speaker had hitherto been enjoying all these advantages. The speaker then does not qualify as עני ואביון ('poor and needy') as he claims in v. 22. Instead it is now the speaker who is accused in v. 16 of lacking חסד ('loving-kindness' or 'loyalty') and hounding the poor to death. In this reading, the identity of the speaker's victim is unstated—the opponents themselves are not claiming to be the injured party; they may be simply exposing the speaker's bad behavior to the community at large.

The speaker's character also suffers from a lack of positive appeals. After such a curse, one expects a denial, a rebuttal, an assertion of innocence or even a conditional self-curse as in Psalm 7—if I have done this, let me be struck by lightning. The speaker does none of these. Instead of defending his treatment of the poor and needy, he simply claims his own place among them. From the speaker's point of view, this reaction may reflect shock at the accusation. On the other hand, identifying oneself as poor and needy after being accused of afflicting the poor and needy comes very close to the classic Yiddish definition of *chutzpah* in which a defendant accused of murdering his father and mother throws himself on the mercy of the court because he is an orphan.

If the speaker is actually a prominent individual in society, then the excess of the curses seems justified. By the talionic principle, the only

---

41. Kitz, 'Effective Simile'.

person who deserves to be hounded to death is someone who has done the same to others. Perhaps, then, the only one who deserves to have a wicked judge appointed against him is a wicked judge! A wicked judge would have many opportunities to cause the families of the needy or the falsely accused to suffer. The opponents of such a judge might well need to resort to cursing because a corrupt judge might otherwise be beyond the reach of a judicial proceeding. The speaker's final subversion of justice in v. 28—to have God intervene in the court system—may show that the speaker has simply switched sides to unduly favoring the poor without learning the lesson of judging with justice.

In addition to its excessiveness, the unusual length of the curse may be consistent with a rhetorical situation in which a prominent speaker is repeating under duress what has been dictated to him. Accounting for the length of the curse is important because it is this very length that has led various scholars to reject the opponent-as-curser reading. Jacobson, in his book on reported speech, rejects the opponent-as-curser reading of Psalm 109 because such a lengthy quote would be 'unprecedented'.[42] Wright, while conceding that the opponent-as-curser reading is 'not lightly dismissed', ends up finding the arguments in its favor 'unconvincing'.[43] Cottrill agrees with Wright that such a lengthy quotation from a hostile source is 'unlikely' and agrees with Gerstenberger that it would disqualify using the psalm in any religious liturgy. Laney rejects this reading in part because of length and in part because the same strategy cannot be used to 'solve' problematic imprecations in other psalms.[44]

According to Christopher Faraone, self-curses and self-blessings in the ancient Near East and Greece often balanced each other in situations of equal social standing or power. A speaker swore to perform some act for a fellow, calling down equal amounts of curses should he fail and blessings should he succeed. However, 'lopsided' oaths with many vivid curses and few or no blessings were common in so-called 'promissory' oaths, such as for a soldier being inducted into the army, an athlete swearing to obey the rules of sportsmanship or a vassal swearing fealty to an overlord. Faraone reports that some 'lopsided, coercive oaths', while rarer, occurred in 'the realm of private oaths by individuals in legal trials or other situations of high social tension in which perjury would have dire consequences for the entire city'.[45] None of Faraone's examples exactly matches the situation described here. However, if Psalm 109 represents a public ordeal testing the character of prominent officials, it makes sense that it includes a curse that

42. Jacobson, *Many are Saying*, p. 27 n. 2.
43. Wright, 'Ritual Analogy', p. 394.
44. Laney, 'A Fresh Look', p. 38.
45. Christopher A. Faraone, 'Curses and Blessings in Ancient Greek Oaths', *Journal of Ancient Near Eastern Religion* 5 (2006), pp. 140-58 (141).

outweighs in length and intensity anything that the speaker can say on his own behalf.

Neither the speaker-as-curser reading nor the opponent-as-curser reading is decisively supported in this analysis. Both readings are plausible. According to the speaker-as-curser reading, Psalm 109 is a act of denunciation and call for violent retribution, like Psalm 35, but the speaker's case is rather unpersuasive due to its excess and inconsistency. Adopting the opponent-as-curser reading of Psalm 109 reveals striking parallels to the oath-challenge situation in Psalm 7. In both cases, the speaker's situation is precarious. He is confronted with a credible accusation from an opponent and is forced either to pronounce a conditional self-curse or to repeat the opponent's curse, with little opportunity to make a positive case. In both psalms, the merits of the case are left to God to settle in God's own good time.

Conclusion

As this chapter has shown, speakers use curses in the psalms in order to besmirch the characters of their opponents. However, a curse can call the speaker's own character into question. As a persuasive strategy, then, curses carry considerable risk, a fact that was recognized at the time. Aristotle quotes an 'already apparently sceptical sixth-century Ionian philosopher Xenophanes, who points out that an oath-challenge by an impious man to a pious man is uneven, rather like a big man challenging a small man to take the first punch in a fight'.[46] The attitude to oaths in Israelite and Judaic culture may have been similar. The Essenes were noted by Josephus for their rejection of oaths: 'whatever [the Essenes] say also is firmer than an oath; but swearing is avoided by them, and they esteem it worse than perjury for they say that he who cannot be believed without [swearing by] God is already condemned'.[47]

As opposed to cursing, the strategy of denunciation is on firmer persuasive ground. Denouncing someone else is a good way to raise one's own moral standing in the eyes of the public. Social psychologists Derek Rucker and Anthony Pratkanis use the term 'projection' for the tactic of distracting the public from one's own possible guilt by deflecting it onto someone else with an accusation of the same misdeeds.[48] Studies show that projec-

---

46. Mirhady, 'The Oath-Challenge', p. 78, citing Aristotle's *Rhetoric* 1.15 1377a19-21.
47. Josephus, *The New Complete Works of Josephus* (trans. William Whiston; Grand Rapids, MI: Kregel, rev. and expanded edn, 1999), 2.8.6.
48. Derek D. Rucker and Anthony R. Pratkanis, 'Projection as an Interpersonal Influence Tactic: The Effects of the Pot Calling the Kettle Black', *Personality and Social Psychology Bulletin* 27 (2001), pp. 1494-507.

tion works: the accuser is seen more favorably while the reputation of the accused opponent is harmed. However, projection only works when the accuser is seen as flawed, capable of the same offense. Under these circumstances, hearers are led to believe that 'the accuser values what he accuses others of not valuing'.[49] However, for someone who is considered beyond reproach, resorting to accusing others actually damages his or her own reputation along with that of the accused. Although Rucker and colleagues would prefer 'that accusations would damage those using them for ulterior motives', their research suggests that 'accusations sometimes benefit the wicked and harm the righteous'.[50]

---

49. Derek D. Rucker and Richard E. Petty, 'Effects of Accusations on the Accuser: The Moderating Role of Accuser Culpability', *Personality and Social Psychology Bulletin* 29 (2003), pp. 1259-271 (1261).

50. Rucker and Petty, 'Effects of Accusations on the Accuser', p. 1269.

Chapter 6

RECOVERING FROM GUILT

In their important study of the persuasive bent of the lament psalms, Dale Patrick and Ken Diable compare the psalms to the prayer-letters of the ancient Mesopotamians. When the Mesopotamians found themselves in a crisis, they used prayer-letters to the gods to confess to 'blatant sinfulness, neglected ritual observances, and ignorance of duties and responsibilities' and to plead for forgiveness.[1] One speaker asks the Akkadian high god Marduk, 'Absolve my guilt, remit my punishment, clear me of confusion, free me of uncertainty…'; another asks Ishtar, 'Absolve my crime, misdeed, sin, and wrong doing! Forget my sin, accept my plea, loose my fetters, set me free'.[2] In some cases, the speaker asks another god to intercede with the offended god who is inflicting the punishment and is apparently too angry to deal directly with the speaker.

The Hebrew psalms resemble the prayer-letters in several ways but not in this readiness of the Mesopotamians to confess guilt. Patrick and Diable write: 'Quite the converse is true of the individual lament in the Hebrew Bible; only rarely does the psalmist admit guilt; in fact, the general stance of the psalmist is that of an innocent sufferer.'[3] Most first-person speakers in the psalms presume or proclaim their innocence of any act that would warrant their troubles; they admit guilt in only a handful of psalms. Speakers acknowledge wrong-doing in Psalms 32, 38, 39, 51, 130 and 143; speakers mention sins in several other first-person psalms.[4] Patrick and Diable suggest that the absence of other gods gave Israelites the freedom to proclaim their innocence and challenge the justness of their suffering.

> When a Mesopotamian experienced the abandonment of one deity, rarely did the suppliant challenge that deity or complain about the deity's unresponsiveness. There were always other deities to address to seek help with the offended deity. For the Mesopotamian, on the one hand, freedom in

---

1. Patrick and Diable, 'Persuading the One and Only God to Intervene', p. 21.
2. Patrick and Diable, 'Persuading the One and Only God to Intervene', pp. 21-22.
3. Patrick and Diable, 'Persuading the One and Only God to Intervene', p. 21.
4. Sins are also mentioned in Psalms 25, 31, 40, 65, 69 and 102. Seven psalms (Psalms 6, 32, 38, 51, 102, 130 and 143) are designated as 'penitential psalms' in Christian liturgy.

prayer life was the latitude to explore various deities to meet the suppliant's needs, either through the power of that deity or through that deity's intercession on behalf of the suppliant. As we have seen above, a variety of deities can be invoked to help the suppliant in time of need. By contrast, for the Israelite, freedom in prayer life was the ability to challenge the deity and complain to the deity in such a way that the petitioner could make a case before YHWH to change and respond positively to the petitioner, even if YHWH was angry.[5]

Patrick and Diable suggest that the discourse of guilt and contrition did not make up a significant portion of Israelite prayer practice. This seems highly unlikely. Israelites clearly had numerous other venues for confessing. The rarity of confession in the psalms is important because it underscores that the normal goal is persuading God of the speaker's innocence and worthiness for rescue. If a speaker is prepared to admit to guilt, what persuasive task is left? This chapter examines three guilt-centered psalms (Psalms 130, 38 and 51) to show how the shape of the argument shifts with certain moves rendered superfluous or inappropriate. In particular, challenges drop away and opponents rarely appear. The guilty seem to lack the standing to enter into the give-and-take of favor-and-praise negotiation. Instead, they acknowledge God's justice and plead for relief using a variety of persuasive strategies: in Psalm 130, the speaker relies on indirection; in Psalm 38, on vivid emotional appeals; and in Psalm 51, on candor.

The Discourse of Guilt

The lopsided ratio of innocence- to guilt-centered psalms surely did not arise from the rarity of sinning in ancient Israel. Rather, speakers had other forums for confessing their sins and requesting expiation. Confession is explicitly commanded as part of the קרבן חטאת ('sin-offering'), both for ordinary Israelites (Lev. 5.5; Num. 5.7) and for the High Priest on the Day of Atonement (Lev. 16.21). But few explicit confessions are preserved; in one narrative, Achan admits to having looted the spoils in Josh. 7.18-21—but only after having been identified by the casting of lots. The discourse of guilt may have involved specific formulas; a legal text in Deut. 21.1-9 spells out an expiation ritual including the exact words for denying guilt that officials must pronounce if they find a murdered corpse outside their town. Perhaps we have no 'Book of Confessions' in the Hebrew Bible because preserving confessions would be an endless task, because they would embarrass a true penitent or because the rituals for expiating sins obviated the need for poetic persuasion.

---

5. Patrick and Diable, 'Persuading the One and Only God to Intervene', p. 23.

Confession may have been considered inappropriate for the elaborate artistry of poetry and music involved in the psalms. Confession involves becoming conscious, pointing out, acknowledging and bringing evil deeds into the open. Even speakers who admit guilt use the language of confession sparingly. The roots ידע and ידה in the sense of 'confess' occur only in Pss. 32.5 and 51.5.

Ps. 32.5   I said, 'I shall confess my sins to the LORD' and You forgave my offending crime.
Ps. 51.5   For my crimes I know, and my offense is before me always.

These activities do not seem to be the primary province of the psalms; even when they do occur, the primary purpose of the guilt-centered psalms is to persuade God to move on.

The Temple ritual most associated with the psalms is not the sin-offering but rather the זבח ('slaughter-offering'), including the זבח תודה ('thanks-offering'), the זבח שלמים ('peace' or 'good-will offering') and the זבח נדבה ('free-will offering'). In contrast to the sin-offering, the flesh of which was given entirely to the Temple staff, the slaughter-offering provided only a cut to the priests (usually the right shoulder according to Lev. 7.32), with the offerer receiving in return enough goat, lamb or beef for a family feast, setting up a public occasion for music and poetry.[6] On these occasions, it seems understandable that individuals would complain and plead for rescue but tend not to admit guilt.

Psalm 130: Proclaiming Patience

Psalm 130 has long been considered difficult to classify. As Harry Nasuti has noted, it has neither the qualities of a lament, in which an innocent speaker complains of undeserved problems, nor the qualities of a thanksgiving, in which a rescued speaker recapitulates a past crisis in order to give public thanks and praise to God for a rescue. In Psalm 130, no problem or complaint is described at all. And no vow of praise is offered in exchange for rescue.[7] Nevertheless, Kraus considers Psalm 130 to be classifiable either as a lament—by reading the last two lines as standing in for an

---

6. Rainer Albertz and Rüdiger Schmitt posit that vows could be made either in private or public contexts but that fulfilling the vow with the זבח ('slaughter-offering') took place in public communal sanctuaries. See *Family and Household Religion*, p. 404. They also distinguish vows from atonement rituals based on inscriptions for fulfilling vows with money offerings in the Gerizim sanctuary (p. 414).

7. Harry Nasuti, 'Plumbing the Depths: Genre Ambiguity and Theological Creativity in Psalm 130', in Hindy Najman and Judith Newman (eds.), *The Idea of Biblical Interpretation: Essays in Honor of James L. Kugel* (Leiden: Brill, 2004), pp. 95-124.

expression of praise or comfort—or as a didactic wisdom-like psalm from a prayer-leader bringing his own experience to the community.[8] In contrast, I see the psalm as a persuasive effort to reclaim the speaker's good character as a patient and even stoical person who is committed to waiting for God's forgiveness. The weight given to the speaker's patience is indicated by the unusual length of the reciprocal praise section, as shown in Figure 6.1.

PSALM 130[9]

1   A song of ascents. From the depths I called You, LORD.
2   Master, hear my voice. May Your ears listen close to the voice of my plea.
3   Were You, O Yah, to watch for wrongs, Master, who could endure?
4   Forgiveness is Yours, so that You may be feared.
5   I hoped for the LORD, my being hoped, and for His word I waited.
6   My being for the Master—more than the dawn-watchers watch for the dawn.
7   Wait, O Israel, for the LORD, for with the LORD is steadfast kindness, and great redemption is with Him.
8   And He will redeem Israel from all its wrongs.

While Psalm 130 does begin with an address, a plea for hearing in vv. 1-2, the speaker does not take the opportunity to identify himself as a faithful—or formerly faithful—follower of God. While the speaker asks God to listen attentively to a plea, no explicit plea is forthcoming.

Title/Address		
	1	Title and Address: Plea for hearing
Address	2	Address: Plea for hearing
	3	*Divine Action*: Indirect plea to suspend fault-detection
	4	Indirect plea for forgiveness
	5	*Reciprocal Action*: Speaker waits for a response
	6	Speaker waits for a response
	7	Speaker recommends waiting to others
Proposal	8	Speaker anticipates God's redemption

Figure 6.1. *Structure of Psalm 130*

The speaker voices no complaint. Whatever pains the speaker is suffering go undescribed; spelling them out would be inconsistent with this speaker's overall stoicism. Instead, the speaker indirectly admits guilt and the need for forgiveness in vv. 3-4. The admission comes by way of a potent rhetorical question, 'Were You, O Yah, to watch for wrongs, Master, who could endure?' By implying that no one on earth could pass God's scrutiny,

---

8. Kraus, *Psalms 60–150*, pp. 465-66. Psalm 32 provides a clear case of a speaker describing a confession for didactic purposes rather than out of current need.
9. Alter, *The Book of Psalms*, p. 455.

the speaker includes himself among the guilty without actually confessing to anything. The speaker also subtly reduces the egregiousness of whatever wrong he has committed by lumping it in with the lesser and possibly greater wrongs committed by others. The question also suggests that God let the sins go. The nature of the suggestion turns on the translation of the verb תשמר that Alter translates as 'watch for' but that is normally translated as 'guard', 'keep' or 'preserve'. While conceding that the verb 'has the particular sense of "keep track of" in the question in v. 3', Alter prefers to play up the repetition of the same verbal stem in 'more than dawn-watchers watch for the dawn' in v. 5.[10] Alter's translation, however, can be read as suggesting that God overlook wrongs entirely. The more conventional translation 'keep track of' allows God to notice the sins but then let them go by forgiving them.

The speaker also omits any request for divine intervention. Rather than describing the desired rescue, the speaker makes an indirect request for forgiveness in v. 4, by declaring that it is in God's nature and self-interest to be forgiving. The motive clause למען תורא ('so that You may be feared') may be an allusion to 1 Kgs 8.38-40.

> 1 Kgs 8.38-40   in any prayer or supplication offered by any person among all Your people Israel—each of whom knows his own affliction—when he spreads his palms toward this House, oh hear in Your heavenly abode, and pardon and take action! Render to each man according to his ways as You know his heart to be—for You alone know the hearts of all men—so that they may revere You all the days that they live on the land that You gave to our fathers.

In this prayer, Solomon lists a variety of occasions on which Israelites (and even non-Israelite sojourners in the land) may offend God, repent and call out in prayer to God. When Israelites repent, God forgives למען יראוך ('that they may revere You'). Because of his offense, the speaker in Psalm 130 cannot accuse God of injustice and refrains even from Solomonic imperatives in asking for forgiveness. Perhaps no more needs to be said: God as the agent of suffering already knows what to do to stop it.

The rest of the psalm, amounting to half the verses (vv. 5-8), describes the speaker's current actions and recommendations to his listeners. The section resembles a reciprocal action even though it says nothing about singing God's praises. In vv. 5-6, the speaker commits to waiting and hoping, expectant that God's forgiveness must come eventually, just as the sun must rise, but with the dark interval of uncertainty stretching out the anxiety. As

---

10. Alter, *The Book of Psalms*, p. 455. The NJPS translates the verse as 'if You keep account of sins'. Kraus (*Psalms 60–150*, p. 464) translates the term more strongly as 'impute'.

Nasuti notes, the verbs in v. 1 and v. 5 allow for either a past or an iterative present reading which leaves the situation unresolved. Correspondingly, in vv. 7-8, the speaker ends not by calling on his listeners to praise, but simply by advising them that when they do wrong, they should accept God's punishment and wait it out as he is doing. Both halves of the psalm end by emphasizing God's forgiving/redeeming nature.

The modifications of the usual shape of a lament—omission of identification among the faithful, of complaint, of request for divine action—reflect the speaker's weaker standing with God and a corresponding shift in the representation of the problem and its causes. Perhaps the speaker had already performed a sin-offering with an explicit confession but has not yet seen any relief. In the circumstances, the best the speaker can do is keep the lines of communication open, assure God of continued faithfulness and show readiness for better future behavior.

Psalm 38: Eloquently Inarticulate

In contrast to the restrained indirection of Psalm 130, the speaker in Psalm 38 vividly portrays the suffering God has inflicted and pleads directly and immediately for relief. The suffering even extends to speech, making speech—appropriate and inappropriate—a central theme of the psalm. Over the course of the psalm, the speaker contemplates the physical, psychological and social consequences of his wrong-doing and resolves at last to confess.

PSALM 38[11]

1   A David psalm, to call to mind.
2   LORD, do not rebuke me in Your fury nor chastise me in Your wrath.
3   For Your arrows have come down upon me, and upon me has come down Your hand.
4   There is no whole place in my flesh through Your rage, no soundness in my limbs through my offense.
5   For my crimes have welled over my head, like a heavy burden, too heavy for me.
6   My sores make a stench, have festered through my folly.
7   I am twisted, I am all bent. All day long I go about gloomy,
8   For my innards are filled with burning and there is no whole place in my flesh.
9   I grow numb and am utterly crushed. I roar from my heart's churning.
10   O Master, before You is all my desire and my sighs are not hidden from You.
11   My heart spins around, my strength forsakes me, and the light of my eyes, too, is gone from me.
12   My friends and companions stand off from my plight and my kinsmen stand far away.

---

11. Alter, *The Book of Psalms*, pp. 134-36.

13	They lay snares, who seek my life and want my harm. They speak lies, deceit utter all day long.
14	But like the deaf I do not hear, and like the mute whose mouth will not open.
15	And I become like a man who does not hear and has no rebuke in his mouth.
16	For in You, O LORD, I have hoped. You will answer, O Master, my God.
17	For I thought, 'Lest they rejoice over me, when my foot slips, vaunt over me'.
18	For I am ripe for stumbling and my pain is before me always.
19	For my crime I shall tell, I dread my offense.
20	And my wanton enemies grow many, my unprovoked foes abound.
21	And those who pay back good with evil thwart me for pursuing good.
22	Do not forsake me, LORD. My God, do not stay far from me.
23	Hasten to my help, O Master of my rescue.

A confessional mood is set at the very outset of Psalm 38 with the unusual expression להזכיר ('to call to mind') in the superscription, which as Alter notes, only occurs here and Psalm 70. Alter suggests that the expression draws a connotation of confession from two narratives where the root זכר is associated with offending: the Egyptian royal cupbearer recalling having offended Pharaoh in Gen. 41.9 and the widow from Zarephath attributing her son's illness to Elijah's calling attention to her sins in 1 Kgs 17.18.[12]

As shown in Figure 6.2, the address (v. 2) is brief, consisting entirely of a plea to God to cease a shower of angry rebukes. As in Psalm 130, the speaker makes no effort to identify himself and even refrains from asking God to hear. Presumably, neither is needed in this situation; the speaker is suffering not from God's neglect but from a surfeit of God's attention.

The bulk of the psalm is devoted to the speaker's complaint, which is divided into three sections (physical distress, vv. 3-9; cognitive impairment, vv. 11-15; and vulnerability, vv. 17-21), each bounded by appeals to God to understand his motives (v. 10 and v. 16). The speaker's physical distress (vv. 3-9) stretches from head to toe and distorts him inside and out, an image that contrasts with the straightness, uprightness and wholeness associated with the righteous. He forthrightly attributes his suffering to עונתי ('my crimes') in v. 5 and, in v. 6, אולתי ('my folly'). The pain reduces the speaker to making noises—שאגתי ('I roared') in v. 9 and אנחתי ('my groans' or 'sighs') in v. 10—as he lays before God only inchoate desire.

In vv. 11-15, the speaker's cognitive impairment causes further distress and danger. The speaker becomes increasingly isolated, first shunned by friends and family in vv. 12-13 and then by acquaintances who turn against him, taking advantage of his vulnerability to make false accusations against

---

12. Alter, *The Book of Psalms*, p. 134. Kraus, however, draws on other occurrences of the root to relate the superscription to an offering with frankincense (*Psalms 1–60*, p. 29).

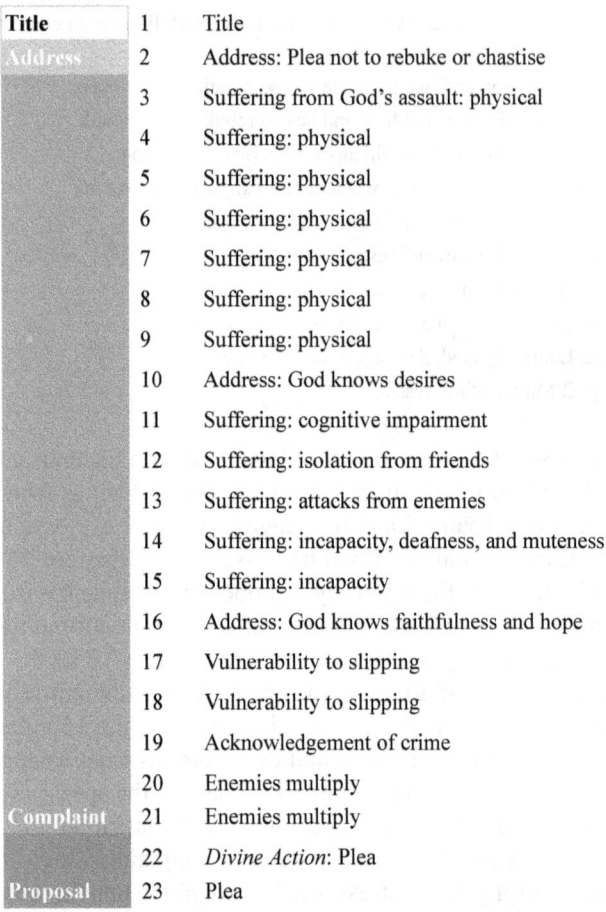

Figure 6.2. *Structure of Psalm 38*

him—perhaps to justify ritual ostracism.[13] While the opponents have full command of their voices, the speaker is in shock, incapable of hearing or speaking out against them. For his own sake and to correct his neighbors, he should rebuke them, as commanded in Lev. 19.17 and as God has been rebuking him. But he cannot—he has no rebuke in his mouth. Finally, in v. 16, the speaker becomes capable of articulating a commitment to waiting and hoping for God's rescue.

In the final section of the complaint, vv. 17-21, the speaker describes his growing vulnerability to his opponents, but still seems unable to take

13. Kraus, *Psalms 1–60*. Kraus believes that the speaker feigns deafness in vv. 14-15 as a step to showing faithfulness and leaving the entire problem to God. But Kraus admits difficulty reconciling the mixture of claims to innocence and guilt in the next section.

decisive action. At this point, he seems capable of coherent thought or speech—the verb אמרתי in v. 17 is sometimes translated as 'I thought' but also as 'I said', or even 'I pray'. Yet, even as he resolves to confess his sin, he seems to have second thoughts, perhaps dreading the public aftermath in vv. 17-18. Finally the speaker haltingly acknowledges sinning in v. 19— the sound pattern of the verse leaves a speaker choking on his words. As in Alter's translation of v. 19, the two nouns for sinning ('crime' and 'offense') bracket the two verbs ('tell' and 'dread'), but phonetically, these adjacent verbs are tongue twisters: 'I will tell, I dread' אגיד אדאג *agid edag*.[14] The imperfect verb forms leave the confession in the planning stages, as compared with the forthright confession of Psalm 51. The speaker's dread may arise from the speaker's mixed status; he may be guilty of ritual sins against God but innocent of the charges laid by the opponents, as he claims in vv. 20-21. Confessing to the former may hurt his chances of being cleared of the latter.

The final verses of the psalm, vv. 22-23, are a brief plea for divine aid that corresponds imperfectly with either physical suffering or looming opponents. It contains none of the usual calls for public vindication, such as the destruction or humiliation of the opponents. The absence of terms for judging between the speaker and the opponents signals that the speaker's main concern is not the opponents but God. Yet the call to God not to neglect the speaker suggests that God has now withdrawn—as opposed to God's over-active engagement in the opening. God's removal may be consistent with the speaker's relative recovery over the course of the psalm. The lack of a reciprocal vow of praise, however, suggests that the speaker still lacks standing to ask for favors regarding the opponents that would be repaid with praise.

Taken as a whole, the psalm is clearly devoted to eliciting sympathy through appeals to pathos or emotion, the most powerful appeals in the rhetorical repertoire. Among emotional appeals, the use of vivid descriptive language—*enargeia*—is especially effective because it leads hearers/readers to imagine or 'actualize' the physical sensations and emotions of real-world experience.[15] Neuropsychologists have found that imagining sensations and motor activity activates the same areas of the brain as actual perception and movement.[16] Identifying with the speaker's suffering may alter the mood or

---

14. The term 'dread' seems the antithesis of the sense of verbalization in the adjacent verb 'tell'; the root דאגה ('dread') contrasts with a speech term דבר ('word') in Prov. 12.25, 'Worry in a man's heart brings him low but a good word will gladden him'. Alter, *The Wisdom Books*, p. 247.

15. Burke (*Rhetoric of Motives*, pp. 78-81) notes that Aristotle classes actuality among the three most effective devices with antithesis and metaphor (*On Rhetoric* III.10.35 1410a).

16. Mikhail Zvyagintsev *et al.*, 'Brain Networks Underlying Mental Imagery of

disposition of the audience and may increase its willingness to entertain new ideas and opinions. While Psalm 38 is certainly not unique in using vivid emotional appeals—they are prominent in Psalm 22, for example—they are exceptionally varied and dominant in Psalm 38, ranging from bodily pains to sensory organs and cognitive capacity, including the power of speech itself. The paradox of such eloquent poetry describing such utter inarticulateness is inescapable, especially given the psalm's sense of immediacy. While the persuasive thrust of the psalm seems to be to convince God that the speaker has suffered enough, it may also be a rationale for some delay or inadequacy in the speaker's confession of wrong-doing.

Psalm 51: An Action-Oriented Confession

Psalm 51 takes a strikingly different approach to recovering from guilt from either Psalm 130 or Psalm 38. The speaker in Psalm 51 is explicit in confessing sins, comprehensive in laying out a plan for divine action and even holds out the possibility of reciprocal action. What is absent from the psalm is any complaint of suffering, physical or psychological.[17] As shown in Figure 6.3, the confession in effect replaces the complaint.

While some commentators treat the superscription as contemporaneous with the psalm's composition, most agree with Alter that 'in all likelihood, this psalm is a general penitential psalm composed centuries after David', in part because the reference to rebuilding the walls of Jerusalem makes it more likely to date from the exile or Second Temple period.[18]

PSALM 51[19]

1   For the lead player, a David psalm,
2   upon Nathan the prophet's coming to him when he had come to bed with Bathsheba.
3   Grant me grace, God, as befits Your kindness, with your great mercy wipe away my crimes.
4   Thoroughly wash my transgressions away and cleanse me from my offense.
5   For my crimes I know, and my offense is before me always.
6   You alone have I offended, and what is evil in Your eyes I have done. So You are just when You sentence, You are right when You judge.

Auditory and Visual Information', *European Journal of Neuroscience* 37 (2013), pp. 1421-34.

17. Kraus, *Psalms 1–59*, p. 500, makes some effort to read illness into the reference to bones in v. 10 but admits that guilt does not always bring on physical suffering.

18. Alter, *The Book of Psalms*, p. 180. See also Kraus, *Psalms 1–59*, p. 500. For a general discussion of editorial addition and movement of the titles, see Sarna, 'The Psalm Superscriptions and the Guilds', pp. 281-300; and Bruce K. Waltke, 'Superscripts, Postscripts, or Both', *JBL* 110 (1991), pp. 583-96.

19. Alter, *The Book of Psalms*, pp. 180-83.

7	Look, in transgression was I conceived, and in offense my mother spawned me.
8	Look, You desired truth in what is hidden; in what is concealed make wisdom known to me.
9	Purify me with a hyssop, that I be clean. Wash me, that I be whiter than snow.
10	Let me hear gladness and joy, let the bones that You crushed exalt.
11	Avert Your face from my offenses, and all my misdeeds wipe away.
12	A pure heart create for me, God, and a firm spirit renew within me.
13	Do not fling me from Your presence, and Your holy spirit take not from me.
14	Give me back the gladness of Your rescue and with a noble spirit sustain me.
15	Let me teach transgressors Your ways, and offenders will come back to You.
16	Save me from bloodshed, O God, God of my rescue. Let my tongue sing out Your bounty.
17	O Master, Open my lips, that my mouth may tell Your praise.
18	For You desire not that I should give sacrifice, burnt-offering You greet not with pleasure.
19	God's sacrifices—a broken spirit. A broken, crushed heart God spurns not.
20	Show goodness in Your pleasure to Zion, rebuild the walls of Jerusalem.
21	Then shall You desire just sacrifices, burnt-offerings and whole offering, then bulls will be offered up on Your altar.

The opening (vv. 3-4) omits any call for hearing as well as any identifying phrase; despite the absence of suffering, the speaker may be assuming that his sin has already attracted God's attention. Instead, the speaker calls on a trio of God's attributes, חן ('grace'), חסדך ('your kindness') and רחמיך ('your mercy'), before making a trio of requests, מחה פשעי ('wipe away my crimes'), כבסני מעוני ('wash me of my transgressions') and טהרני מחטאתי ('cleanse me from my offense'). These terms for malfeasance have different senses; the use of a variety of terms may be designed for emphasis or may make this an all-purpose confessional psalm.

These requests lead into the confession (vv. 5-7), the most direct admission of wrong-doing in the entire book of Psalms.[20] The confession further reduces the character of the speaker. It reuses all three of the previous terms for malfeasance and adds a couple of others. In v. 5, the speaker knows פשעי ('my crime') and is constantly aware of חטאתי ('my offense'). In v. 6, the speaker admits that these acts offended God, saying that he עשיתי הרע בעיניך ('did what is evil in your eyes'). Rather than challenging God, he acknowledges that God's judgment is just. In v. 7, he even traces his sinfulness back to his birth. The verbs in v. 7 are unusual: חוללתי

---

20. Tull ('Bakhtin's Confessional', p. 48) notes that Bakhtin's application of confessional self-accounting to the penitential psalms is hampered by the lack of admissions of guilt apart from Psalm 51. She instead applies it to the first-person laments more generally.

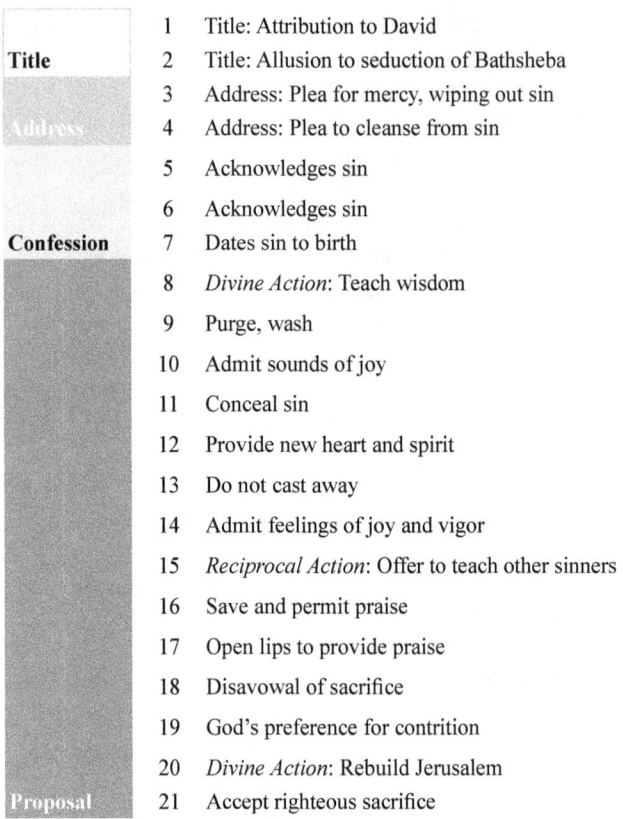

Figure 6.3. *Structure of Psalm 51*

('I was conceived') that refers to the writhing of child-birth and יחמתני ('I was spawned') that refers to the heat of estrus in female sheep or cattle. The main intent seems not to cast aspersions on the speaker's mother, nor to refer to original sin.[21] Rather, it reduces the status of the speaker from human to animal, the opposite direction of the progression in Psalm 22 from less-than-human worm to new-born infant for whom God served as midwife (see Chapter 4).

The proposal takes up two-thirds of the psalm. The divine-action half of the proposal (vv. 8-14) describes a thorough rehabilitation of the speaker's character. The structure is a verse-by-verse alternation of requests to God to remove sullying qualities (and their consequences) and to instill positive qualities. In the positive requests, the speaker asks to be instilled with wisdom (v. 8), to hear joyful sounds and experience bodily pleasure (v. 10),

---

21. Alter (*The Book of Psalms*, p. 181) also rejects interpreting the verse as a reference to a 'general doctrine of Original Sin' as does Kraus (*Psalms 1–59*, p. 503).

to be recreated with a pure heart and firm spirit (v. 12) and to re-experience joy and a sustaining spirit (v. 14). In the cleaning requests, the speaker asks for cleansing and purification (v. 9), for his sins to be concealed or erased (v. 11) and not to be cast away or deprived of God's spirit (v. 13). The terms for cleansing from the opening (vv. 3-4) recur with more specific detail as to method ('purifying with hyssop') and results ('becoming whiter than snow'). Commentators are divided on whether the passage refers to a specific ritual or to an internal spiritual exercise. However, the speaker's active engagement in the process seems slight as compared to the steps for overcoming temptation laid out in Psalms 4 and 62 (see Chapter 2) or those involving self-persuasion (see Chapter 7).[22]

In the reciprocal-action section, vv. 15-19, the speaker promises to put into practice the positive qualities that he has just asked God to instill: to teach, make sounds of joy, to tell praises and to offer the right kind of sacrifices: a broken heart and spirit. As shown in Figure 6.4, the positive qualities in vv. 8-14 align with the speaker's proposed actions in vv. 15-19.

A	v. 8 'make wisdom known to me'	
B	v. 10 'let me hear gladness and joy'	
C	v. 12 'a pure heart' and 'a firm spirit'	
D	v. 14 'gladness' and 'noble spirit'	
A'	v. 15 'let me teach transgressors'	
B'	v. 16 'let my tongue sing Your bounty'	
C'	v. 17 'open my lips that I may tell Your praise'	
D'	vv. 18-19 'a broken spirit', 'a broken, crushed heart'	

Figure 6.4. *Parallel Structure of Divine and Reciprocal Action in Psalm 51*

The reciprocal actions describe the speaker's reform as well as his future influence on the community. By rescuing the speaker, God enables the community as a whole to reform its actions, not only through praise but also through appropriate teaching and appropriate sacrifice. Teaching is the explicit focus of v. 15 but it may also resonate in v. 16. In v. 16, the speaker emphasizes that it is God's rescuing him from 'bloodguilt' (NJPS translation) or 'bloodshed' (Alter's translation) that would allow him to sing of God's bounty. Some commentators see the term reflecting on the nature of the speaker's sin. However, John Goldingay sees the reference to 'bloodguilt' in Ps. 51.16 as alluding to Ezekiel (Ezek. 3.17-19; 33.7-9) who is concerned

---

22. Bakhtin ('Author and Hero', p. 147-49) notes that the performed act of confession, as in Psalm 51, can turn the solitary speaker outward in a movement from consciousness to remorse to trust in God. However, only subsequent readers engaging with the text for their own self-accounting may create 'an answering act' that produces spiritual growth and 'enrichment through accumulated spiritual experience'.

about avoiding bloodguilt by turning a sinner away from the wrong path. In Goldingay's reading, Ezekiel compares himself in his relations to Israel to a watchman who must warn a resident of danger:

> A concern with deliverance from bloodguilt in these passages in Ezekiel, then, is connected with an obligation to pass on God's call to repentance and his offer of grace. Failure to deliver this testimony may lead to the death of the sinner, and the responsibility for this death belongs to the neglectful 'watchman'.[23]

The implication of vv. 15-16, then, is that God, by forgiving the speaker's sins and teaching him wisdom, enables him to become a teacher who rescues other sinners; God thereby also prospectively rescues the speaker from the bloodguilt of the other sinners' possible bad ends. The process of divine and reciprocal action is recursive: the speaker's own reform involves taking in wisdom and hearing sounds of joy from the community; as a reformed character, the speaker imparts wisdom and elicits sounds of praise and joy.

Appropriate sacrifice is the focus of vv. 18-21. Interestingly, making appropriate 'righteous' sacrifice is also the final step in the reform of sinners in Psalm 4 (see Chapter 4). Most commentators read vv. 18-19 as alluding to prophetic denunciations of the sacrificial system for carelessness and hypocrisy. While the speaker does not explicitly promise to offer sacrifices, this is the implication of the connection back to v. 12 and v. 14 in which God was requested to instill a new heart and spirit. Presumably the old heart and spirit were arrogant, while the new ones are appropriately humble and contrite. Marjorie O'Rourke Boyle emphasizes that a broken heart does not signify grief or unrequited love but punishment for sin that can be healed through repentance.[24]

Most commentators view vv. 20-21 as a late addition to affirm the validity of the Second Temple ritual. Alter, for example, sees everything up to v. 20 as 'entirely concerned with the remorseful confession of an individual, so this prayer for the rebuilding of Jerusalem looks suspiciously like a conclusion added by an editor'.[25] Kraus also sees these verses as 'a later accretion'.[26] However, it is also possible that the repudiation of animal sacrifice may be a rationale for confessing with a psalm instead of as part of a sin-offering. Perhaps the speaker has not made a sin-offering because an appropriate altar is not available (i.e., the speaker is in exile) or as part of a larger rejection of the current incarnation of the sacrificial system as a

---

23. John Goldingay, 'Psalm 51:16a (English 51:14a)', *CBQ* 40 (1978), pp. 388-90 (389).

24. Marjorie O'Rourke Boyle, 'Broken Hearts: The Violation of Biblical Law', *JAAR* 73 (2005), pp. 731-57.

25. Alter, *The Book of Psalms*, p. 183.

26. Kraus, *Psalms 1–59*, p. 506.

whole in favor of prayer and action. It is also possible that the speaker had made such a sacrifice but concluded that God had repudiated it because his heart and spirit were not appropriately chastened. In this case, the psalm is an additional effort to persuade God. If, however, the reciprocal action is focused on reforming the community, then the speaker may be positioning himself to critique the conduct of sacrifices as well. For a speaker to propose leaping from a frank admission of guilt to a position of social reformer bespeaks great confidence in his powers of persuasion.

Conclusion

The guilt-centered psalms in this chapter depart structurally and thematically from more typical laments. Aware that their suffering derives from God's notice of their faulty actions, the speakers omit self-characterizations in their brief opening addresses. I have suggested that the brevity of these address sections derives from the speakers' consciousness that God is all too aware of their cases. This reading is consistent with the findings of Alan Lenzi, who has compared addresses in the lament psalms to the generally lengthier addresses in Mesopotamian prayers. Lenzi notes that the briefest addresses among Akkadian prayers come in 'supplications for abatement of a personal god's wrath' when there is a 'familiar connection' between the supplicant and the deity.[27] In the psalms in general, Israelites assume a closer connection with God than Akkadians do with their deities; both cut back on the addresses even further when attributing their suffering to their own offending acts.

The complaints sections of the guilt-centered psalms, if they exist at all, seek only to evoke God's pity, not to challenge God's commitment to justice. The proposals are also modified. Lacking the status of an innocent sufferer who can bargain for rescue in exchange for praise, these speakers seek first to soften God's wrath and then to rehabilitate their characters. The speaker in Psalm 130 reminds God that all humans are imperfect and constructs an ethos of patience and faith by commiting to waiting for God to act. The speaker in Psalm 38 attempts to soften God's wrath by evoking pity for intense suffering and vulnerability to undeserved attacks from opponents; his willingness and ability to confess to his actual crimes increase across the psalm but are left unresolved. Finally, the speaker in Psalm 51 confesses explicitly and immediately submits his character to a complete reconstruction, after which he proposes not only to praise God but to lead others out of sin. The unusual nature of these psalms underscores the usual presumption of innocence noted by Patrick and Diable. However,

---

27. Alan C. Lenzi, 'Invoking the God: Interpreting Invocations in Mesopotamian Prayers and Biblical Laments of the Individual', *JBL* 129 (2010), pp. 303-15 (304).

the analysis in this chapter does not support their rationale that Israelites avoided confession in the psalms because monotheism left them freer to challenge God. Rather, it seems likely that Israelites simply used a separate forum for dealing with guilt and reserved the artistry of the psalms for less clear-cut situations where persuasion was required.

Chapter 7

SELF-PERSUASION AND WISDOM

As public discourse, the psalms address multiple audiences. God, of course, is usually the direct addressee, but speakers often turn to address by-standers and opponents, an assembly that stands in for the community at large. Another key audience member is the speaker; composing or performing a psalm enables persuading one's self. At the outset of this book, I objected to approaches that reduce the purpose of the psalms to the therapeutic, that portray the psalms as a moment-by-moment flow of thoughts and feelings leading to revived faith and praise. Self-persuasion is a more complex process than expression. Working out the reasons for God to intervene on one's behalf rehearses and strengthens one's commitment to the community's core values and standards of behavior. The effects of self-persuasion are also more complex than relief of tension. Considering possible objections from hearers and selecting among the available arguments improves one's ability to take and judge alternative perspectives. As the psalms in this chapter will show, internal deliberation may supplant rather than supplement a direct appeal to God.

The process of self-persuasion and its moral consequences were well-known in ancient Athens. In her book on classical self-persuasion, Jean Nienkamp points to Isocrates as the first rhetorician to spell out 'a causal connection between internal rhetoric and ethical, wise behavior'.[1] Isocrates founded the first rhetoric academy with a fixed location in Athens in the early fourth century BCE. In his 'Hymn to Logos', Isocrates equates the ability to argue internally with arguing in public:

> With this faculty [logos] we both contend against others on matters which are open to dispute and seek light for ourselves on things which are unknown; for the same arguments which we use in persuading others when we speak in public, we employ also when we deliberate in our own thoughts; and, while we call eloquent those who are able to speak before a crowd, we regard as sage those who most skillfully debate their problems in their own minds (15.256).[2]

1. Jean Nienkamp, *Internal Rhetorics: Toward a History and Theory of Self-Persuasion* (Carbondale, IL: Southern Illinois University Press, 2001), p. 20.
2. Isocrates, *Isocrates with an English Translation in Three Volumes* (trans. George Norlin; Cambridge, MA: Harvard University Press; London: William Heinemann, 1980).

For Isocrates, eloquence, a matter of verbal fluency and style, is of lesser value than sagacity which takes discipline and judgment. As Nienkamp explains, an eloquent public speaker may be ready instantly to respond to the demands of the immediate situation. But sagacity takes a 'mental habit' that goes beyond this mere opportunism: 'mental discipline is required for grasping the larger significance of the situation—its possible consequences and moral import'.[3] A key aspect of self-persuasion is the ability to consider the merits of alternative perspectives, alternative explanations, alternative courses of action.

Like persuasion of other people, self-persuasion combines appeals to rationality (logos) with varying degrees of passion (pathos). It may have a calm rational quality or the intense agonism of wrestling with an adversary. As a way to gain wisdom, James Crosswhite sees a calm process as most enlightening:

> What we are at one moment, with our present desires and attainments and perspectives, can be challenged by other desires and attainments and perspectives, and the process can be one not of dissonance and fragmentation and psychic violence but one of conversation and transcendence toward our selves. This capacity for being hospitable to a rhetorical interaction of competing perspectives is associated with wisdom itself, and is a kind of peace.[4]

In the psalms considered in this chapter, internal debate yields wisdom but the process described is far from peaceful, being brought on by fundamental doubts about God's faithfulness and commitment to justice. In Psalm 77, the speaker overcomes physical suffering by mentally rehearsing God's deeds; in Psalm 73, the speaker conquers anger that God allows the wicked to prosper. In both cases, the turn in the speakers' attitudes results from internal deliberation rather than appeals to God to intervene.

Psalm 77: Reimagining the Past

Psalm 77 has received little scholarly attention, in part because it resists easy classification and in part because it appears rough-edged—both its opening and ending seem abrupt and its two halves seem to shift in character. The first part has all the earmarks of a lament of an individual, a vivid expression of distress and distance from God. However, unlike most laments, the speaker says nothing of the source or nature of the problem, makes no call on God for rescue and makes no vows of public praise. The second part of the psalm has the character of a communal lament or hymn alluding to the narrative of the exodus from Egypt. However, the psalm concludes without calling on God to continue faithful action in the future.

---

3. Nienkamp, *Internal Rhetorics*, p. 134.
4. James Crosswhite, *Deep Rhetoric: Philosophy, Reason, Violence, Justice, Wisdom* (Chicago: University of Chicago Press, 2013), pp. 141-42.

Most commentators see the two parts reflecting a shift in the speaker's outlook from despair to praise. In contrast, I will suggest that the speaker is throughout recounting, enacting and modeling an active form of self-persuasion. Rather than asking God to intervene to relieve his distress, the speaker actively calls to mind thoughts and images that change his own disposition and lead him to focus on God's historic faithfulness. In this way, the speaker uses both first-hand experience and imaginative recreations of such experiences as a way to build moral character, as a form of self-discipline or *habitus*.

PSALM 77[5]

1 For the lead player on [*y'du-tun*], an Asaph psalm.
2 My voice to God—let me cry out. My voice to God—and hearken to me.
3 In the day of my straits I sought the Master. My eye flows at night, it will not stop.[6] I refused to be consoled.
4 I call God to mind and I moan. I speak and my spirit faints. Selah.
5 You held open my eyelids. I throbbed and could not speak.
6 I ponder the days of yore, the years long gone.
7 I call to mind my song in the night. To my own heart I speak, and my spirit inquires.
8 Will the Master forever abandon me, and never again look with favor?
9 Is His kindness gone for all time, His word done for time without end?
10 Has God forgotten to show grace, has He closed off in wrath His compassion? [selah]
11 And I said, it is my failing, that the High One's right hand has changed.
12 I call to mind the acts of Yah when I recall Your wonders of old.
13 I recite all your works, Your acts I rehearse.
14 God, Your way is in holiness. Who is a great god like God?
15 You are the god working wonders. You made known among peoples Your strength.
16 You redeemed with Your arm Your people, the children of Jacob and Joseph. Selah
17 The waters saw You, O God, the waters saw You, they trembled, the depths themselves shuddered.
18 The clouds streamed water. The skies sounded with thunder. Your bolts, too, flew about.
19 Your thunder's sound under the wheel—lightning lit up the world. The earth shuddered and shook.
20 In the sea was Your way, and Your path in the mighty waters, and Your footsteps left no traces.
21 You led Your people like a flock by the hand of Moses and Aaron.

---

5. Alter, *The Book of Psalms*, pp. 268-71.
6. In v. 3, Alter (p. 268) emends 'my hand' to 'my eye', reading it as an allusion to Lam. 3.49, 'My eye flowed and was silent, without stop'. In a similar vein, the NJPS assumes more textual corruption and incorporates both hand and eye, 'with my hand [uplifted]; [my eyes] flow all night without respite'.

As shown in Figure 7.1, the psalm opens with an extremely brief address in v. 2. It includes three calls to God and one request for hearing. However, reconnecting with God does not seem to be the primary goal. The speaker mainly uses third person rather than second person to address God and does nothing to remind God of his or her character or their previous relationship. These elements are also absent from the complaint.

In the complaint (vv. 3-7), the speaker describes inconsolable, inarticulate, restless distress. The proximal cause for the suffering, whether defeat by enemies or physical illness, is left unstated. It may be God's absence itself that is keeping the speaker awake weeping all night. The speaker's effort to recall past times and past songs in vv. 6-7 enables him to start questioning what is happening.

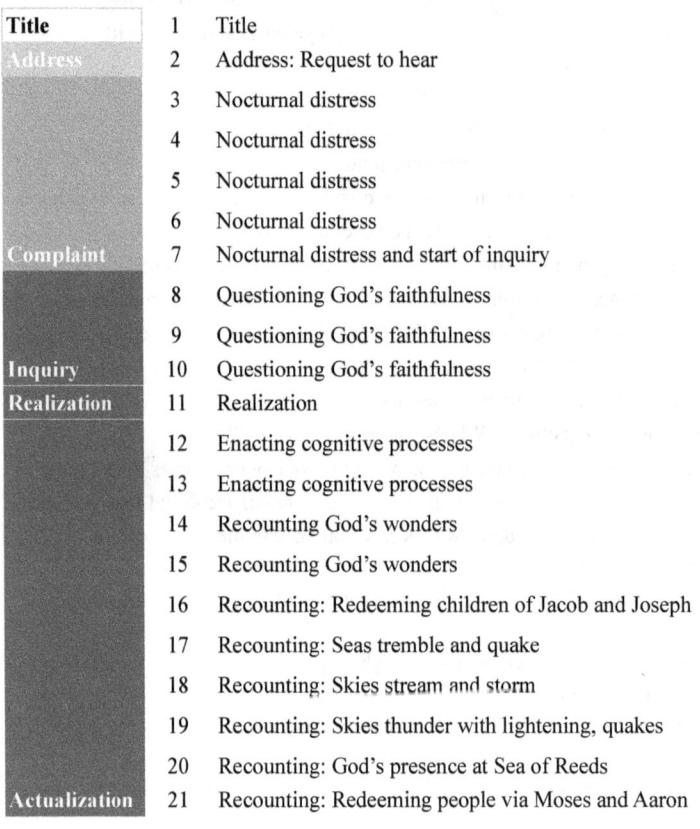

Figure 7.1. *Structure of Psalm 77*

In the final two-thirds of the psalm, the speaker engages in a self-directed recovery composed of an inquiry, a realization and an inner process of actualizing the realization. In vv. 8-10, the speaker asks whether God's very essence has changed, raising the horrific possibility that God has closed off

7. Self-Persuasion and Wisdom

all positive interaction—favor, kindness, grace, compassion. John Kselman sees allusions here to God's self-proclaimed attributes in Exod. 34.6: 'compassionate and gracious, slow to anger, abounding in kindness and faithfulness, extending kindness to the thousandth generation'.[7]

Coming after such a vivid depiction of personal suffering, the questions may seem entirely personal. Brueggemann reads them as emerging 'out of an overriding self-concern. They appear to ask about God's faithfulness. But they really ask, what about me?'; Brueggemann views the speaker at this stage as consumed by narcissism.[8] Alter's translation also treats the questions as personal; he goes so far as to insert 'me' into the translation of v. 8 as the object of abandonment. But there is good reason to reject this insertion and read the complaint in broader terms. The direness of the crisis is amplified if the object of God's neglect is the entire community. The phrasing certainly points well beyond the concerns of a single lifetime, with לעולמים ('for all worlds') in v. 8 and לנצח ('altogether'/'in perpetuity') and לדור ודר ('for all generations') in v. 9. Together with the absence of personal information in the address and complaint, these elements weigh against seeing the speaker as self-absorbed. Rather, this is a speaker inquiring into the implications of God's apparent absence from the community at large.

The turning point comes at the psalm's half-way point in v. 11; the speaker realizes that he is responsible for the perception that God has changed. Commentators have debated just what onus the speaker has taken on. The obscure term חלותי that Alter translates as 'my failing' is translated as 'my fault' by the NJPS; as 'my grief/sorrow' by Kraus, the RSV, Kselman and Brueggemann; and as 'my infirmity' in the KJV. Rendering the term as 'grief' or 'sorrow' carries least blame, portraying the speaker as simply continuing to express dismay over the change in God without conveying a sense of self-criticism. On the other hand, the NJPS translation of the term as 'my fault' casts the verse as a confession of sinful wrong-doing that could justify God's abandonment. Alter's choice of 'failing' fits best with the speaker's cognitive focus; the speaker is critiquing his own assumptions, realizing that the line of questioning is deluded.

The continuation of v. 11 with its reference to God changing is also obscure. Though Alter, like most commentators, translates the term שנות as 'has changed', grammatically it might be translated as 'repeated' or even as 'years of' (an option taken in the KJV).[9] Commentators have over-looked the

---

7. John S. Kselman, 'Psalm 77 and the Book of Exodus', *JANES* 15 (1983), pp. 51-58 (53).
8. Walter Brueggemann, 'Psalm 77: The "Turn" from Self to God', *Journal for Preachers* 6 (1983), pp. 8-14 (9); Brueggemann and Bellinger, *Psalms*, pp. 332-33.
9. Alter, *The Book of Psalms*, p. 269.

co-occurrence of the same two problematic verb forms (חלל and שנות) in the perfectly clear Ps. 89.35, in which God renounces the possibility of changing toward the line of David, even if the people fall into sin:

Ps. 77.10-11	And I said, it is my failing [חלותי], that the High One's right hand has changed [שנות].
Ps. 89.34-35	Yet My steadfast kindness I will not revoke for him, and I will not betray My faithfulness. I will not profane [אחלל] My pact and My mouth's utterance I will not alter [אשנה].

Psalm 89 is another admixture of personal with communal, hymn with lament; it goes on to accuse God of violating this very promise and to plead for restoring the pact. Further connections between Psalm 89 and Psalm 77 will be discussed below. At this point, I am suggesting that Ps. 77.11 is a deliberate twist on the terms of Ps. 89.35. The speaker takes responsibility for impugning God's faithfulness by imagining that God's right hand could change. This realization leads into a cycle of recollection and rehearsal of God's historical relationship to the community, a recursive process that began early in the psalm.

Verses 12-13 focus on the speaker's thought processes, repeating many of the same verbs as in the early part of the complaint:

v. 4	אזכרה 'I call to mind' [God] and אשיחה 'I speak'
v. 5	לא אדבר 'I can't speak'/'I can't say a word'
v. 6	חשבתי 'I ponder' [the past]
v. 7	אזכרה 'I call to mind' [my song], אשיחה 'I speak' [to my own heart], and יחפש רוחי 'my spirit inquires'
v. 11	אמר 'I said'
v. 12	אזכור 'I call to mind' [God's acts] and אזכרה 'I recall' [God's wonders]
v. 13	הגיתי 'I recite' [God's works] and אשיחה 'I speak'/'I rehearse' [God's acts]

The second time around, the process of recalling the past leads not to questioning but to reaffirmation. The intentional act of recalling God's wonders, God's works and God's acts in vv. 12-13 leads the speaker in vv. 14-15 to ask who can compare to God in greatness and holiness, working wonders to rescue the people, echoing the triumphant question of the Song of the Sea:

Exod. 15.11-13	Who is like You, O LORD, among the celestials; who is like You, majestic in holiness, awesome in splendor, working wonders! You put out Your right hand, the earth swallowed them. In Your love You lead the people You redeemed; in Your strength You guide them to Your holy abode.

For Kselman, the references to the Song of the Sea are central to the meaning of the psalm, which he represents with a rather misshapen chiasm, as shown in Figure 7.2:[10]

A   vv. 9-10 questioning God's attributes
B   v. 11 questioning whether God's hand changed
C   vv. 12-14 allusion to Song of Sea
B'   vv. 15-16 reaffirming that God still redeems with mighty arm
A'   vv. 17-21 reaffirming God's attributes through hymnic theophany

Figure 7.2 *Kselman's Chiastic Structure of Questions and Answers in Psalm 77*

In Kselman's view, the fact that his chiasm cuts across the border usually drawn between the lament portion and the hymnic portion speaks to the overall unity of the psalm. What matters is the historical material rather than the speaker's mental struggle. As a result, he has little to say about the opening portion of the psalm. In contrast, Herbert Levine sees the unity of the psalm arising from the profusion of cognitive verbs; after a repeated cycle of meditation, the speaker can contemplate both lament and hymn at the same time.[11] My view aligns with Levine's. As the structure in Figure 7.1 suggests, this reading preserves the coherence of the complaint portion while placing the realization in v. 11 (rather than an allusion to the Song of the Sea) at the center of the psalm. My reading also suggests a larger purpose for the closing verses describing God's presence at the sea.

Verses 17-21 are filled with evocative description and poetic imagery. The theme—God's appearance at the edge of the sea with dramatic reactions from nature—is certainly relevant to the Song of the Sea but does not exactly reflect its imagery or the imagery of the narrative of the crossing. God appeared there in the form of a pillar of fire and cloud (Exod. 14.19-29). The imagery of a sky filled with thunder bolts and lightning and of the earth quaking more closely reflects the revelation at Sinai (Exod. 19.16-20). Kraus, while drawing connections to Psalm 29 among others, sees this theophany as a 'special independent element' that incorporates the 'essential characteristics of Baal' in Canaanite mythology.[12] Whatever its source, the passage is a further stage of mental action, starting from the initial intention of recalling God's wonders, works and acts in vv. 12-13, moving through the explicit declaration of God's historical wonders, works and acts in vv. 14-16, and culminating in an imaginative enactment of God's wonders, works and acts on earth.

---

10. Kselman, 'Psalm 77', p. 58.
11. Levine, *Sing unto God*, pp. 146-47.
12. Kraus, *Psalms 60–150*, pp. 116-17.

By activating the imagination, the speaker enlists emotion to support the previous rational efforts to cope with the loss of faith.[13] Appeals to *pathos* (emotion) have been recognized since ancient times as among the powerful aids to persuasion. Among the emotional appeals, the most powerful is the use of *enargeia*, vivid description and imagery that evokes in hearers/readers the physical sensations and emotions of real-world experience. Psalm 77.17-21 evokes the sound of thunder, the flash of lightning, the feel of the earth quaking—awe-inspiring experiences shared by the waters themselves. Imagining and visualizing are powerful because, as neuro-psychologists have found, they activate areas of the brain associated with perceptual organs and motor activities.[14] Yet the persuasive function of vivid passages such as this often goes unrecognized. They are treated as expressive, as a release or articulation of the speaker's feeling, rather than as persuasive, as a move to change the disposition or mood of a hearer, a reader, or even one's self. Changing the mood or disposition of an audience goes a long way toward increasing their willingness to entertain new ideas and opinions. Thus the final verses of Psalm 77, framed as they are by God's commitment to the community's patriarchs (Jacob and Joseph in v. 16) and leaders (Moses and Aaron in v. 21), cap the speaker's self-guided reintegration into stoic faithfulness. God's absence in the immediate crisis does not signal an essential change; rather the speaker's attitude to God's absence is transformed.

The nature of the immediate crisis cannot be pinned down but it is reasonable to take it as communal rather than entirely personal. Richard Clifford sees a connection between the extended hymnic portions of three psalms, Pss. 77.12-21; 78.52-54; and 89.2-38, going so far as to propose that they along with Psalm 44 belong in a subgenre that he calls the 'communal lament'.[15] Clifford argues for the textual integrity of these psalms, which like Psalm 77 have been read as redactional agglomerations of communal hymns with individual laments. Clifford argues that a clue to the nature of the current crisis is the choice of ancestral triumphs to recite. He therefore takes the hymnic part of Psalm 77 as a sign that the speaker is responding to a national disaster.

Matthew Mitchell agrees with Clifford on the textual unity of these psalms and their thematic connections. However, he questions whether they

---

13. The appreciation of Classical rhetoricians for the tight connection between imagination and emotion is elaborated by Ruth Webb, 'Imagination and the Arousal of the Emotions in Greco-Roman Rhetoric', in Susanna Morton Braund and Christopher Gill (eds.), *The Passions in Roman Thought and Literature* (New York: Cambridge University Press, 1997), pp. 112-27.

14. Zvyagintsev *et al.*, 'Brain Networks'.

15. Richard J. Clifford, 'Psalm 89: A Lament over the Davidic Ruler's Continued Failure', *HTR* 73 (1980), pp. 35-47; cited by Croft, *The Identity of the Individual*, p. 194.

fit a new form-critical type as closely as Clifford claims. Mitchell suggests that 'there are, within this "tightly defined" genre of "communal laments", accusatory as well as self-effacing types, and very different understandings of what the "communal" identity supposed to characterize them means'.[16] Psalms 44 and 89 both use recitals of God's past behavior and claims of current faithfulness to convince God to return to form; Psalm 78 uses its recital to warn the community to shun the behavior of ancestors whose rebellions and straying led to their punishment and defeat. Unlike the other psalms in the group, Psalm 77 lacks any specific reference to enemies or battle, so Mitchell sees Clifford's claim that it relates to a national disaster as speculative.

Following Mitchell's lead, I suggest that these psalms offer a range of ways to respond to God's absence: by claiming innocence, by blaming subgroups or by eschewing blame to focus on maintaining faithfulness despite God's apparent abandonment. Like Levine, I see Psalm 77 as a didactic model of an extended process of meditation for listeners. However, whereas Levine argues that an individual's story of deliverance has 'far more lasting impact [on hearers] if it is aligned with a national story of deliverance',[17] I see the story of national deliverance as a powerful tool for an individual seeking to achieve a personal sense of deliverance.

Psalm 73: Speaking Internally and Externally

Whatever it was that triggered the speaker's crisis of doubt in Psalm 77 is never identified. However, what roils the speaker's faith in Psalm 73 is quite clear: the absence or at least the deferral of judgment on the wicked. Rather than being punished, the wicked live at ease, achieve material success and lead the people into apostasy. They make no effort to hide their deeds and even mock God's failure of omniscience. The speaker feels envious and sorely tempted to deny God's power. Dealing with these doubts is vital but voicing them would be a betrayal. Self-persuasion provides the way out.

No consensus has been reached about the setting and purpose of Psalm 73; though McCann notes that more than half a dozen possibilities have been advanced, most commentators identify it either as a didactic psalm—despite the lack of public address, or as a thanksgiving psalm—despite the absence of explicit thanks.[18] Kraus sees it as 'an autobiographical stylization' rather than a real event in the speaker's life; for didactic purposes,

---

16. Matthew W. Mitchell, 'Genre Disputes and Communal Accusatory Laments: Reflections on the Genre of Psalm LXXXIX', *VT* 55 (2005), pp. 511-27 (26).

17. Levine, *Sing unto God*, p. 147.

18. J. Clinton McCann, Jr, 'Psalm 73: A Microcosm of Old Testament Theology', in K.G. Hoglund *et al.* (eds.), *The Listening Heart: Essays in Wisdom and the Psalms in*

the speaker describes, reports and confesses doubts but ends up giving thanks for achieving a level of 'certainty' that 'overcame all affliction and temptation'. The didactic purpose is signaled by the psalm's framing in which doubts are 'embedded in the full certainty of salvation'.[19]

PSALM 73[20]

1. An Asaph psalm. Only (אך) good to Israel is God, to the pure of heart.
2. As for me, my feet had almost strayed, my steps had nearly tumbled.
3. For I envied the revelers, I saw the wicked's well-being:
4. 'For they are free of the fetters of death, and their body is healthy.
5. Of the torment of man they have no part, and they know not human afflictions'.
6. Thus haughtiness is their necklace, outrage, their garment, bedecks them.
7. Fat bulges round their eyes, imaginings spill from their heart.
8. They mock and speak with malice, from on high they speak out oppression.
9. They put their mouth up to the heavens, and their tongue goes over the earth.
10. Thus the people turn back to them, and they lap up their words.
11. And they say, 'How could God know, and is there knowledge with the Most High?'
12. Look, such are the wicked, the ever complacent ones pile up wealth.
13. But (אך) in vain have I kept my heart pure and in innocence washed my palms.
14. For I was afflicted all day long, and my chastisement, each new morning.
15. If I said, Let me talk like them. Look, Your sons' band I would have betrayed.
16. When I thought to know these things, it was a torment in my eyes.
17. Till I came to the sanctuaries of God, understood what would be their end.
18. Yes (אך), You set them on slippery ground, brought them down to destruction.
19. How they come to ruin in a moment, swept away, taken in terrors!
20. Like a dream upon waking, O Master, upon rising You despised their image.
21. When my heart was embittered, and my conscience stabbed with pain,
22. I was a dolt and knew nothing, like cattle I was with You.
23. Yet I was always with You, You grasped my right hand.
24. You guarded me with Your counsel, and toward glory You took me.
25. Whom else do I have in the heavens, and beside You whom would I want upon the earth?
26. Though my flesh and my heart waste away, God is my heart's rock and my portion forever.
27. For, look, those far from you perish, You demolish all who go whoring from You.
28. But I—God's closeness is good to me, I make the Master the LORD my shelter, to recount all Your works.

Honor of Roland E. Murphy, O. Carm (JSOTSup, 58; Sheffield: JSOT Press, 1987), pp. 247-57.
  19. Kraus, *Psalms 60–150*, p. 85.
  20. Alter, *The Book of Psalms*, pp. 252-56.

Kraus thus reads Ps. 73.1 as a confident declaration of God's commitment to the good. He even reveals a parallelism underscoring the point; by breaking ישראל ('Israel') into the two words ישר ('upright') and אל ('El'), he reveals the verse as a chiasm: 'good to the upright [*yashar*] is El, God, to the pure of heart'. Given the absence of other communal references, Alter considers this a plausible option, though he retains 'Israel' in his translation.

The speaker's certainty in this declaration, however, is undermined by the term אך (*ach*) which as noted in the discussion of Psalm 62 usually has an adversative rather than an emphatic effect. This effect is not conveyed by Alter as he translates אך (*ach*) in Ps. 73.1 as 'only' as he did throughout Psalm 62 (though he does not follow suit in Ps. 17.13, 18). Reading אך (*ach*) as an adversative in Ps. 73.1, Snaith sees it as a signal that the speaker is opening with a hard-won conclusion.[21] Even to serve this purpose, however, v. 1 must also be recognized as the claim that is at stake throughout the psalm; v. 1 states the premise that the speaker's recent experiences have called into doubt. At present, God seems to be good to the wicked.

As indicated in Figure 7.3, the brief opening is followed by a complaint describing the speaker's crisis of faith (vv. 2-12) that takes up nearly half the psalm.[22] The speaker focuses on the opponents' appearance, behavior and material wealth but does not specify any harms they have inflicted on the speaker himself. Rather, the arrogant evil-doers simply flaunt their well-being, stirring the envy and emulation of others including the speaker. The speaker is led to the brink; in v. 3 he reports narrowly resisting straying, though he admits giving in to envy.

Psalm 17, discussed in Chapter 4, makes an interesting contrast to Psalm 73. In both psalms, the speaker dwells on the opponents' prosperity. However, the opening in Psalm 17 was far longer, including a confident assertion of the speaker's righteousness and innocence. There, the speaker associated himself with God by interposing his physical features with God's, setting up a contrast to the gross and beast-like appearance of the opponents. In Psalm 73, however, the speaker feels distant from God, omitting any direct address and depicting the opponents not as beastly but as otherworldly, even approaching the divine. They seem immune to death (v. 4), avoid the troubles of a mere mortal—אנוש 'man' or אדם 'human' (v. 5) and even speak from on high, with פיהם 'their mouths' and לשונם 'their tongues' in the heavens (vv. 8-9). The speaker dwells on their appearance, weaving their arrogance and violence into their garments but he barely describes any evil they do. Their worst comes in the form of thoughts and speeches: imaginings spilling from their hearts (v. 7), mockery, malicious and extortionate

---

21. Snaith, 'The Meaning of the Hebrew "אך"', p. 223.
22. As McCann does ('Psalm 73', p. 249), I take אך (*ach*) to signal section boundaries.

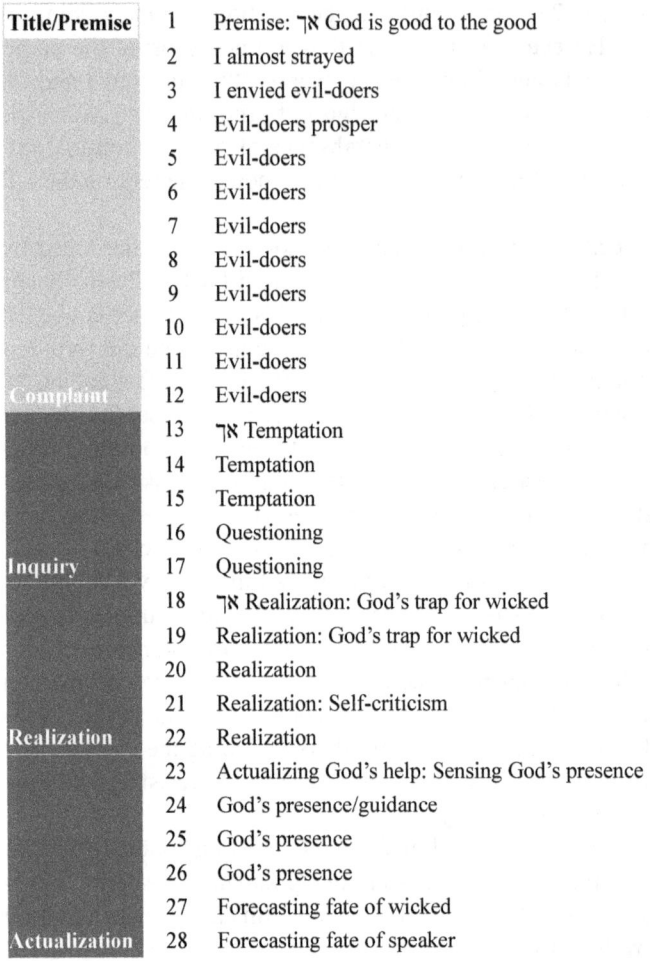

Figure 7.3. *Structure of Psalm 73*

speech (v. 8) and open challenges to God's omniscience (v. 11). No wonder people are drawn towards them, away from God's path.

The speaker's own drift is described in vv. 13-14. He becomes cynical towards his own behavior, seeing his efforts to remain pure as a waste and feeling constant anguish over the conflict between his beliefs; the doctrine that God reserves goodness for the good is undermined by his first-hand observation that God seems to have rewarded the wicked. In vv. 15-16, he describes exactly what he was tempted to do—not to join in wicked deeds but to speak out his loss of faith in righteous behavior. But he realizes that even so little would be a betrayal. As Levine notes, speech in these verses is an act with consequences; even adopting speech like the opponents' would have corrupted the speaker.²³ Yet Levine maintains that considering such speech even hypothetically enables a process of self-persuasion to begin, opening a dialogue not only with the words of the wicked but with the almost-spoken words of the speaker's own. To explain this effect, Levine quotes Bakhtin:

> A conversation with an internally persuasive word that one has begun to resist may continue, but it takes on another character: it is questioned, it is put in a new situation in order to expose its weak side, to get a feel for its boundaries, to experience it physically as an object.²⁴

Rather than voicing his loss of faith aloud, in v. 16 the speaker applies his mind to understand the conflict between his beliefs and his experience, perplexing though it is. Alter and Kraus translate v. 16 as a continuation of the anguish that such thoughts cause the speaker; others however translate it as a contemplation of the difficulty of the inquiry:

Ps. 73.16	Alter	When I thought to know these things, it was a torment in my eyes.
	Kraus	And I pondered how I should understand this—it was torment in my eyes!
	NJPS	So I applied myself to understand this, but it seemed a hopeless task.
	Crenshaw	But when I pondered the way to understand this, it was burdensome in my sight.²⁵

Insight comes next in v. 17 when the speaker enters God's holy precincts. From a place of ultimate closeness to the divine, he comprehends how distant from God his opponents must eventually end up. The location and nature of this insight are key to appreciating the speaker's struggle. Like most critics, Kraus and Crenshaw locate the speaker within the Jerusalem temple and identify the insight as an act of God that reveals some aspect of eternal redemption. For Kraus, 'the psalmist either received a divine revelation or was confronted by the reality of God in a theophany'; the speaker's inquiry is taken out of his hands: 'what in this world can no longer be demonstrated empirically is cleared up prophetically'.²⁶ While Crenshaw poses the possibilities less assertively using question form, he too sees the source of enlightenment as external, whether from 'a priestly oracle

---

23. Levine, *Sing unto God*, p. 124.
24. Mikhail Bakhtin, *The Dialogic Imagination: Four Essays* (ed. Michael Holquist; trans. Caryl Emerson and Michael Holquist; Austin, TX: University of Texas Press, 1981), p. 348.
25. James L. Crenshaw, *The Psalms: An Introduction* (Grand Rapids, MI: Eerdmans, 2001), p. 110.
26. Kraus, *Psalms 60–150*, p. 89.

of salvation', 'a prophetic mediator' or an 'assurance come directly to the worshipper'.[27]

Levine agrees that the location at the Temple is key, but not because of the greater availability of priests, prophets or Godhead. Rather, he emphasizes the effect on the individual of such a change in place. By entering a sacred space, the speaker 'momentarily assumes God's perspective on timespace'; 'the shift from human to divine temporal perspective, from profane to sacred ground, allows this psalmist to make his peace with the world in which he lives for as long as he can remain connected to God'. In contrast to Kraus and Crenshaw, Levine attributes the insight to the speaker's ongoing cognitive efforts, not to a certainty implanted by revelation. For Levine, the life of ritual observance within a community prepares the way for connecting with the divine at sacred places through 'patient meditative mindfulness'.[28]

In many ways, Levine's reading is akin to that of Martin Buber, who is probably the most influential modern interpreter of Psalm 73. Levine and Buber both focus on the mindful work of the individual. They differ, not surprisingly, on the role of ritual observance and on the referent of God's sanctuaries in v. 17. For Buber, the location is not 'the Temple precincts in Jerusalem, but the sphere of God's holiness, the holy mysteries of God'.[29] An individual with a heart in the right frame can connect to the divine anywhere. For Buber, לבב ('heart') which occurs six times, is the key term in Psalm 73; the speaker starts out merely going through the motions of innocence and purity (v. 13) but after affliction and struggle, his heart is purified enough to enter into communion with the divine and realize God's continual presence.

Interpreting the nature of the insight has strong implications for identifying the purpose of the remainder of the psalm. Kraus and Crenshaw see the major work of the psalm as over as soon as the revelation occurs in v. 17—the rest is proclamation of the good news. In Kraus's terms, as the speaker 'inquires about God's final dispositions, this unveiling has dawned so impressively, so immediately, that he announces, in prophetic style, in the form of a funeral song, the downfall of the רשעים ["wicked ones"] as already accomplished'. Kraus sees vv. 21-22 as rejecting human efforts at comprehension as delusory and painful. For Crenshaw, too, once the revelation occurs in v. 17, 'the burden of trying to understand vanishes'; the

---

27. Crenshaw, *The Psalms*, p. 123.
28. Levine, *Sing unto God*, p. 173.
29. Martin Buber, 'The Heart Determines (Psalm 73)', in Nahum Glatzer (ed.), *On the Bible: Eighteen Studies by Martin Buber* (Syracuse, NY: Syracuse University Press, 2000), pp. 199-210 (203-204). Buber is cited by Brueggemann, Kraus, Levine and McCann, among others.

speaker 'as it were, takes a deep breath and shouts the discovery. The key is their fate.'[30]

From another perspective, however, the speaker's mental work is far from done at the moment of insight. The speaker has yet to work through its implications. The adversative אך (*ach*) in v. 18 signals the rejection of old assumptions about the stability of the wicked. A new view of the opponents becomes potent, real and actualized as he visualizes them slipping away, crumbling in destruction, evaporating as in an interrupted dream (vv. 18-20). Their seeming stability is illusory, liable to disappearing in an instant. It is only at this point in the psalm that the speaker begins to address God directly, using the second person. The previous view now appears to the speaker as doltish and bovine (vv. 21-22)—the speaker realizes that he was previously incapable of clear thought regarding either the opponents or God. The point is not that attempts to comprehend are useless; rather, once understanding is achieved, the previous view seems vastly inferior.

In the final section of the psalm (vv. 23-28), the speaker articulates his new understanding of what his relationship with God has been all along. It is not that God has changed proximity; God is always there, even during periods of struggle. It is the speaker whose perceptions and attitudes have changed. Struggling can now be seen as an aspect of God's presence and guidance, a positive step on the road to renewed faith. In a similar way, struggle served as a prescription to the errant in Ps. 4.5 (as discussed in Chapter 2) and as a request to God for refinement in Ps. 26.2 (as discussed in Chapter 1). Buber emphasizes that God's guidance does not take the form of 'a constant oracle, who would exonerate [the speaker] from the duty of weighing up and deciding what he must do'.[31] The speaker must still take and direct his own steps.

In the final verses, the speaker contrasts the inevitable destruction of those far from God with the constant security of God's presence. As in Psalm 17, closeness to God is treasured above all else. After a long process of self-persuasion, the speaker is able to move on and, in the psalm's final words, take on the task of telling God's deeds—a task fulfilled through the psalm itself.

The power of the psalm derives from the public articulation of a dangerous internal debate. The crux of the psalm is not revelation but speech—speech that has been overheard, speech that has been contemplated but stifled, speech that is uttered only internally, and finally speech that is planned.

---

30. Kraus, *Psalms 60–150*, p. 89; Crenshaw, *The Psalms*, p. 123.
31. Buber, 'The Heart Determines (Psalm 73)', p. 206. For another reading that underscores the continuation of struggle in Psalm 73, see Carolyn Sharp, *Irony and Meaning in the Hebrew Bible* (Bloomington, IN: Indiana University Press, 2009), pp. 221-39.

Discipline and Persuasion

Psalms 73 and 77 have been difficult to fit into the usual categories of psalms because the speakers do not call on God directly for rescue. Rather, they rely on their own mental efforts. They struggle, they examine their beliefs, they question and they initiate an inquiry to understand the situation. They recall or envision God's deeds; they go to a place where God can be encountered. And their perspective is altered.

The depiction of self-persuasion in these psalms may have been intended to model mental processes within a scribal group or for the public at large. The ancient Greeks inculcated such habits much more actively through both physical and mental training. As Jeff Walker describes it, *meletê* 'practice' in the sense of 'exercise' or 'rehearsal' is

> the cultivation of an acquired 'nature', *physis*, or indeed a *thymos* or 'heart' endowed with potentialities for emotions, intentions, and behaviors that will seem 'natural' or intuitive to the person acting but that also may be consciously, deliberately invoked and performed—or examined.[32]

Debra Hawhee emphasizes that this kind of habit formation is 'intensely demanding'; it 'requires intensive attention and disciplined, painful, repeated exercise'.[33] More than most, Psalms 73 and 77 illustrate that the purpose of composing, performing and hearing the psalms is part of Israelite moral education.

Ultimately, admitting to a crisis in faith in public actually enhances the speakers' authority within the community rather than dissolving it. In a similar way to hearers of Psalms 4 and 62 discussed in Chapter 2, hearers can identify even more closely with someone who suffers doubts and temptations similar to their own. They learn from the psalms how to become more active in maintaining their own faith. In the case of Psalms 73 and 77, it is God who serves as by-stander, one whose eternal presence alone enables faith in the face of apparent absence.

---

32. Walker, *Rhetoric and Poetics*, p. 148.
33. Hawhee, *Bodily Arts*, p. 146.

BIBLIOGRAPHY

Albertz, Rainer, and Rüdiger Schmitt, *Family and Household Religion in Ancient Israel and the Levant* (Winona Lake, IN: Eisenbrauns, 2012).
Alexander, Elizabeth Shanks, *Transmitting Mishnah: The Shaping Influence of Oral Tradition* (New York: Cambridge University Press, 2006).
Alter, Robert, *The Book of Psalms: A Translation with Commentary* (New York: W.W. Norton, 2007).
—*The Wisdom Books: Job, Proverbs, and Ecclesiastes: A Translation with Commentary* (New York: W.W. Norton, 2010).
Anderson, Jeff S., 'The Social Function of Curses in the Hebrew Bible', *ZAW* 110 (1998), pp. 223-37.
Aristotle, *On Rhetoric: A Theory of Civic Discourse* (trans. George A. Kennedy; New York: Oxford University Press, 1991).
Assmann, Jan, 'When Justice Fails: Jurisdiction and Imprecation in Ancient Egypt and the Near East', *JEA* 78 (1992), pp. 149-62.
Bakhtin, Mikhail, *The Dialogic Imagination: Four Essays* (ed. Michael Holquist; trans. Caryl Emerson and Michael Holquist; Austin, TX: University of Texas Press, 1981).
—'Author and Hero in Aesthetic Activity', in Michael Holquist and Vadim Liapunov (eds.), *Art and Answerability: Early Philosophical Essays by M.M. Bakhtin* (Austin, TX: University of Texas Press, 1990), pp. 4-256.
Barré, Michael L., 'Hearts, Beds, and Repentance in Psalm 4,5 and Hosea 7,14', *Bib* 76 (1995), pp. 53-62.
Bechtel, Lyn M., 'The Perception of Shame within the Divine-Human Relationship in Biblical Israel', in Henry Neil Richardson and Lewis M. Hopfe (eds.), *Uncovering Ancient Stones* (Winona Lake, IN: Eisenbrauns, 1994), pp. 79-92.
Bellinger, William H., Jr, 'Psalms of the Falsely Accused: A Reassessment', *SBL Seminar Papers* 25 (1986), pp. 463-69.
Berlin, Adele, 'Psalms and the Literature of Exile: Psalms 137, 44, 69, and 78', in Peter W. Flint and Patrick D. Miller (eds.), *Book of Psalms: Composition and Reception* (VTSup, 109; Leiden: Brill, 2005), pp. 65-86.
Bialostosky, Don, 'Aristotle's Rhetoric and Bakhtin's Discourse Theory', in Walter Jost and Wendy Olmsted (eds.), *A Companion to Rhetoric and Rhetorical Criticism* (Malden, MA: Blackwell, 2007), pp. 392-408.
Bitzer, Lloyd, 'The Rhetorical Situation', *Philosophy and Rhetoric* 1 (1968), pp. 1-14.
Blackburn, Bill, 'Psalm 71', *RevExp* 88 (1991), pp. 241-45.
Bland, Dave, 'Exegesis of Psalm 62', *ResQ* 23 (1980), pp. 82-95.
Botha, Phil J., 'To Honour Yahweh in the Face of Adversity: A Socio-Critical Analysis of Psalm 131', *Skrif En Kerk* 19 (1998), pp. 525-33.
Boyle, Marjorie O'Rourke, 'Broken Hearts: The Violation of Biblical Law', *JAAR* 73 (2005), pp. 731-57.

Brown, William P., 'The Psalms and "I": The Dialogical Self and the Disappearing Psalmist', in Joel S. Burnett, W.H. Bellinger and W. Dennis Tucker (eds.), *Diachronic and Synchronic: Reading the Psalms in Real Time* (Proceedings of the Baylor Symposium on the Book of Psalms; New York: T. & T. Clark, 2007), pp. 26-44.

Broyles, Craig C., *Psalms* (Peabody, MA: Hendrickson, 1999).

—'Psalms Concerning Temple Entry', in Peter W. Flint and Patrick D. Miller (eds.), *Book of Psalms: Composition and Reception* (VTSup, 109; Leiden: Brill, 2005), pp. 248-87.

Brueggemann, Walter, 'Psalms and the Life of Faith: A Suggested Typology of Function', *JSOT* 17 (1980), pp. 3-32.

—'Psalm 77: The "Turn" from Self to God', *Journal for Preachers* 6 (1983), pp. 8-14.

—'Psalm 109: Three Times "Steadfast Love"', *WW* 5 (1985), pp. 144-54.

—'The Costly Loss of Lament', *JSOT* 36 (1986), pp. 57-71.

—'The Psalms in Theological Use: On Incommensurability and Mutuality', in Peter W. Flint and Patrick D. Miller (eds.), *Book of Psalms: Composition and Reception* (VTSup, 109; Leiden: Brill, 2005), pp. 581-602.

Brueggemann, Walter, and William H. Bellinger, Jr, *Psalms* (New York: Cambridge University Press, 2014).

Buber, Martin, 'The Heart Determines (Psalm 73)', in Nahum Glatzer (ed.), *On the Bible: Eighteen Studies by Martin Buber* (Syracuse, NY: Syracuse University Press, 2000), pp. 199-210.

Burke, Kenneth, *A Rhetoric of Motives* (Berkeley: University of California Press, 1969).

—'The Rhetorical Situation', in Lee Thayer (ed.), *Communication: Ethical and Moral Issues* (New York: Routledge, 1973), pp. 263-74.

Carr, David M., *Writing on the Tablet of the Heart: Origins of Scripture and Literature* (New York: Oxford University Press, 2005).

Carter, Michael, 'Stasis and Kairos: Principles of Social Construction in Classical Rhetoric', *Rhetoric Review* 7 (1988), pp. 97-112.

Charney, Davida, 'Performativity and Persuasion in the Hebrew Book of Psalms: A Rhetorical Analysis of Psalms 22 and 116', *Rhetoric Society Quarterly* 40 (2010), pp. 247-68.

—'Maintaining Innocence before a Divine Hearer: Deliberative Rhetoric in Ps. 22, Ps. 17, and Ps. 7', *BibInt* 21 (2013), pp. 33-63.

Charney, Davida, and Christine Neuwirth, *Having your Say: Reading and Writing Public Arguments* (New York: Pearson/Longman, 2006).

Clifford, Richard J., 'Psalm 89: A Lament over the Davidic Ruler's Continued Failure', *HTR* 73 (1980), pp. 35-47.

—*Psalms 1–72* (AOTC; Nashville, TN: Abingdon Press, 2002).

Consigny, Scott, 'Rhetoric and its Situations', *Philosophy and Rhetoric* 7 (1974), pp. 175-86.

Cottrill, Amy C., *Language, Power, and Identity in the Lament Psalms of the Individual* (New York: T. & T. Clark, 2008).

Craigie, Peter C., *Psalms 1–50* (Nashville, TN: Thomas Nelson, 2nd edn, 2005).

Crenshaw, James L., *The Psalms: An Introduction* (Grand Rapids, MI: Eerdmans, 2001).

Croft, Steven J.L., *The Identity of the Individual in the Psalms* (JSOTSup, 44; Sheffield: JSOT Press, 1987).

Crosswhite, James, *Deep Rhetoric: Philosophy, Reason, Violence, Justice, Wisdom* (Chicago: University of Chicago Press, 2013).

Crow, Loren D., 'The Rhetoric of Psalm 44', *ZAW* 104 (1992), pp. 394-401.
Davis, Ellen F., 'Exploding the Limits: Form and Function in Psalm 22', *JSOT* 53 (1992), pp. 93-105.
deClaissé-Walford, Nancy, 'The Theology of the Imprecatory Psalms', in Rolf Jacobson (ed.), *Soundings in the Theology of the Psalms: Perspectives and Methods in Contemporary Scholarship* (Minneapolis: Fortress Press, 2011), pp. 77-92.
Dolson-Andrew, Stephen L., 'An Exegesis of Psalm 13', *Chafer Theological Seminary Journal* 10 (2004), pp. 49-71.
Eaton, John H., 'Psalm 4:7', *Theology* 67 (1964), pp. 355-57.
—*Psalms: A Historical and Spiritual Commentary* (New York: Continuum International, 2005).
Fahnestock, Jeanne, *Rhetorical Style: The Uses of Language in Persuasion* (New York: Oxford University Press, 2011).
Faraone, Christopher A., 'Molten Wax, Spilt Wine and Mutilated Animals: Sympathetic Magic in Near Eastern and Early Greek Oath Ceremonies', *JHS* 113 (1993), pp. 60-80.
—'Curses and Blessings in Ancient Greek Oaths', *Journal of Ancient Near Eastern Religion* 5 (2006), pp. 140-58.
Fisch, Harold, *Poetry with a Purpose: Biblical Poetics and Interpretation* (Bloomington, IN: Indiana University Press, 1988).
Foster, Robert, and David M. Howard, Jr (eds.), *My Words are Lovely: Studies in the Rhetoric of the Psalms* (New York: T. & T. Clark, 2008).
Frank, David A., 'Arguing with God, Talmudic Discourse, and the Jewish Countermodel: Implications for the Study of Argumentation', *Argumentation and Advocacy* 41 (2004), pp. 71-86.
Frijda, Nico H., 'The Lex Talionis: On Vengeance', in Stephanie H.M. van Goozen, Nanne E. Van de Poll and Joseph A. Sergeant (eds.), *Emotions: Essays on Emotion Theory* (New York: Psychology Press, 1994), pp. 263-90.
Gagarin, Michael, 'The Nature of Proofs in Antiphon', *Classical Philology* 85 (1990), pp. 22-32.
Gentili, Bruno, *Poetry and its Public in Ancient Greece: From Homer to the Fifth Century* (trans. A. Thomas Cole; Baltimore, MD: Johns Hopkins University Press, 1988).
Gerstenberger, Erhard S., 'Theologies in the Book of Psalms', in Peter W. Flint and Patrick D. Miller (eds.), *Book of Psalms: Composition and Reception* (VTSup, 109; Leiden: Brill, 2005), pp. 603-25.
Gitay, Yehoshua, 'Prophetic Criticism—"What are They Doing?": The Case of Isaiah—A Methodological Assessment', *JSOT* 96 (2001), pp. 101-27.
Goldingay, John, 'Psalm 51:16a (English 51:14a)', *CBQ* 40 (1978), pp. 388-90.
—'Psalm 4: Ambiguity and Resolution', *TynBul* 57 (2006), pp. 161-72.
Greenberg, Moshe, 'On the Refinement of the Conception of Prayer in Hebrew Scriptures', *AJS Review* 1 (1976), pp. 57-92.
Grice, Paul, 'Logic and Conversation', in Heimir Geirsson and Michael Losonsky (eds.), *Readings in Language and Mind* (Cambridge, MA: Blackwell, 1996), pp. 121-33.
Grohmann, Marianne, 'Jewish and Christian Approaches to Psalm 35', in Marianne Grohmann and Yair Zakovitch (eds.), *Jewish and Christian Approaches to Psalms* (Freiburg im Breisgau: Herder, 2009), pp. 13-29.
Gunkel, Hermann, and Joachim Begrich, *Introduction to Psalms: The Genres of the Religious Lyric of Israel* (trans. James Nogalski; Macon, GA: Mercer University Press, 1998).

Halpern, Baruch, 'YHWH the Revolutionary: Reflections on the Rhetoric of Redistribution in the Social Context of Dawning Monotheism', in Alice Ogden Bellis (ed.), *Jews, Christians, and the Theology of the Hebrew Scriptures* (Atlanta, GA: SBL, 2000), pp. 179-212.

Hawhee, Debra, *Bodily Arts: Rhetoric and Athletics in Ancient Greece* (Austin, TX: University of Texas Press, 2005).

Isocrates, *Isocrates with an English Translation in Three Volumes* (trans. George Norlin; Cambridge, MA: Harvard University Press; London: William Heinemann, 1980).

Jacobson, Rolf, *Many are Saying: The Function of Direct Discourse in the Hebrew Psalter* (New York: T. & T. Clark, 2004).

—'The Altar of Certitude', in R. Foster and D.M. Howard, Jr (eds.), *My Words are Lovely: Studies in the Rhetoric of the Psalms* (New York: T. & T. Clark, 2008), pp. 3-18.

Josephus, *The New Complete Works of Josephus* (trans. William Whiston; Grand Rapids, MI: Kregel, rev. and expanded edn, 1999).

Kennedy, George A., *Classical Rhetoric and its Christian and Secular Tradition from Ancient to Modern Times* (Durham, NC: University of North Carolina Press, 2nd rev. edn, 1999 [1980]).

Kessler, Martin, 'Psalm 44', in Janet W. Dyk *et al.* (eds.), *Unless Some One Guide Me...* (Festschrift Karel A. Deurloo; Maastricht: Shaker, 2001), pp. 193-204.

Kitz, Anne Marie, 'The Hebrew Terminology of Lot Casting and its Ancient Near Eastern Context', *CBQ* 62 (2000), pp. 207-14.

—'Effective Simile and Effective Act: Psalm 109, Numbers 5, and KUB 26', *CBQ* 69 (2007), pp. 440-56.

Knohl, Israel, 'Between Voice and Silence: The Relationship between Prayer and Temple Cult', *JBL* 115 (1996), pp. 17-30.

Kock, Christian, 'Constructive Controversy: Rhetoric as Dissensus-Oriented Discourse', *Cogency* 1 (2009), pp. 89-111.

Kraus, Hans-Joachim, *Psalms 1–59* (trans. H.C. Oswald; Minneapolis: Augsburg Fortress, 1988).

—*Psalms 60–150* (trans. H.C. Oswald; Minneapolis: Augsburg Fortress, 1989).

Krugman, Paul, 'Boring Cruel Romantics', *New York Times* (20 November 2011), p. A29.

Kselman, John S., '"Why have you abandoned me": A Rhetorical Study of Psalm 22', in David Clines, David M. Gunn and Alan J. Hauser (eds.), *Art and Meaning* (Sheffield: JSOT Press, 1982), pp. 172-98.

—'Psalm 77 and the Book of Exodus', *JANES* 15 (1983), pp. 51-58.

Kwakkel, Gert, *'According to my Righteousness': Upright Behaviour as Grounds for Deliverance in Psalms 7, 17, 18, 26, and 44* (Leiden: Brill, 2006).

Laney, J. Carl, 'A Fresh Look at the Imprecatory Psalms', *BibSac* 138 (1981), pp. 35-45.

Lee, Sung-Hun, 'Lament and the Joy of Salvation in the Lament Psalms', in Peter W. Flint and Patrick D. Miller (eds.), *Book of Psalms: Composition and Reception* (Leiden: Brill, 2005), pp. 224-47.

LeMon, Joel, *Yahweh's Winged Form in the Psalms: Exploring Congruent Iconography and Texts* (Fribourg: Academic Press, 2010).

—'Saying Amen to Violent Psalms', in Rolf Jacobson (ed.), *Soundings in the Theology of the Psalms: Perspectives and Methods in Contemporary Scholarship* (Minneapolis: Fortress Press, 2011), pp. 93-109.

Lenzi, Alan C., 'Invoking the God: Interpreting Invocations in Mesopotamian Prayers and Biblical Laments of the Individual', *JBL* 129 (2010), pp. 303-15.

Leveen, Jacob, 'Textual Problems of Psalm 17', *VT* 11 (1961), pp. 48-54.
Levine, Herbert, *Sing unto God a New Song: A Contemporary Reading of the Psalms* (Bloomington, IN: Indiana University Press, 1995).
Lichtenstein, Murray H., 'The Poetry of Poetic Justice: A Comparative Study in Biblical Imagery', *JANES* 5 (1973), pp. 255-65.
MacDowell, D.M., *Gorgias: Encomium of Helen* (Bristol: Bristol Classical Press, 1982).
Mandolfo, Carleen, 'Finding their Voices: Sanctioned Subversion in Psalms of Lament', *HBT* 24 (2002), pp. 27-52.
— *God in the Dock: Dialogic Tension in the Psalms of Lament* (JSOTSup, 357; London: Sheffield Academic Press, 2002).
—'Dialogic Form Criticism: An Intertextual Reading of Lamentations and Psalms of Lament', in Roland Boer (ed.), *Bakhtin and Genre Theory in Biblical Studies* (Atlanta, GA: SBL, 2007), pp. 69-90.
—'Psalm 88 and the Holocaust: Lament in Search of a Divine Response', *BibInt* 15 (2007), pp. 151-70.
Martin, Troy, 'Apostasy to Paganism: The Rhetorical Stasis of the Galatian Controversy', *JBL* 114 (1995), pp. 437-61.
McCann, J. Clinton, Jr, 'Psalm 73: A Microcosm of Old Testament Theology', in K.G. Hoglund *et al.* (eds.), *The Listening Heart: Essays in Wisdom and the Psalms in Honor of Roland E. Murphy, O. Carm* (JSOTSup, 58; Sheffield: JSOT Press, 1987), pp. 247-57.
Miller, Carolyn R., and Davida Charney, 'Audience, Persuasion, and Argument', in Charles Bazerman (ed.), *Handbook of Research on Writing: History, Society, School, Individual, Text* (New York: Routledge, 2007), pp. 583-98.
Miller, Patrick D., '"Enthroned on the Praises of Israel": The Praise of God in Old Testament Theology', *Int* 39 (1985), pp. 5-19.
—'Prayer as Persuasion: The Rhetoric and Intention of Prayer', *WW* 13 (1993), pp. 356-62.
—'The Hermeneutics of Imprecation', in Wallace M. Allston, Jr (ed.), *Theology in the Service of the Church: Essays in Honor of Thomas Gillespie* (Grand Rapids, MI: Eerdmans, 2000), pp. 153-63.
Mirhady, David Cyrus, 'The Oath-Challenge in Athens', *ClQ* 44 (1991), pp. 78-83.
Mitchell, Matthew W., 'Genre Disputes and Communal Accusatory Laments: Reflections on the Genre of Psalm LXXXIX', *VT* 55 (2005), pp. 511-27.
Morrow, William S., *Protest against God: The Eclipse of a Biblical Tradition* (Sheffield: Phoenix Press, 2006).
Mosca, Paul G., 'Psalm 26: Poetic Structure and the Form-Critical Task', *CBQ* 47 (1985), pp. 212-37.
Muilenberg, James, 'Form Criticism and Beyond', *JBL* 88 (1969), pp. 1-18.
Nasuti, Harry, 'Plumbing the Depths: Genre Ambiguity and Theological Creativity in Psalm 130', in Hindy Najman and Judith Newman (eds.), *The Idea of Biblical Interpretation: Essays in Honor of James L. Kugel* (Leiden: Brill, 2004), pp. 95-124.
Nienkamp, Jean, *Internal Rhetorics: Toward a History and Theory of Self-Persuasion* (Carbondale, IL: Southern Illinois University Press, 2001).
Patrick, Dale, and Kenneth Diable, 'Persuading the One and Only God to Intervene', in Robert Foster and David M. Howard (eds.), *My Words are Lovely: Studies in the Rhetoric of the Psalms* (London: T. & T. Clark, 2008), pp. 19-32.

Peels, Hendrick G.L., 'Sanctorum communio vel idolorum repudiatio? A Reconsideration of Psalm 16,3', *ZAW* 112 (2000), pp. 239-51.
Perelman, Chaïm, and Lucie Olbrechts-Tyteca, *The New Rhetoric: A Treatise on Argumentation* (trans. J. Wilkinson and P. Weaver; Notre Dame, IN: University of Notre Dame Press, 1969).
Pernot, Laurent, *Epideictic Rhetoric: Questioning the Stakes of Ancient Praise* (Austin: University of Texas Press, 2015).
Pratt, Jonathan, 'The Epideictic *Agōn* and Aristotle's Elusive Third Genre', *AJP* 133 (2012), pp. 177-208.
Raabe, Paul R., 'Deliberate Ambiguity in the Psalter', *JBL* 110 (1991), pp. 213-27.
Raj, J.R. John Samuel, 'Cosmic Judge or Overseer of the World-Order? The Role of Yahweh as Portrayed in Psalm 7', *Bangalore Theological Forum* 34 (2002), pp. 1-15.
Rom-Shiloni, Dalit, 'Psalm 44: The Powers of Protest', *CBQ* 70 (2008), pp. 683-98.
Rucker, Derek D., and Richard E. Petty, 'Effects of Accusations on the Accuser: The Moderating Role of Accuser Culpability', *Personality and Social Psychology Bulletin* 29 (2003), pp. 1259-1271.
Rucker, Derek D., and Anthony R. Pratkanis, 'Projection as an Interpersonal Influence Tactic: The Effects of the Pot Calling the Kettle Black', *Personality and Social Psychology Bulletin* 27 (2001), pp. 1494-1507.
Sarna, Nahum, 'The Psalm Superscriptions and the Guilds', in Siegfried Stein and Raphael Loewe (eds.), *Studies in Jewish Religious and Intellectual History* (Tuscaloosa, AL: University of Alabama Press, 1979), pp. 281-300.
Schiappa, Edward, and David M. Timmerman, 'Aristotle's Disciplining of Epideictic', in Edward Schiappa (ed.), *The Beginnings of Rhetorical Theory in Ancient Greece* (New Haven, CT: Yale University Press, 1999), pp. 185-206.
Schuele, Andreas, '"Call on me in the day of trouble…": From Oral Lament to Lament Psalms', in Annette Weissenrieder and Robert B. Coote (eds.), *Interface of Orality and Writing: Speaking, Seeing, Writing in the Shaping of New Genres* (Tübingen: Mohr Siebeck, 2010), pp. 322-34.
Sharp, Carolyn, *Irony and Meaning in the Hebrew Bible* (Bloomington, IN: Indiana University Press, 2009), pp. 221-39.
Shoemaker, H. Stephen, 'Psalm 131'. *RevExp* 85.1 (1988), pp. 89-94.
Snaith, Norman Henry, 'The Meaning of the Hebrew "אך"', *VT* 14 (1964), pp. 221-25.
Staton, Cecil, '"How long, O Yahweh?" The Complaint Prayer of Psalm 13', *Faith and Mission* 7 (1990), pp. 59-67.
Sternberg, Meir, 'The Bible's Art of Persuasion: Ideology, Rhetoric, and Poetics in Saul's Fall', *HUCA* 54 (1983), pp. 45-82.
Stewart, Susan, 'What Praise Poems are For', *PMLA* 120 (2005), pp. 235-45.
Tayler, Christopher, 'In the Vale of Death's Shadow', review of *The Book of Psalms* by Robert Alter, in *The Guardian* (London, 21 December 2007).
Tull, Patricia K., 'Bakhtin's Confessional Self-Accounting and Psalms of Lament', *BibInt* 13 (2005), pp. 41-55.
van Rees, M.A., 'Indicators of Dissociation', in Franz H. van Eemeren and Peter Houtlosser (eds.), *Argumentation in Practice* (Amsterdam: John Benjamins, 2005), pp. 53-67.
Walker, Jeffrey, 'Enthymemes of Anger in Cicero and Thomas Paine', in Marie Secor and Davida Charney (eds.), *Constructing Rhetorical Education* (Carbondale, IL: Southern Illinois University Press, 1996), pp. 357-81.

—*Rhetoric and Poetics in Antiquity* (New York: Oxford University Press, 2000).
Waltke, Bruce K., 'Superscripts, Postscripts, or Both', *JBL* 110 (1991), pp. 583-96.
Webb, Ruth, 'Imagination and the Arousal of the Emotions in Greco-Roman Rhetoric', in Susanna Morton Braund and Christopher Gill (eds.), *The Passions in Roman Thought and Literature* (New York: Cambridge University Press, 1997), pp. 112-27.
Westermann, Claus, *Praise and Lament in the Psalms* (trans. Keith R. Crim and Richard N. Soulen; Atlanta, GA: John Knox Press, 1981).
Wright, David P., 'Ritual Analogy in Psalm 109', *JBL* 113 (1994), pp. 385-404.
Zulick, Margaret D., 'The Active Force of Hearing: The Ancient Hebrew Language of Persuasion', *Rhetorica* 10 (1992), pp. 267-380.
Zvyagintsev, Mikhail, Benjamin Clemens, Natalya Chechko, Krystyna A. Mathiak, Alexander T. Sack and Klaus Mathiak, 'Brain Networks Underlying Mental Imagery of Auditory and Visual Information', *European Journal of Neuroscience* 37 (2013), pp. 1421-34.

INDEXES

INDEX OF REFERENCES

HEBREW BIBLE

Genesis
20.5-6	34
32.24-32	13
37.26	23
41.9	117

Exodus
14.19-29	133
15.11-13	132
18.13-26	1
19.16-20	133
22.23-25	97
24.7	45
34.6	131

Leviticus
5.5	112
7.32	113
16.21	112
19.15	104
19.17	118
19.18	97

Numbers
5.7	112
6.24-26	46
11.1-34	80

Deuteronomy
1.17	104
21.1-9	112

Joshua
7.18-21	112

2 Samuel
15.11	34

1 Kings
3.16-28	87
8.31-32	86-87, 105
8.32	87
8.38-40	115
17.18	117
22.34	34

Isaiah
8.18	27
20.3	27

Jeremiah
2.11	43
11.20	34
17.10	34
20.12	34

Ezekiel
3.17-19	123
12.6	27
12.11	27
24.24	27
24.27	27
33.7-9	123

Psalms
3.3	74
4	5, 15, 37, 39, 41-52, 54, 123-24, 142
4.2	42-43, 45
4.3-7	43
4.3	44
4.4-6	45
4.4	44-45
4.5-6	44
4.5	37, 44-46, 60, 141
4.6	44
4.7-9	45
4.8-9	42, 45-46
4.7	45-46
4.8	46
4.9	46
5.9-10	24
6	111
6.6	21
7	7, 9, 15, 43, 84, 86-92, 102, 106-107, 109
7.1	94
7.2-3	88
7.2	88
7.3	89
7.4-6	89
7.4	88, 106
7.6	89
7.7-18	89
7.7-11	89
7.7-8	89
7.9-17	91
7.12-17	90
7.12	90
7.13-14	90
7.13	90
7.18	90
8.5	81
9.14-15	22
10.3-7	24
12.7	34
13	15, 36, 58-61, 63

Index of References

13.2-3	59, 60-61	22.2-12	71, 77		104, 107,
13.3	60	22.2-3	72		109
13.4-5	23, 61	22.4-6	72	35.1-10	92, 97
13.4	60-61	22.7-9	72	35.1-8	93
13.5	61	22.8-9	73	35.1-3	93
13.6	5, 61	22.8	74	35.4-8	94
15	33	22.9	74	35.7	94
16	30-32, 37,	22.10-11	74	35.8	94, 106
	60	22.10	74	35.9-10	93
16.1-2	30	22.12	72, 75	35.10	94
16.1	30	22.13-22	71	35.11-18	93, 95
16.2	30	22.13-19	75	35.11	95
16.3-4	31	22.14-16	75	35.12-16	96
16.3	31	22.17-19	75	35.13-14	83, 96
16.5-6	31	22.20-22	75	35.13	107
16.6	31	22.22	75	35.14	96
16.7-8	31	22.23-32	71, 75	35.15-16	96
16.7	32, 34, 44,	22.23-26	75	35.15	96
	60	22.23-24	25	35.18	93
16.8	32	22.23	75	35.19-28	92, 96
16.9-11	32	22.30-32	75	35.19-26	93
17	15, 43, 65,	22.31-32	25	35.19	96
	76-82, 86,	23	20	35.22	97
	88, 137,	24	33	35.25	96
	141	25	111	35.26	96
17.1-8	77	25.16	94	35.27-28	93
17.2	77	26	32-35, 37	35.27	97
17.3-4	77	26.1-3	33	37	69
17.3	77	26.1	35	37.7	37
17.4	77-78	26.2	34, 141	38	15, 20,
17.5-8	78	26.4-5	33, 35		111-12,
17.5	78	26.5	35		116-20,
17.6	78	26.6-8	33, 35		125
17.7	78	26.7	34	38.2	117
17.8	78	26.9-10	33, 35	38.3-9	117
17.9-12	77-78, 80	26.11-12	33, 35	38.5	117
17.10	78, 80	26.12	35	38.6	117
17.12	78	27	43, 86	38.9	117
17.13-14	77, 79	28	43, 83, 86	38.10	117
17.13	79, 137	28.3	24	38.11-15	117
17.14	79-81	29	133	38.12-13	117
17.15	77, 80	30.10	21, 23	38.14-15	118
17.18	137	30.12	38	38.16	117-18
18.9	44	31	43, 86, 111	38.17-21	117-18
18.5-6	31	32	111	38.17-18	119
22	15, 22, 25,	32.5	113	38.17	119
	65, 71-77,	35	15, 24, 48,	38.19	119
	80-83, 88,		84, 86, 92-	38.20-21	119
	120, 122		100, 102,	38.22-23	119

Psalms (cont.)		51.17	17	71.8	27
39	111	51.18-21	124	71.9	27
40	111	51.18-19	124	71.10-13	27
40.7-11	17	51.20-21	124	71.14-16	27
40.18	94	51.20	124	71.14	27
41.7	83	52	39	71.15	28
42.4	74	54	15, 36, 58-	71.17-19	28
42.11	24, 74		59, 61, 63	71.20-24	28
44	15, 65-71,	54.3-4	58, 61	71.22	28
	81-83, 134-	54.5	24, 58, 61	71.23	28
	35	54.6-7	58, 61	73	15, 128,
44.2-9	66	54.6	58		135-42
44.9	68	54.8-9	58, 61	73.1	137
44.10-17	67	55	24	73.2-12	137
44.10	68	55.13-15	83	73.3	137
44.15	68	57.4	24	73.4	137
44.16	68	58	39, 84	73.5	137
44.18-23	68-70	59	84	73.7	137
44.18-20	69	59.6	83	73.8-9	137
44.18	69-70	62	5, 15, 37,	73.8	138
44.21-22	69-70		39, 41-42,	73.11	138
44.21	69		47-52, 54-	73.13-14	138
44.23	68-69		55, 123,	73.13	140
44.24-27	69		137, 142	73.15-16	138
44.24	69			73.16	139
44.25	69	62.2-3	48	73.17	140
44.27	69	62.2	50	73.18-20	141
50.13	17	62.3	50	73.18	141
51	15, 111-12,	62.4-5	48	73.21-22	140-41
	119-20,	62.4	50, 102	73.23-28	141
	123, 125	62.5	37, 50	77	15, 128-34,
		62.6-8	48		142
51.3-4	121, 123	62.9-11	48-50	77.2	130
51.5-7	121	62.9	49-51	77.3-7	130
51.5	113, 121	62.10	49	77.3	129
51.6	121	62.11	49	77.6-7	130
51.7	121	62.12-13	48-49	77.8-10	130
51.8-14	122, 123	62.12	51	77.8	131
51.8	122	64	43, 48, 86	77.9	131
51.9	123	65	111	77.10-11	132
51.10	122	66.10	34	77.11	131-33
51.11	123	69	70, 84, 111	77.12-21	134
51.12	123-24	69.30	94	77.12-13	132-33
51.13	123	69.31	17	77.14-16	133
51.14	123-24	70.6	94	77.14-15	132
51.15-19	123	71	21, 25-29	77.16	134
51.15-16	124	71.1-4	26	77.17-21	133-34
51.15	54, 123	71.5-9	27	77.17	44
51.16-17	22	71.6	27	77.19	44
51.16	123	71.7	27	77.21	134

Index of References

78	70, 135	109.6	102-104,	119.61	31
78.52-54	134		106	130	15, 38,
78.55	31	109.8	106		111-17,
82	15, 39, 52-	109.9	106		125
	54	109.12	102	130.1-2	114
82.1-2	53	109.15	102	130.1	116
82.3-4	53	109.16	102, 106-	130.3-4	114
82.5	54		107	130.3	115
83	84	109.17-20	103, 106-	130.4	115
86.1	94		107	130.5-8	115
86.10	37	109.17-19	103	130.5-6	115
88	7	109.17	107	130.5	115-16
88.11-13	21	109.20-31	106	130.7-8	116
89	132, 135	109.20	103, 106	130.7	38
89.2-38	134	109.21-25	101	131	35-38
89.34-35	132	109.21	102	131.1	36
89.35	132	109.22	94, 101,	131.2	36-37, 44
99.1	44		102, 107	131.3	36, 38
102	111	109.23-24	102	137	70, 84
105.11	31	109.25	102	139	84
106.19-20	43	109.26-31	104	139.6	37
109	5, 9, 15,	109.26	102	139.14	37
	84, 86, 98-	109.27	106	140	48
	109	109.28	104, 106-	140.6	31
109.1-5	101, 102,		108	143	111
	106	109.29	106		
109.1	99	109.30-31	104	*Proverbs*	
109.2	100, 106	111.2	37	12.25	119
109.3	106	115.17-18	21		
109.4	102	116	9, 22-23	*Job*	
109.5	100	116.1-2	22	31.33-34	38
109.6-20	102	116.3	31		
109.6-19	98, 105	116.12-14	22	*Lamentations*	
109.6-7	103	116.17-19	22	3.49	129

CLASSICAL GREEK AND ROMAN SOURCES

Aristotle		Gorgias		Josephus	
	2, 11, 18,		40-41		109
	29, 56, 63,				
	81, 85, 98,	Isocrates			
	109, 119		11, 127-28		

Index of Rhetorical Terms

Aeschylus 28
ambiguity 24, 46, 80
amplitude 15, 39-41,45, 48, 61, 63, 71, 75
appeal 40, 61, 75, 81, 107, 112, 119-20,
    128, 134
  ethical 8, 57, 61, 64, 74, 81, 125
  logical 57, 61, 81, 127-28
  pathetic 57, 61, 71, 81, 119, 128, 134
Aristophanes 89
audience 2, 4, 15, 18-19, 29, 35-36, 39-40,
    52-54, 57, 81, 120, 127, 134

Cicero 98
claim 2, 9, 21-22, 27, 30, 36, 40-41, 51,
    54, 57, 62-63, 65, 68-69, 72, 76-77,
    81-83, 86-87, 94, 102, 107, 118-19,
    135, 137
  rebuttal 9, 49, 68-69, 104-105, 107
curse 3, 15, 24, 83-109

deliberative discourse 11, 15, 18, 29, 56,
    57
  problem in 2, 15, 44, 56-59 61-62 67,
    71, 75, 78, 80, 85, 113, 116, 128
  proposal in 15, 56-57, 61, 63, 66, 71,
    75, 77, 89, 93, 96-99, 102, 104-105,
    122, 125
  solution in 2, 15, 57-58, 61-62, 71, 79
dispute 1, 9, 13, 24, 62, 68, 83, 86-87, 89-
    90, 102, 105

emotion 18, 32, 57, 61, 72, 75, 81, 97,
    112, 119-20, 134, 142
epideictic discourse 11, 18-19, 29-30, 32,
    35

forensic/judicial discourse 9, 11, 13, 18,
    29, 43, 47, 85-89, 91, 97, 102, 108
forum 11-12, 29, 56, 81, 112, 126

identification 15, 22, 41, 45-48, 50, 52-53,
    78, 81-82, 107, 114, 116, 119, 142

Hesiod 28
Homer 28

kairos 9, 13, 99

narrative 1, 75, 78, 112, 117, 128, 133

oaths 43, 77-78, 85-86, 89, 91, 105, 107-
    109

persuasion 1-3, 11, 15, 17-18, 29, 32, 35,
    39-41, 44, 48, 52, 54, 56-57, 63, 65, 75,
    81, 89, 91, 96, 98, 112-13, 123, 125-29,
    134-35, 139, 141-42
Plato 11, 19

rhetorical situation 2, 9, 13-14, 39, 52-53,
    67, 81, 88, 98-99, 108

Socrates, 11, 19
stasis/stases 62, 81, 87
  action/jurisdiction 11, 44, 49, 53-54,
    56-63, 66,69-71, 75, 77, 79, 89, 90,
    93-94, 96, 104, 115-16, 120, 122-24
  cause 41, 57, 62, 65, 116, 130
  definition 41, 62, 82
  existence 15, 57, 62, 68, 87
  value 4, 8, 12, 15, 18-19, 24, 27, 29-30

INDEX OF AUTHORS

Albertz, R. 10, 113
Alexander, E.S. 89
Alter, R. 1, 16, 36, 50, 74, 77-78, 80, 81,
    90, 96, 99, 106, 115, 117, 119, 120,
    122, 123, 124, 129, 131, 137, 139
Anderson, J. 85
Assmann, J. 84-85

Bakhtin, M. 6, 12, 121, 123, 139
Barré, M. 44, 60
Bechtel, L.M. 98
Bellinger, W.H. 31, 42-43, 48, 86, 92
Berlin, A. 70
Bialostosky, D. 12
Bitzer, L. 39
Blackburn, B. 27
Bland, D. 36, 47, 50
Botha, P.J. 36, 44
Boyle, M.O. 124
Brown, W. 9
Broyles, C. 33, 42
Brueggemann, W. 4, 7, 14, 20, 31, 42, 48,
    86, 99, 103, 131, 140
Buber, M. 140-41
Burke, K. 40-41, 119

Carr, D. 28
Carter, M. 62
Charney, D. 2, 9, 23, 40, 62, 67, 68, 71
Clifford, R. 42, 134-35
Consigny, S. 39
Cottrill, A. 11, 21, 99, 108
Craigie, P.C. 80
Crenshaw, J.L. 139-40
Croft, S. 42, 47, 92, 134
Crosswhite, J. 128
Crow, L.D. 68-69

Davis, E. 22, 75
deClaissé-Walford, N. 84

Diable, K. 11, 14, 65, 74, 111-12, 125
Dolson-Andrews, S. 60

Eaton, J.H. 46, 80

Fahnestock, J. 40
Faraone, C. 84, 85, 108
Fisch, H. 8
Foster, R. 10
Frank, D. 1
Frankel, D. 54
Frijda, N.H. 97

Gagarin, M. 85
Gentili, B. 12
Gerstenberger, E. 10, 108
Gitay, Y. 10
Goldingay, J. 42, 46, 123, 124
Greenberg, M. 17-18, 36
Grice, P. 63
Grohmann, M. 94
Gunkel, H. 59

Halpern, B. 4, 7
Han, J.H. 50
Hawhee, D. 12, 142
Howard, D.M. 10

Jacobson, R. 42, 46, 54, 55, 99, 108

Kennedy, G. 11
Kessler, M. 68-69
Kitz, A.M. 31, 99, 103, 107
Knohl, I. 34
Kock, C. 56
Kraus, H.-J. 26, 27, 42, 47, 74, 78-79, 86,
    88-89, 90, 92, 96, 99, 103, 113, 114,
    115, 117-118, 120, 122, 124, 131, 133,
    135, 136, 137, 139-40
Krugman, P. 41

Kselman, J.S. 71, 74, 131, 133
Kwaakel, G. 77, 79, 86, 89-90

Laney, J.C. 84, 99, 108
Lee, S.-H. 102
LeMon, J. 79, 84
Lenzi, A. 125
Leveen, J. 79
Levine, H. 3, 5, 6, 133, 135, 138, 139, 140
Lichtenstein, M. 94

Mandolfo, C. 4, 6-8, 47, 91
Martin, T. 62
McCann, J.C. 135, 137, 140
Miller, C. 2
Miller, P.D. 17, 83, 84
Mirhady, D.C. 85, 109
Mitchell, M.W. 134-35
Morrow, W. 5, 10, 13, 14
Mosca, P. 33-34
Muilenburg, J. 10

Nasuti, H. 113, 116
Nienkamp, J. 127-28

Patrick, D. 11, 14, 65, 74, 111-12, 125
Peels, H.G.L. 31
Perelman, C. 3, 10, 29, 30, 40-41, 63
Pernot, L. 18
Petty, R. 110
Pratkanis, A.R. 109-110
Pratt, J. 18-19

Raabe, P. 24, 44, 90
Raj, J.R.J.S 90
Rees, M.A. van 41
Rom-Shiloni, D. 68-69
Rucker, D.D. 109-10

Sarna, N. 13, 120
Schiappa, E. 18
Schuele, A. 4, 5, 9, 62
Sharp, C. 141
Shoemaker, H.S. 44
Snaith, N.H. 51, 137
Staton, C. 5, 61
Sternberg, M. 10
Stewart, S. 28

Tayler, C. 1
Timmerman, D. 18
Tull, P. 6-7, 13, 121

Walker, J. 12, 16, 52, 97-98, 142
Waltke, B.K. 120
Webb, R. 134
Westermann, C. 19
Wright, D.P. 99, 103-104, 106, 108

Zulick, M. 2
Zvyagintsev, M. 119, 120, 134

www.ingramcontent.com/pod-product-compliance
Lightning Source LLC
Chambersburg PA
CBHW071432160426
43195CB00013B/1872